Praise for earlier editions of

Maine
Off the Beaten Path®

"It's to Curtis's great credit that *Maine: Off the Beaten Path*® ... not only gets us to the very top of the state but gives us good reasons for going."
　　—*Maine Times*

"Lives up to its modest boast ... a guide to unique places [and] a good read as well."
　　—*The Quoddy* (ME) *Tides*

"Describes overlooked attractions."
　　—*Coast Star* (Kennebunk, ME)

"For anyone interested in what's to be seen in Maine this book is a must."
　　—*Maine in Print*

"Informal and very friendly ... doesn't pretend to be the end-all guide to the state, just the guide to the stuff you'd miss otherwise.... For historical fun, interesting, delicious, beautiful, out-of-the-way things to see and do—and eat—check out this guidebook."
　　—*Lincoln* (ME) *News*

Help Us Keep This Guide Up to Date

Every effort has been made by the author and editors to make this guide as accurate and useful as possible. However, many things can change after a guide is published—establishments close, phone numbers change, facilities come under new management, etc.

We would love to hear from you concerning your experiences with this guide and how you feel it could be made better and be kept up to date. While we may not be able to respond to all comments and suggestions, we'll take them to heart and we'll also make certain to share them with the author. Please send your comments and suggestions to the following address:

The Globe Pequot Press
Reader Response/Editorial Department
P.O. Box 480
Guilford, CT 06437

Or you may e-mail us at:

editorial@globe-pequot.com

Thanks for your input, and happy travels!

OFF THE BEATEN PATH® SERIES

Maine

FOURTH EDITION

by
Wayne Curtis

The
Globe
Pequot
Press

Guilford, Connecticut

The area code for the entire state is 207.
The prices and rates listed in this guidebook were confirmed at
press time. We recommend, however, that you call establishments before traveling to obtain current information.

Copyright © 1992, 1995, 1998, 2000 by Wayne Curtis

Maps created by Equator Graphics © The Globe Pequot Press
Illustrations by Carole Drong
Cover and text design by Laura Augustine
Cover photo by Kindra Clineff/Index Stock

Off the Beaten Path is a registered trademark of The Globe Pequot Press.

Library of Congress Cataloging-in-Publication Data

Curtis, Wayne, 1957–
        Maine : off the beaten path / Wayne Curtis. —4th ed.
        p. cm. (Off the beaten path series)
     Includes index.
     ISBN 0-7627-0644-9
     1. Maine—Guidebooks. I. Title. II. Series.
     F17.3.C87   2000
     917.4'4104'43—dc21   00-028435

Manufactured in the United States of America
Fourth Edition/Second Printing

To Susanne and Caleb

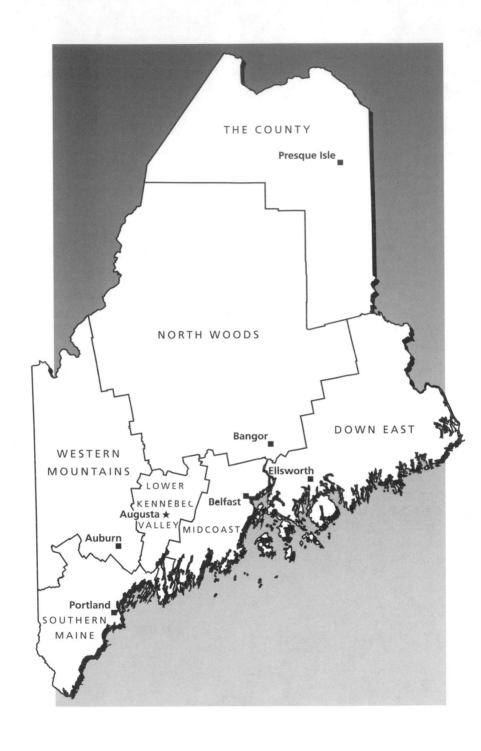

THE COUNTY

Presque Isle ■

NORTH WOODS

DOWN EAST

Bangor ■

WESTERN
MOUNTAINS

Ellsworth ■

LOWER

KENNEBEC   Belfast ■

Augusta ★

VALLEY   MIDCOAST

Auburn ■

Portland ■

SOUTHERN
MAINE

Contents

Acknowledgments

Thanks are due to many people for tips, advice, and encouragement in researching and writing this book. Among those deserving thanks: Louise Klaila for her company and good ideas; Cody Klaila and Dallas and Addie Rolnick for letting me take their mother away so often; and Janice Brand, Jody Alesandro, Mel Allen, and David Lyon for hiring me to write about Maine at one time or another. Special thanks go to the Maine State Historic Preservation Commission and the Maine Office of Tourism, both of which kindly provided information and assistance.

Introduction

An acquaintance from Boston drove up to Maine one weekend a while back looking for some of that remote, storm-tossed coast he had heard all about. He crossed the bridge at Kittery, got off the interstate, and headed resolutely up Route 1. After a couple of hours of driving, he decided that Maine, in fact, looked a lot like suburban Boston. The rugged coast and small villages, he concluded, were figments of an effective if misleading advertising campaign. He turned around and went home, rather pleased with himself for having deflated a pernicious myth.

In truth, my friend was right. Maine's beaten path isn't that much different from the sprawl outside of Boston. There are boxy Wal-Marts and Rite-Aid drugstores, U-store-it centers ringed with chain link fencing, and plenty of those now-ubiquitous gas station/convenience stores huddled under squarish canopies and illuminated with eye-searing klieg lights.

Finding the other Maine—the Maine that looms large in the popular imagination—takes a bit more creativity and ingenuity than simply charging up Route 1. You'll need to wander farther afield, getting off primary arteries to explore the winding back roads. And even that is sometimes not enough. Every so often you'll need to trade your car for canoe, windjammer, or hiking boots to reach Maine's most appealing areas.

Rest assured that the other Maine—the off-the-beaten-path Maine—does still exist. You still can find unspoiled coastal villages without a single T-shirt or ice cream shop. And pristine lakes deep in the spruce and fir forest, with lakeside campsites accessible only by canoe. And intriguing small museums where you're the only visitor present, allowing for undistracted browsing. You'll also find there's little in the way of extravagance or outlandishness in Maine—no Elvis museums, nor much in the way of garish architecture. Even the twenty-bedroom summer "cottages" dating from the nineteenth century seem understated and subdued. To my mind, the most alluring attractions in the state reflect its flinty New England roots: a sweep of unadorned coastline, a magnificently simple Federal-era house, an undisturbed five-acre pond accessible only by foot.

The state is often divided into two regions: the Coast and the North Woods. But that view simplifies things a bit much. For one, coastal areas often bear little resemblance to one another. Other than the frosty waters that wash both shores, the long, sandy beaches of York County have little in common with the bold headlands near Cutler or with the oceanside farms of the Midcoast.

Likewise with the North Woods. The generally flat terrain around the popular canoe route down the Allagash River is reminiscent of Minnesota, with the horizon defined by the sharp spires of spruce trees at water's edge. In contrast, brawny and broad Carrabasset Valley seems to have more in common with Montana, with distant, open views of rounded, rocky mountains. And then there are the vast, rolling farmlands of Aroostook County, which categorically defeat all attempts to pigeonhole Maine. For those willing to wander off the main track, Maine's breadth and diversity rarely fail to impress.

Did You Know?

- *Maine is the only state that shares a border with just one other state?*

- *Maine is the only state with just one syllable?*

Exploring back-road Maine requires a high degree of conviction, because places to eat and stay aren't always easy to locate. Before you set off exploring the state's secondary road network, be aware that it was not created with tourism in mind. At times it seems not to have been created with transportation in mind: Why else would early residents put all those roads down dead-end peninsulas along the coast, and timberland owners erect barricades across perfectly serviceable logging roads in the North Woods? The old Maine chestnut that ends with the punch line "You can't get there from here" didn't germinate in a fertile imagination. It had a solid basis in reality. Those who do best in their endeavor of scouting back-road Maine tend to be well endowed with patience and possessed of a finely honed sense of adventure.

They also tend to have a copy of DeLorme's *Maine Atlas and Gazetteer*. First published in 1976, the atlas breaks the state down into some seventy road atlas–sized maps. If cut out and assembled, DeLorme's map of the state would measure about 8 by 12 feet, providing more than enough detail on back roads and byways, right down to dirt lanes that peter out into jeep tracks and foot trails. Updated frequently, the atlas is essential for anyone intent on getting seriously off the main track. It's available for $16.95 at many Maine stores as well as at DeLorme's Map Store on Route 1 in Yarmouth. For more information call (888) 227–1656, or visit the company's Web site at www.delorme.com.

Even with your atlas in hand, be prepared for some geographic surprises. Maine is fairly massive by New England standards. The geographic center of the state is near Katahdin Iron Works, deep in the North Woods and a long, long drive from the South Coast. Travelers often charge into the state from New Hampshire and fail to notice that the map scale has changed; an inch, which earlier covered 10 miles, now covers 20. They can't figure out why it suddenly takes so long to get everywhere. When planning a trip to the northern part of the state, keep one fact in mind: Portland is closer to Manhattan than it is to Fort Kent.

There's also the issue of access. Maine has one of the smallest percentages of publicly owned land of any state in the country. Much of the dramatic coastline featured on wall calendars and placemats is privately owned. It's nice to look at, but if you try to visit you'll be cited for trespassing. As a result, those few coastal areas that are publicly owned—such as Acadia National Park—tend to be overrun. One way to circumvent this is to view the coast from the water, where private property and trespass is less of an issue. In addition, the state owns and maintains dozens of islands that are open to public use. Windjammer trips, naturalist expeditions, and sea kayak tours all offer a means to visit these salty wildernesses, even if you don't have your own oceangoing vessel.

The North Woods also are privately owned for the most part, but access is less of an issue. Timber companies own much of the woodlands in inland Washington County and from Rangeley Lake northward to Fort Kent. They maintain an extensive network of logging roads for their daily operations, but allow the public to use these to visit the many lakes and mountains. Some roads are open without charge. Others, particularly those managed by North Maine Woods, Inc., in the northwestern part of the state, are tightly controlled through a network of gatehouses. Daily and overnight fees are levied much as they are at national parks. The main logging roads and gatehouses are all detailed in DeLorme's atlas.

Some of the most distinctive private lands in the state are owned and managed by the Maine chapter of The Nature Conservancy. I've included several Nature Conservancy properties in this book and simply can't say enough favorable things about the organization. Since its founding in 1956 (naturalist Rachel Carson was among the nine organizers), the Conservancy has acquired more than 60,000 acres of Maine, from dramatic islands far offshore to untouched inland lakes and their feeder streams. Conservancy holdings are kept wild and managed for wildlife, but the public is invited to visit many of these preserves for day use. (Overnight camping is prohibited, and groups of twelve or more must have advance permission.) I encourage all readers to support the Conservancy's efforts to preserve the state's natural heritage by becoming members ($25 annual dues). The Conservancy also publishes a helpful guide to the more than sixty preserves it currently manages. Write to Maine Chapter, The Nature Conservancy, 14 Maine Street, Suite 401, Brunswick 04011, or call (207) 729–5181.

What's the best season to travel? "Summer" is often used as a verb in Maine, and the state naturally tends to be more crowded during the glorious summer season, when the weather is most reliable. (Summer, incidentally, runs precisely from July 4 to Labor Day.) By coming at another time, you can avoid the crowds and have the place more to yourself. June is an agreeable month to visit Maine's towns and cities, but those with outdoor inclinations will likely find themselves fighting a losing battle against black flies and mosquitoes. The weather and insects tend to be most cooperative in September and early October, when the landscape is at its most spectacular, but these advantages come at a cost. Many of the state's smaller museums and other attractions are open only in July and August.

Visiting in winter also has its benefits. Off-season rates apply throughout much of the state (except near ski areas, of course). Summer tourist destinations, such as Boothbay Harbor and Old Orchard Beach, take on a pleasantly mournful and melancholy look; but the rest of the state displays a local vigor often not visible during the warmer seasons. Greenville and Millinocket become snowmobile meccas, fueling stops for those exploring the state's 3,000-mile snowmobile trail network. Portland's arts and theater season is in full swing. Even Acadia attracts hundreds of visitors who've found John D. Rockefeller's carriage roads an ideal cross-country skiing destination.

No matter when you visit, take your time to enjoy the state fully. The more narrowly you set your sights, the more you're likely to appreciate Maine. Instead of attempting to see all the highlights, pick one or two regions that intrigue you and focus your quest. Find a base and use it to launch unhurried forays into the countryside. You'll be disappointed if you try to view some place like Pemaquid Point through your windshield. Bring a picnic and a book and plan to while away an afternoon. Slowly, the landscape will come alive. You'll begin to notice the patterns in the granite, the lichens on the rocks, the lobstermen working offshore, and the sound of the distant foghorns as the fog begins to roll in. Explorers don't find Maine—Maine finds them. Longtime visitors to the state often return annually to a favorite inn or cabin, developing a rich appreciation of the local natural history and culture year after year. That may be the best way to visit a state that begrudges giving up its best secrets.

Fact Block

- *Maine Tourism Association, P.O. Box 2300, Hallowell 04347, (207) 623–0363, www.mainetourism.com*
- *Major newspapers:* Portland Press Herald, Bangor Daily News
- *Recommended reading for kids:* Charlotte's Web, *by E. B. White;* Blueberries for Sal, *by Robert McCloskey;* Island Boy, *by Barbara Cooney;* Lost on a Mountain in Maine: A Brave Boy's True Story of His Nine-Day Adventure Alone in the Mount Katahdin Wilderness, *by Donn Fendler*
- *Public transportation: Concord Trailways (800) 639–3317 or (617) 426–8080, Vermont Transit (800) 451–3292*
- *Climate overview: average high/low temperatures in Portland: January 31/16, February 32/16, March 40/27, April 50/36, May 61/47, June 72/54, July 76/61, August 74/59, September 68/52, October 58/43, November 45/32, December 34/22*
- *Population: 1,227,928 (1990 Census)*
- *Size: 33,265 square miles (about the size of the rest of New England combined)*
- *Famous Mainers: Vice President Hannibal Hamlin, movie director John Ford, retailer L. L. Bean, poet Henry Wadsworth Longfellow, poet Edna St. Vincent Millay, painter Marsden Hartley, novelist Stephen King, marathoner Joan Benoit*
- *State bird: chickadee*
- *State tree: eastern white pine*
- *State animal: moose*
- *Maine's claim to trivia: only state that borders just one other state; only state with one syllable*
- *Highest point: Mount Katahdin (5,267 feet)*

Southern Maine

You could look for a greater range of terrain and regional character than you'll find in Southern Maine, but there's not much point in it. The region has everything from small coastal harbors to gentle, wooded mountains; from the state's largest city to quiet backwoods hamlets. As with much of the state, the bulk of the population lives along a narrow crescent near the coast. This area was where the ships first deposited early settlers, and where later highway construction made it easiest to live. The main arteries—such as Route 1 and the turnpike—tend to parallel the shoreline, creating a broad transportation corridor with links to Boston and southward. In contrast, traveling east to west (or vice versa) presents something more of a challenge.

Historical attractions are the chief draw of the southern region, and those who delight in early homesteads and cluttered antiques stores will be content here. In addition, this is beach territory, where you can find miles of sandy shorefront to walk and relax on. Of course, you also can swim, but it helps if you're a hardy sort: The ocean temperature tops out at not much more than sixty degrees during the balmiest of days.

York County

A reasonable argument could be made to eliminate coastal York County entirely from this guide. There are few places here that haven't been discovered by tourists, and few places that haven't discovered tourists and oriented themselves to the trade. In fact some years ago one Maine newspaper proposed, presumably in jest, that the state should just give York County to New Hampshire, which would, in exchange, allow Mainers toll-free travel on its turnpike. Maine never acted on this unsolicited advice, but the idea does point up the popular notion that York County has been engulfed by the megalopolis spreading northward from Boston.

This persistent conception notwithstanding, you're likely to find that York County still has plenty to offer, particularly if you take pains to

Southern Maine

117
302
11
107
121
26
495
136
25
302
202
1
Brunswick
Sebago Lake
North Windham
115
95
114
CUMBERLAND CO.
25
302
Gorham
Portland
95
YORK CO.
202
South Portland
4
Scarborough
Old Orchard Beach
Alfred
Biddeford
Saco
Sanford
16
202
Kennebunk
109
4
Kennebunkport
95
Ogunquit
York Village
16
Kittery

NEW HAMPSHIRE
MAINE

ATLANTIC OCEAN

N

0   10 mi
0   10 km

avoid Route 1. The county has a strong historical tradition with roots in the seventeenth and eighteenth centuries, and many of its attractions reflect this early history. Perhaps surprisingly, the inland townships contain inviting hardwood forests as peaceful and remote as you'll find anywhere in the state.

1. **Hamilton House,** Salmon Falls River
2. **Old York Historical Society,** Old York
3. **Laudholm Farm,** Ogunquit area
4. **Seashore Trolley Museum,** north of Kennebunkport
5. **Eastern Promenade Trail,** Portland
6. **Eagle Island,** northern Casco Bay area
7. **Sabbathday Lake Shaker Community,** New Gloucester region

Kittery and Vicinity

Your first encounter with Maine is likely to be at Kittery, which lies just over the I–95 bridge from Portsmouth, New Hampshire. Veer off at exit 3 if you're itching to break out your wallet. A growing number of *factory outlets* cluster along both sides of Route 1, creating a sort of Scylla and Charybdis of consumer culture. More than 120 stores hawk brand-name merchandise ranging from Calvin Klein to Smith and Wesson, and Converse to Crate and Barrel. Bostonians and others searching for bargains throng here throughout the summer, often leading to gridlock and frustration along this stretch of road. Be prepared for long waits if you're trying to make a left turn from a right lane. If you'd rather do your outlet shopping on foot in a village setting, stay on the

Island Wrangle

One of New England's more enduring disputes is the running battle over who owns the Portsmouth Naval Shipyard, which is in Kittery. Or so says Maine. New Hampshire claims otherwise, and efforts to bring the shipyard under its jurisdiction erupt periodically, typically during election years. The dispute dates back to colonial days, when New Hampshire's border was set at the high-water mark of the Piscataqua River on the Maine side. New Hampshire claims the shipyard is on an island and, therefore, in New Hampshire territory. Nonsense, says Maine; it's an extension of the mainland and part of Maine.

It's more than an idle point of debate. New Hampshire workers who commute to the shipyard are required to pay Maine state income tax, something they resent mightily. (New Hampshire has no state income tax.) Wresting control of the shipyard would put an end to this "taxation without representation," Granite Staters say. In one of the more colorful protests a few years ago, disgruntled workers hung a giant tea bag made of bedsheets from the bridge, declaring the start of a new Boston tea party to fight for their rights.

highway and set your sights on Freeport, Maine's other outlet center. It's about an hour north.

One of the shops that launched the Kittery retail boom is the *Kittery Trading Post,* and it's worth a visit if you're coming to Maine for the mountains and lakes. Several levels are filled with rugged merchandise ranging from hiking boots to axes and tents. It's located on Route 1 on your left as you head north up the stripmallplex. Call (888) 587–6246 or 439–2700 for hours and information.

In contrast to the outlet area, Kittery's small downtown has a sleepy, backyard feel, as if it's been overlooked by both travelers and the years. Dominating the town is the venerable Portsmouth Naval Shipyard. The shipyard was established on Dennett's Island in 1806 as the navy's first yard, then expanded to neighboring Seavey Island in 1866. The main entrance is in the middle of Kittery, just beyond the Rice Library, a fine manse of elaborate Victorian brickwork. On the base is the *Naval Shipyard Museum,* which traces the history of the yard. In an immense room in the former enlisted men's barracks, you'll find ship models and naval artifacts from the nineteenth century, including uniforms, shipbuilding tools, and memorabilia from past launchings.

The most interesting exhibits reflect the yard's current central mission of overhauling and rebuilding submarines. Ten large-scale submarine models (up to 6 feet long) are on display, tracing the evolution of the submarine from early concept to advanced seagoing vessel. Other submarine-related items include artifacts recovered from German submarines that surrendered during World War II. The museum is open in the summer Monday through Saturday from 10:00 A.M. to 4:00 P.M. or the rest of the year by appointment. Admission is $3.00 for adults, $1.50 for children; there's a $6 family rate. For more information call 439–3080.

A pair of historic coastal forts on the Maine side of Portsmouth harbor invite exploration as you continue along Route 103. *Fort McClary* has gone through a number of permutations and additions since the bluff was first fortified in 1715. The original fort was expanded and strengthened during the American Revolution, the War of 1812, the Civil War, and then again during the 1898 Spanish-American War. The most prominent building on the twenty-seven-acre site—located amid a labyrinth of earthworks—is a handsome hexagonal wooden blockhouse atop a fieldstone and granite foundation. Built in 1844, it has the distinction of being the last blockhouse constructed in the state. The blockhouse and site are administered as a state memorial and are open daily in summer from 9:00 A.M. to 8:00 P.M. Admission is $1.00; children under 12 are free. For more information call 384–5160.

The remains of **Fort Foster** on nearby Gerrish Island (visible from Fort McClary) are of more contemporary vintage. This early fort was expanded during World War II, when it was used to anchor one end of a massive net stretched across Portsmouth Harbor to keep inquisitive German submarines from prowling around the naval yard. The ninety-acre site, now operated as a park by the town of Kittery, is dotted with hulking concrete walls and towers. Attractive pebbly beaches are set aside for various activities, including scuba diving, windsurfing, and swimming, and a long pier is open to fishing. Picnic tables and sweeping lawns provide dramatic views of lighthouses and an old offshore Coast Guard station, lending the whole area a fine sense of Gothic melodrama.

The town-run park is on the southern tip of Gerrish Island, accessible from the mainland over a small bridge. Look for the sign to Gerrish Island on Route 103 just north of Kittery Point village, then make the first right over the bridge. The park is open daily from June through August from 10:00 A.M. to 7:00 P.M. (weekends only in May and September). Admission is $2.00 for adults and $1.00 for children under 12, plus $2.50 per vehicle. Contact the town parks department for more information at 439–3800.

TOP ANNUAL EVENTS

1. *Old Port Festival,* Portland, early June, 772–6828

2. *La Kermesse Festival,* Biddeford, late June, 282–3909

3. *Yarmouth Clam Festival,* Yarmouth, mid-July, 846–3984

4. *Maine Festival,* Brunswick, late July–early August, 772–9012

5. *Topsham Fair,* Topsham, 725–2735

6. *Sidewalk Art Sale,* Ogunquit, mid-August, 646–2939

7. *Annual Beach Olympics,* Old Orchard Beach, mid-August, 934–2500

8. *Maine Highland Games,* Brunswick, mid-August, 364–3063

9. *Ogunquit Antique Show,* Ogunquit, late September, 646–2939

10. *Maine Brewer's Festival,* Portland, late October, 767–5424

11. *Christmas Prelude,* Kennebunkport, December, 967–0857

Salmon Falls River Valley

Some travelers become so smitten with the coast that they overlook the inland areas. Don't make the same mistake. *Vaughan Woods Memorial,* a 250-acre park 12 miles inland, provides welcome solace from the relative crowding and congestion along the coast. The park is located on a quiet, unspoiled stretch of the Salmon Falls River near South Berwick. Picnic tables are spread about a quiet pine and hemlock grove near the parking area. You can wander the trails down a gentle hill through hemlocks and maples to Cow Cove, where the first cattle in Maine were landed off a ship from Denmark in 1634. (Maine's first permanent settlement was just upstream.) From a riverside bench, take the time to enjoy the picture-perfect view across the cove of what is arguably Maine's most outstanding example of Georgian architecture.

That splendid manor home across the cove is the **Hamilton House.** It's open to the public but not accessible from along the shore. Return to your car and take the first left on Vaughan Lane, then drive to the end and park in the field. Built in 1787 by Colonel Jonathan Hamilton, a successful West Indies trader and merchant from Portsmouth, the house passed through various hands before it was eventually acquired by the Society for the Preservation of New England Antiquities in 1949. With its regal aspect, wonderful proportions, and picturesque setting, the house will impress even those notably uninterested in either architecture or history. The grounds are immaculately maintained and feature a hedge-enclosed garden complete with sundial and unobtrusive bits of classical statuary here and there. Guided tours of the house, offered throughout the summer, reveal a fine collection of Chippendale and Sheraton furniture.

To reach Vaughan Woods and the Hamilton House, turn onto Route 101 (toward New Hampshire) from Route 236, then make an immediate right. Vaughan Woods is 2.7 miles on the left. The park is open daily from 9:00 A.M. to 8:00 P.M. during the summer. Admission is $1.00 for adults; children under 12 are free. For more information call 384–5160 in summer, 624–6075 in the off-season. Hamilton House is open June 1 to October 15 Wednesday to Sunday from 11:00 A.M. to 5:00 P.M. Last tour is at 4:00 P.M. Admission (which includes a guided tour) is $4.00 for adults, $3.50 for seniors, and $2.00 for children ages 6 to 12. Children under 6 are free. For more information call 384–5269.

In the town of South Berwick, stop at the **Sarah Orne Jewett House,** which presides over the main intersection in the middle of town. Jewett died in 1909; she is widely regarded as one of Maine's most accomplished writers and has risen in stature in academia in recent years. Indeed, novelist Willa Cather once wrote that Jewett's *Country of the Pointed Firs* would take its place alongside Mark Twain's *Huckleberry Finn* and Nathaniel Hawthorne's *Scarlet Letter* on the shelf of great American literature. *Country of the Pointed Firs,* a collection of tales of Maine coastal life (Jewett summered in Martinsville in Knox County), remains in print and is available in paperback in many Maine bookstores. Jewett also wrote the novel (now out of print) *The Tory Lover,* which was set at nearby Hamilton House.

The Jewett House, built in 1774, has been fully restored and furnished to reflect the period when the author lived and worked: 1849–1909. It features exceptional detailing, including early wood paneling and some of the original eighteenth-century wallpaper. Like the Hamilton House, the Jewett house is owned by the Society for the Preservation of New England Antiquities, and SPNEA offers tours during the summer. The house is at 101 Portland Street and is open June 1 to October 15 Wednesday to Sunday from 11:00 A.M. to 5:00 P.M. The last tour is at 4:00 p.m. Admission (which includes a guided tour) is $4.00 for adults, $3.50 for seniors, and $2.00 for children ages 6 to 12. Children under 6 are free. For more information call 384–2454.

Be sure also to visit the **Eastman-Jewett House** next door, which is home to the South Berwick Public Library. Except for the addition of dozens of freestanding bookcases, the house has been left largely unchanged from its earlier days. A fire lies kindled in the fireplace, a pendulum clock marks time on the wall, and several rooms have been papered with wallpaper designed after traditional nineteenth-century woodblock prints.

To get your bearings en route back to the coast, consider a detour to the top of **Mount Agamenticus,** a 692-foot hill that may be climbed by foot or ascended by car. Long a navigational landmark for sailors, Agamenticus has a diverse and intriguing history. Aspinquid, a revered Pawtucket Indian who died at the age of 94 in 1692, was said to be buried on this mound in a funeral ceremony that involved the sacrifice of more than 6,000 animals. In recent years the hill has served more prosaic functions as a ski area and a site for radio towers. The state bought most of the hill a few years ago for conservation and recreation. With the communications stations, parking lot, and defunct ski lodge, the summit is a bit cluttered for purists. But never mind that. Scramble up the fire tower and you can enjoy spectacular views westward toward New Hampshire's White Mountains and eastward along the coast from Cape Ann in Massachusetts well up Maine's convoluted shoreline. The summit road is accessible off Agamenticus Road.

The Yorks

Return to the coast and you'll find yourself in the Yorks. Although there's technically only one York, three areas have maintained distinct identities and separate names: York Village, York Harbor, and York Beach. As travelers soon discover, each town has its own particular personality.

Historians are invariably drawn to York Village, where they find one of the finest collections of historic buildings open to the public in the state of Maine. First settled around 1630, York Village is a peaceful town of tree-lined streets, with few intrusions from the modern age. The *Old York Historical Society* maintains seven historic buildings scattered between the York River and York Street, and each has a distinct flavor and intriguing past. Visitors set their own pace in exploring the local history, wandering by foot or car from one building to the next, or taking a break for rubbings of the early tombstones at the Old Burying Ground.

Among the buildings open to the public is the Old Gaol, built in 1719 to house both debtors and hardened criminals. Constructed of fieldstone walls more than 2 feet thick, the jail, which was in use until 1860, is considered the oldest public building in the United States. The building has been a museum since 1900, and today the cells, dungeon, and gaoler's quarters are furnished as they might have been around 1790.

Next door is the Emerson-Wilcox House, the original portion of which was built in the mid-eighteenth century. Over the years additions were built, and you can trace the history of early American architecture during a tour with a knowledgeable guide.

Other historic York buildings include Jefferds Tavern, a public house dating from 1759, and the nearby Old Schoolhouse, with its furnishings circa 1745. Along the York River you'll find the John Hancock warehouse and wharf, once owned by the famous signer of the Declaration of Independence. In the words of one historian, Hancock was "more successful in politics than in business." This wharf, restored in 1950 after a long and lackluster history, is York's only commercial building. Just across the river is the Elizabeth Perkins house, which reopened in 1998 after a yearlong restoration.

The Old York buildings are open Tuesday through Sunday early June through late September (a limited weekend schedule may be offered in spring and late fall; call first). Hours are 10:00 A.M. to 5:00 P.M. (1:00 to 5:00 P.M. on Sundays). One ticket provides admission to all buildings and may be purchased at any of the properties. Adults are $7.00, children $3.00. For more information call 363–4974.

In the village center, look also for *York Village Crafts and Antiques* in the handsome 1834 church at 211 York Street. About 150 antiques dealers and craftspeople maintain booths here, selling a whole array of items. It's open daily April through December from 9:30 A.M. to 5:00 P.M. and January to March Thursday to Sunday from 10:00 A.M. to 5:00 P.M. For more information call 363–4830.

Just downstream from York Village (or a short drive east on Route 1A), you'll come to York Harbor, as gracious and sophisticated as York Village but with a slightly more modern flair in architecture and tone. Take a break from history and stretch your legs along the waterfront walking path. If you head south on Route 103, you'll soon see on your right *"Wiggly Bridge,"* said to be the smallest suspension bridge in the world. Park along the road and follow the path across this unique footbridge to enjoy a quiet walk through the woods on the far bank. The trail loops back along Barrel Mill Pond; or more ambitious hikers may continue on, walking on dirt roads to Lindsay Road near Hancock Wharf in York Village.

Heading along the path the other way will take you along York Harbor's waterfront to Harbor Beach, where the modern Stage Neck Inn occupies a prominent bluff overlooking the harbor's mouth. The path is narrow and quiet, a world removed from the present day. If your appetite demands more historic buildings, visit the *Sayward-Wheeler House,* owned by the Society for the Preservation of New England Antiquities. This fine merchant's home was built in the 1760s and offers a grand view of the harbor. Inside look for the chinaware Captain Jonathan Sayward hauled back from the successful 1745 battle against the French at Louisbourg. The mansion's well-maintained grounds are the first you cross when you head eastward on the path from Route 103. The building also is accessible from Barrel Lane. It's open June through mid-October on Saturdays and Sundays from 11:00 A.M. to 5:00 P.M. Tours are held on the hour (last tour at 4:00 P.M.) and cost $4.00 for adults, $3.50 for seniors, and $2.00 for children. For more information contact the SPNEA regional office in New Hampshire at (603) 436–3205.

If you're enjoying the walking so far, continue past Harbor Beach to the *Cliff Walk,* a dramatic shoreline trail that hugs rocky crags and provides excellent views of the harsh coastline and the splendid nineteenth-century summer homes along the way. The trail crosses private land but is open to the public within certain limitations (e.g., no radio playing, no picnicking, no bus tours). The trail, which may be rough going for those with unsure footing, also provides access to several small, pebbly beaches. The trail begins at the end of Harbor Beach Road, where you'll find parking for about twenty cars.

Northward up the coast, York Beach has a more laid-back feeling than other stretches. The pleasant seaside town draws its history more from the late nineteenth century than from the colonial era, and it is more raucous and less polished. A once popular destination for urban dwellers seeking to elude the summer heat, York Beach still retains a dated honky-tonk flavor, one that has been tempered somewhat by recent gentrification. Long Sands Beach is south of famous **Nubble Light** (look for it as you drive up Route 1A) and offers metered parking along the road. North of the lighthouse is Short Sands Beach, which fronts the town (metered parking is available adjacent to the beach in a lot that tends to fill early). York Beach also offers the usual shorefront amusements, including the Fun-O-Rama arcade, palm readers, and candlepin bowling—all pleasant diversions for sunburnt or restless beachgoers.

A short walk from the beach is York's **Wild Kingdom Zoo and Amusement Park,** which has a small collection of animals and a selection of low-key amusement park rides, including a bumper car pavilion and a small roller coaster. General admission includes the zoo and all rides and costs $13.75 for adults, $9.75 for children 4 to 10, and $3.50 for children 3 and under. Tickets also are available separately for rides and zoo. The park is open Memorial Day to Labor Day. For more information call (800) 456–4911.

Ogunquit Area

North of York Beach is Ogunquit, a pleasant seaside town that was "discovered" by urban artists from New York and Boston, who in turn attracted the gentry. That now-familiar process began over a century ago, but Ogunquit still retains its artistic flavor (galleries abound) and remains an exceedingly popular seaside destination. The town brims with motels, restaurants, souvenir shops, and self-styled "resorts," but to its credit it has managed to retain the character of a more restful era. This notwithstanding, if you come during the peak season, plan to spend a lot of time stewing in traffic and dodging crowds. Ogunquit appears to be on the verge of strangling on its own success as a destination. If you can time it, a visit during the shoulder seasons—spring or fall—will be far more relaxing.

The best way to enjoy Ogunquit is to park your car and leave it for the duration, spending your time traveling by foot. And the best way to see the sea is along **Marginal Way,** a winding footpath donated to the town in 1923 by a farmer who used the route to usher his cattle to summer pasture. Today strollers, sunbathers, and hikers are far more common than cows. Venture out early in the morning or later in the evening to avoid trail gridlock. (Be aware that some two million people walk the trail each year, making this arguably Maine's most beaten path.)

Parking for the trail may be found near the town police station on Cottage Street. More ambitious walkers could make a day of it by parking farther up the coast at Footbridge Beach (turn off Route 1 on Ocean Street). From there ramble your way along the water's sandy edge southward for about a mile to the village's main beach. Cross the bridge on Beach Street into the center of Ogunquit for lunch at any of the town's eateries, then resume your walk after lunch.

Pick up the main pathway across from Seacastles Resort on Shore Road. The route meanders away from the sandy strand and along the twisting, rocky shoreline for the next mile, with benches well placed for reading, relaxing, or restful contemplation. In places you'll find yourself surrounded by wild roses or beneath a delicate canopy of cedar trees. Take the time to scramble down to the shore's edge, where you can explore tide pools and the rugged coastal geology.

The pathway ends at **Perkins Cove,** a picturesque and well-protected harbor clotted with fishing boats and pleasure craft. The cove is a popular tourist destination and boasts more than its fair share of jewelry stores, crafts shops, and restaurants. Parking is a perpetual problem (something not afflicting those arriving by foot). Be sure to investigate the pedestrian footbridge that crosses the harbor's entrance. When a tall-masted sailboat needs to enter or depart, it blasts its horn and whoever happens to be handy raises the narrow bridge by pressing a series of buttons.

For one of the area's finest meals, look around Perkins Cove for **Hurricane,** a classy eatery with one of the better ocean views in the state. The small restaurant serves lunch and dinner (reservations are essential for dinner), but it has an attractive, tiny bar area if you're looking for a sip of something and a light snack. For reservations call 646–6348.

To return to your car, board one of the **trolley buses** that stop frequently at Perkins Cove. These modern gas-powered trolleys are operated as a nonprofit venture by the chamber of commerce and feature detailing of brass, oak, and leather. The fare is $1.00 for adults, 50 cents for children under 12, which you deposit in the wooden box next to the driver. The trolleys run through the center of Ogunquit and as far as Footbridge Beach, with numerous stops in between. Between July and Labor Day the trolley operates from 8:00 A.M. to 11:00 P.M. daily. During the "shoulder" seasons, starting in late May and extending through Columbus Day, the trolley operates until 9:00 P.M.

North of Ogunquit, just past the town of Wells, you'll find the **Wells National Estuarine Research Reserve,** a coastal wildlife refuge that's evolving and growing as new parcels are added. Assembled through local private initiative, the reserve's thousands of acres of coastal marsh and forested uplands are managed as a wildlife sanctuary and for scientific research. The reserve includes 1,600 acres of privately owned land at Laudholm Farm, 4,000 acres of federal land managed as the Rachel Carson National Wildlife Refuge, and additional acreage that supporters hope will someday emerge as Laudholm State Park, but as yet remains undeveloped.

Laudholm Farm provides the setting for an enchanting walk through both complex ecosystems and a long-gone era. Once maintained as a summer residence by George C. Lord, a prominent New England railroad tycoon, this historic saltwater farm is now owned by the Laudholm Trust, which acquired the land in 1986 with donations from nearly 2,500 people. The trust manages the property, maintains research facilities, and offers naturalist programs for students and the public alike. The centerpiece of the property is a majestic Victorian farmhouse with graceful barns and outbuildings. The farm complex perches on a gentle rise amid

From Chippendale to "Chipped"

*T*he 50 miles or so of Route 1 between York and Scarborough are a mecca of sorts for shoppers who aren't happy unless the stuff they buy is a half-century old or older. Along this stretch are some two dozen antiques shops, ranging from the ineffably classy to those just a notch or two above "junk shop."

On the higher end is the wonderful **R. Jorgensen Antiques,** which displays fine examples of early American and European furniture in an unimpeachably restored early home and a modern outbuilding. The shop is at 502 Post Road (Route 1); for more information call 646–9444.

Another great spot for browsing, with a selection less ethereal than at Jorgensen's, is farther north at **Antiques USA,** on Route 1 in Kennebunk. Dozens of dealers stock this sprawling, Wal-Mart–sized shop with all manner of stuff. This is the best destination if you like rooting around for undiscovered deals. It's open all through the year except major holidays. Call 985–7766.

At the northern end of antiques row is the fine **Centervale Farm** on Route 1 in Scarborough. Unlike many other Route 1 shops, which are mini malls offering the merchandise of various dealers, Centervale is a single but sizable shop. The offerings include early American and Mission-style furniture, with a whole mess of other collectibles. It's open daily except Monday; for more information call 883–3443.

open fields, providing views down the coast toward Ogunquit. Nature guides and trail maps are available in the visitor center in the farmhouse.

The farm has 7 miles of trails for wandering through fields, forests, and along boardwalks through coastal wetlands. You even might take a swim at the quiet barrier beach, which is a 0.75-mile walk through meadow and forest and past several summer homes. Pick up an interpretive pamphlet for the Knight Trail, a fine introduction to the local habitat. Bird-watchers will be delighted in the mix of terrain hereabouts: Some 250 species have been observed within the reserve itself. If you're without a clue about the flora and fauna you're looking at, sign up for one of the guided naturalist tours offered throughout the year.

In July and August, parking at the trust is $5.00 per car; the remainder of the year parking is free. There is no charge to enter the grounds, which are open from 8:00 A.M. to 5:00 P.M. daily. The visitor center is open Monday through Saturday from 10:00 A.M. to 4:00 P.M. and Sundays from noon to 4:00 P.M. To reach Laudholm Farm, turn right off Route 1 on Laudholm Farm Road at the blinking light just north of Harding Books. Turn left at the fork and then make the next right into the farm's entrance. For more information call 646–1555.

Just north of Laudholm Farm is the headquarters of the *Rachel Carson National Wildlife Refuge,* named after the crusading biologist and author, who spent many of her summers in Maine exploring tidal waters. Appropriately enough, Carson also worked for the wildlife service, which manages this property. The refuge consists of nine parcels along the southern coast (when acquisitions are complete, more than seven thousand acres will be protected), but very little of it has been developed for visitors.

At the refuge headquarters, you'll find a mile-long nature trail offering a good introduction to the salt-marsh ecosystem. The Carson Trail skirts the edge of a fine marsh, with informative educational stations along the way. Stop at the main kiosk near the parking area and pick up a free trail map and brochure. The refuge headquarters is open from dawn to dusk throughout the year. The trail is located on Route 9 just off Route 1. For more information contact refuge headquarters at 646–9226.

The Kennebunks

Kennebunkport, a slumbering seaside town long known for its elegant inns and bed-and-breakfasts, found itself thrust into the national spotlight when George Bush was elected president in 1988.

Bush, whose family has been part of the Kennebunkport social season for decades, still summers at the house built by his grandfather at Walker Point, a dramatic peninsula jutting out into the Gulf of Maine. The Bush presence continues to draw tourists to the town, and parking is problematic near Dock Square in the center of town. Spaces tend to be available on side streets at some distance from the center.

On Main Street looking down toward Dock Square is **Nott House.** This impressive home, constructed in 1853, will please anyone interested in America during the Victorian era. When Elizabeth Nott gave the house to the local historical society in 1983, it was with the proviso that nothing be changed. Her stipulation was actually a continuation of a policy her family maintained for years. The place still boasts the original wallpaper, carpeting, and furnishings, creating a virtual time capsule of Victorian life. Guided tours last thirty to forty minutes and are offered from mid-June to mid-October between 1:00 and 4:00 P.M. Tuesday through Saturday from 10:00 A.M. to 1:00 P.M. The cost is $5.00 for adults, $2.00 for children under 18. The historical society also offers walking tours of Kennebunkport Thursday at 1:30 P.M. These last about one hour and cost $3.00 per person. For more information contact the historical society at 967–2751.

The handsome inland town of Kennebunk, located 3.5 miles from the port on Routes 35 and 9A, offers a slower pace and less of a seasonal ebb and flow. Between the port and the town, on Summer Street, you'll pass through the Kennebunk Historic District with its fine examples of grand nineteenth-century architecture. Be sure to note the "wedding cake house," a flamboyant building that resembles, well, a wedding

Tom's Better Tube of Toothpaste

*W*hen American troops invaded Panama some years ago to oust dictator Manuel Noriega, they found in the general's palace a tube of toothpaste from **Tom's of Maine.** Word does get around. This small, socially responsible firm, founded and still run by Tom and Kate Chappell, specializes in natural toothpastes made without artificial sweeteners (Chappell also makes natural mouthwashes, dental ribbon, shampoos, and deodorants). The toothpaste flavors tend toward the offbeat and include "cinnamint," spearmint, and fennel. Commoners and dictators alike often find it hard to go back to their old brands once they've tried Tom's. The outlet shop, located downtown in a rehabbed factory building called the Lafayette Center, sells factory seconds (read: slightly crumpled toothpaste tubes) at a healthy discount. It's open Monday through Saturday from 10:00 A.M. to 5:00 P.M. For more information call 985–3874.

cake. The story is that a local sea captain rushed to sea before a proper cake could be baked for his new bride. This ornate house, which he had built upon his return, was his way of making amends. You'll know which one it is when you pass by.

The Brick Store Museum, located at 117 Main Street, was founded in 1936 by Edith Cleaves Barry on the second floor of an 1825 brick store. The modest museum showcasing local history since has expanded down the block and now includes the adjacent three buildings. Despite its growth the place remains quite intimate and personal. Three or four special historical exhibits are presented each year in the first-floor galleries. Permanent collections are housed on the second floor and include maritime paintings, ship models, and early-nineteenth-century portraits and furnishings. The museum is open June through December Tuesday through Friday from 10:00 A.M. to 4:30 P.M. Admission is $5.00 for adults, $2.00 for students; children under 7 are free. For more information call 985–4802.

The *Seashore Trolley Museum,* located just north of Kennebunkport, may sound a bit dull to the uninitiated. It's easy to imagine a handful of well-polished, lifeless streetcars housed in a trim building on a well-scrubbed, concrete floor. But do yourself a favor and check this out. It's anything but clean and trim. The museum is a lively, thriving scrap yard where operating streetcars wind their way through heaps of rusting metal and piles of railroad ties. Wandering the grounds induces a sense of continual wonderment.

The museum, founded in 1939, contains the world's largest collection of streetcars, most of which have been restored and now are maintained by a cadre of two hundred volunteers, including many local retirees with a

Seashore Trolley Museum, Kennebunkport

penchant for tinkering. The museum owns streetcars from New Orleans, Glasgow, Montreal, Rome, San Francisco, Budapest, and a number of towns in Maine. Each of the two hundred or so cars on the lot (of which forty run regularly) evokes a subtle nostalgia, even in those of us too young to remember the era when you could travel the entire eastern seaboard connecting one trolley line with the next. Some of the early cars still have the old advertising posters mounted inside. Most are housed in two corrugated metal sheds that produce a wonderfully cacophonous rattle when a breeze kicks up.

Admission includes unlimited rides along a 2-mile track through the woods. Be sure to visit the restoration shop, where new cars are overhauled when they arrive. (Average restoration time is four to seven years.) The gift shop offers an unrivaled selection of postcards, books, and other items related to streetcars.

The museum is 3.2 miles north of Kennebunkport on North Street; it's open from early May through mid-November. During peak season (July and August) the museum is open daily from 10:00 A.M. to 5:00 P.M.; limited hours during the shoulder seasons. Admission is $7.00 for adults, $4.50 for children ages 6 to 16, and free for children under 6. Maximum charge per family is $22. For more information call 967–2712.

Old Orchard Beach and Vicinity

Traveling anywhere in northern Maine or New Hampshire, you're likely to come across a sign pointing the way to *Old Orchard Beach,* located near the twin towns of Saco and Biddeford. This aggressive signing isn't the result of a hyperactive chamber of commerce. Thousands of French Canadians conduct annual pilgrimages to this lively beach town and its 7 miles of sandy oceanfront, and you're as likely to hear French spoken here as English. Old Orchard is best known for its profusion of amusements, nausea-inducing rides, games of chance and skill, and foods cooked in oil. Among the attractions just off the beach is *Palace Playland,* which claims to be New England's largest pinball and video arcade. If you're an aficionado of the garish, plan to stroll after dark, when the beachfront fully displays its brilliant neon plumage.

Just over a mile to the south of Old Orchard on Route 9, you'll come to a suburb that has a decidedly different disposition. *Ocean Park* was founded in 1880 by the Centennial Conference of Free Will Baptists as an educational summer resort. In a stately grove of pines several blocks from the ocean, you'll find the three pleasing buildings from the colony's early days clustered on the north side of Temple Street near the intersection of Royal Street. Of particular interest is the Temple, an octagonal wooden structure representing an architectural style that was once highly popular. The building, based on plans purchased for $27, was dedicated in August 1881 and has been in continuous use by congregants ever since.

Nearby in Saco is the **York Institute,** one of the region's best small museums. Well-designed displays highlight early life in Southern Maine, with a particular emphasis on the late eighteenth and early nineteenth centuries. Founded in 1870, the museum features a colonial kitchen, an eighteenth-century bedroom, and an early printing press. An exceptional collection of paintings is also on display, including a fine selection of portraits. The museum is located at 371 Main Street in Saco, and admission is $4.00 for adults, $3.00 for seniors, $1.00 for students, and $10.00 for families. Children under 6 are free. Open year-round Sunday, Tuesday, Wednesday, and Friday from noon to 4:00 P.M., Thursday from noon to 8:00 P.M. For more information call 283–0684.

Carousel Lost

Until 1996 Old Orchard Beach was famed for its antique carousel, which was the centerpiece of Palace Playland, the amusement park on the beach. The vintage 1910 merry-go-round was built in Philadelphia and provided endless hours of amusement for the very young, the very old, and just about everyone in between. In the end, the attraction succumbed to the mania for collecting. Given the skyrocketing price for circus memorabilia, the owners realized that it was just too valuable to earn its keep at $1.00 a ride. If split up and sold individually, the handsome wooden horses could bring as much as $600,000. Happily the old building remains, and it is now home to a new herd of fiberglass animals that have all the color—if only a fraction of the character—of the old horses.

Inland York County

F ar from the coast, in a wooded valley in the northwest part of the county, you'll find **Willowbrook at New-field,** a historic village that offers visitors a glimpse of late-nineteenth-century Maine. The museum opened in 1970 and consists of thirty-seven structures, including original homes and replicas of early buildings. The collections are extensive and broad, with virtually everything originating within 100 miles of the museum. Many of the items on display have been splendidly restored and refinished to their original luster, as if just from the shop of the craftsman.

The displays include sixty carriages and horse-drawn sleighs, an opulent 1849 Concord coach commissioned by a Bath sea captain, and an 1894 Armitage-Herschell carousel with the original organ. (The carousel operates, but rides aren't allowed.) A fine bicycle collection includes a curious tandem bicycle; it allows both front and back riders to steer, a mechanism that gives some pause. The centerpiece of the village is the 1835 William Duggin house, furnished in that fussy Victorian style preferred by better families everywhere in the late nineteenth century. There's also a late-nineteenth-century ice-cream parlor and a general store with penny candy.

The emphasis at Willowbrook is on the late nineteenth century, but the one exhibit that may stick in your mind longest is Frank Skrobach's "roadable and garageable airplane," dating from the 1930s. Skrobach was an upstate New York inventor who keenly perceived that the main flaw of the airplane was its large wingspan: A pilot couldn't land on a highway since another plane might be coming the other way and they'd clip one another. Skrobach set about to remedy that. The result was an airplane with a 6-foot wingspan. Attached to a 21-foot zeppelin-shaped fuselage are not one but six pairs of wings. Diagrams show how the aerodynamics are supposed to work. In several early trials with a forty-five-horsepower engine, however, Skrobach's dream never got off the ground. Engineering students who've looked it over in recent years think the prototype would fly if equipped with a ninety-horsepower engine, but no flight tests are scheduled.

Willowbrook at Newfield is located just off Route 11 in Newfield. (The turn is well marked.) The village is open between May 15 and September 30, from 10:00 A.M. to 5:00 P.M. daily. Admission is $8.00 for adults, $4.00 for students, free for children under 6. For more information call 793–2784.

Cumberland County

Cumberland County is the most populous (around 250,000 residents), the wealthiest, and the most densely settled of Maine's counties. In some areas Cumberland flirts with a suburban tone, but generally it manages to retain its essential woodland character. In this the county is aided and abetted by miles of wooded shoreline along Casco Bay and by the dense forests in the hills around Sebago Lake, the state's second largest body of water.

Greater Portland

Portland, you'll read here and elsewhere, is the state's largest city. Don't be fooled by this "state's largest" business. It's still a small city, a pleasure to visit, and a fine place to live. The city proper has a population

Horse-drawn milk wagon, Willowbrook at Newfield

of only 65,000 or so, making it about one-fifth as populous as Toledo, Ohio. If you count the surrounding communities, the metropolitan area climbs to only about 125,000, still small by national standards. Despite the relatively low head count, Portland has a brisk urban feel that eludes many cities several times its size. That's due in large part to its location on a peninsula, which forced early builders to grow upwards rather than outwards. And Portland's urbanity transcends mere appearances. Today the city boasts its own symphony, a superb art museum, several theater groups, and an array of art galleries and excellent restaurants.

Visitors invariably gravitate first to the *Old Port* near the waterfront, an area of brick sidewalks and cobblestoned streets chock-full of boutiques, bars, T-shirt shops, and ice cream emporiums. These narrow streets blossomed during rediscovery and renewal in the late 1970s, when the run-down area was spruced up from sidewalk to cornice. Take some time to walk around the Old Port and investigate the extravagant late-nineteenth-century brickwork on the buildings. If it seems somewhat uniform, it is; Portland's downtown was devastated by fire in 1866 and rebuilt shortly afterwards. Note that the dates on many of the buildings read 1867 or thereabouts.

The Old Port wears its charm on its sleeve, but the rest of the city's intrigue is somewhat more subtle. On upper Congress Street, Portland's main artery of commerce, visit the *Neal Dow Memorial,* a wonderful 1829 brick home preserved in memory of the man instrumental in bringing prohibition to Maine. Dow, who was born in Portland, grew up in a town that thrived on the rum trade with the West Indies. The obvious ill effects of "demon rum" on the city streets led Dow to become a lifelong temperance leader, and over time he became a surprisingly effective lobbyist. In 1851, virtually singlehandedly, Dow managed to usher through the state legislature a bill that effectively banned the sale of spirits in Maine. The campaign brought him political prominence and propelled him into the office of mayor of Portland. Not surprisingly his actions also brought him a number of enemies. When touring the house, ask to see where local agitators tried to beat down the rear door to discuss some of their grievances with Mr. Dow.

When he died in 1897 (long after surviving a Civil War ordeal as a captured Union general at the age of 58), Dow bequeathed the mansion and its contents to the Maine Women's Christian Temperance Union, which still maintains offices on the second floor. The union offers free tours of the first floor, which is kept up much as it was when Dow lived here. The shelves are lined with Dow's books on the evils of alcohol, and the several rooms are graced with a fine collection of priceless antiques. Another small room contains relics and artifacts from Dow's Civil War days.

The Dow Memorial, at 714 Congress Street, is open Monday through Friday from 11:00 A.M. to 4:00 P.M. Call 773–7773.

If the city's range of architecture intrigues you, consider a walking tour through one of several historic neighborhoods. *Greater Portland Landmarks,* a nonprofit group credited with curbing many of the excesses of urban renewal in recent decades, has produced a series of brochures highlighting four historic areas. One area is the Western Promenade, where the city's grandest homes stand on a bluff looking westward toward the White Mountains. The mansions range from Gothic to Italianate to shingle style, making the area a virtual catalog of nineteenth-century architectural styles. Around Bowdoin Street, note the grand shingle-style homes designed by renowned Portland architect John Calvin Stevens, including numbers 36, 40, 44, and 52.

Other walking tour brochures are available for the Old Port, State Street, and Congress Street. The cost is $1.00 each. Greater Portland Landmarks' headquarters is at 165 State Street and is open from 9:00 A.M. to 5:00 P.M. Monday through Friday. For more information call 774–5561.

Easily the most extravagant home in Portland is the *Morse-Libby House,* known locally as the Victoria Mansion. Built of brownstone in an exuberant interpretation of the Italianate villa style, the mansion was constructed between 1859 and 1863 for Ruggles Sylvester Morse, a Maine native who made his fortune in the New Orleans hotel trade. The exterior is solid and imposing, a layered grouping of towers and blocks with overhanging eaves. Inside, virtually no space has been left unadorned. Eleven Italian artists were employed to paint murals and trompe l'oeil scenes on the walls and ceilings; the staircases contain 400 hand-carved mahogany balusters. The dark, brooding rooms are filled with marble fireplaces and ornate chandeliers; stained glass brightens some of the darkness. Preservationists managed to forestall demolition of this gem (to make room for a gas station, no less) in 1940; the house is now administered by the Victoria Society of Maine.

Guided tours are offered between May and October Tuesday through Saturday from 10:00 A.M. to 4:00 P.M. and Sunday from 1:00 to 5:00 P.M. Tours begin at fifteen and forty-five minutes past the hour. Admission is $6.00 for adults and $3.00 for children under 18. The mansion is at 109 Danforth Street between State and High Streets. For more information call 772–4841.

A decidedly less opulent homestead is located not far away on busy Congress Street near Monument Square. The *Wadsworth-Longfellow House* was built in 1785–1786 by General Peleg Wadsworth, a Revolutionary War officer and grandfather of Portland's most celebrated native son, Henry Wadsworth Longfellow. The poet spent his childhood in this house, which is as austere and simple as the Victoria Mansion is unrestrained. This was originally a two-story house, but its gabled roof was destroyed and a third story and hip roof were added in 1815, creating a solid Federal appearance. Both the house and the gardens behind it are open to the public. The rooms are filled with furniture and documents related to the lives of the Wadsworths and the Longfellows.

Immediately behind the home are the library and offices of the Maine Historical Society, where you can indulge in genealogical research (there's a small fee for nonmembers). The *Center for Maine History* is in the boxy, modern structure on the other side of the home. (Built in the 1980s by a bank, it tends to crop up in surveys of Portland's least favorite buildings.) The center has changing exhibits of artifacts and documents related to Maine's rich history.

The Longfellow House and Center for Maine History are at 485–489 Congress Street and are open June through October from 10:00 A.M. to

4:00 P.M. The cost to tour the house and visit the gallery is $5.00 for adults, $1.00 for children under 12. The gallery alone is $2.00 for adults. For more information call 772–1807.

Continuing eastward on Congress Street you'll begin a climb up Munjoy Hill and soon see the unique *Portland Observatory,* on the crest near a fire station. This handsome conical building with a cupola atop was constructed in 1807 by Captain Lemuel Moody, and today it is the last signal tower remaining on the East Coast. Manned for many years by Moody himself, the wooden observatory was used to sight incoming cargo ships well before they pulled into the harbor. Once the ships were spotted, the observer would hoist the ship's flags atop the building to alert the town of its impending arrival. When it was built, the 86-foot-high observatory occupied an open, treeless hill used for political rallies, circuses, and public hangings. Today it is surrounded by an unassuming neighborhood of low apartment buildings and small shops.

The observatory is at 138 Congress Street. Sadly, voracious insects have gotten to the building and have seriously weakened the supporting timbers. It's been closed to the public in recent years, but plans call for it to reopen following a campaign to save it. Check with Portland Landmarks at 774–5561 to find out if it has reopened by the time you visit.

The view from atop the observatory is the best in town, but lacking that, head to the *Eastland Hotel* at 157 High Street, at the corner of Congress Street. This old brick hotel dates back to the early twentieth century and has since been marketed under various national franchises, including Radisson and Sonesta, and has suffered from financial woes. If it's open, head to the rooftop lounge for a libation and a panoramic view of the city. It's nice at sunset, when you can watch the sun sink over the distant White Mountains, and the islands in Casco Bay take on a coppery glow.

The view from above may have stirred some curiosity about those islands just off Portland's docks. Although several of the islands with year-round inhabitants—including Great and Little Diamond, Peaks, and Cliff—are within Portland city limits, the pace is decidedly slower and the landscapes are far more rural than urban.

Most of the islands enjoyed their heyday as summer destinations for middle-class vacationers a century ago, and the architecture reflects that heritage. There's typically a general store and maybe a small restaurant on each island, but little else. Most are still predominantly summer destinations with the exception of Peaks Island, which has become something of an island suburb; many of its inhabitants commute twenty minutes by ferry to jobs in the city. Chebeague Island, at 2,400 acres, is the largest and offers fine bicycling terrain. Cliff Island is the farthest from town (over an hour by ferry) and has the most convincing lost-in-time atmosphere.

Frequent ferry service is offered throughout the summer to all islands; visitors can disembark with a picnic lunch to wander about and return on a later boat, or they can simply enjoy the passing water view from benches on the upper deck. The ferry terminal is located at the State Pier at the corner of Franklin and Commercial Streets. For more information call Casco Bay Lines at 774–7871.

Along the waterfront on the city's eastern end is a striking recreational pathway. The *Eastern Promenade Trail* departs from near the ferry terminal and curves a little over a mile around the base of flinty cliffs with great views out toward the islands and Fort Gorges, that hulking stone fortress that rises out of the harbor just offshore. It's a popular spot for strolling or bike riding; plans call to link this pathway with the equally popular *Back Cove Pathway.* That pathway loops around a tidal cove for 3.5 miles; it's teeming with runners and power walkers after work.

If you're wondering about the train tracks that parallel the promenade trail, that's part of the *Maine Narrow Gauge Railroad Co. and Museum.* The museum features a collection of locomotives and coaches dating from earlier in this century, when a number of "two-footer" rail lines were built to link communities that couldn't justify a full-sized train line. You can learn about the history of the small trains in the equally small museum, then take a short ride out along the tracks for views of the bay while gently rocking along.

The museum is open daily from 10:00 A.M. to 4:00 P.M. year-round; trains run daily in summer starting at 11:00 A.M. Admission to the museum is free; train rides are $5.00 for adults, $3.00 for children.

The Old Port is your best bet for browsing boutiques, where you can find everything from old stained glass to new books. Among the notable shops is *Maine Potters Market* at 376 Fore Street smack in the middle of the Old Port. This artists' cooperative sells a variety of beautiful handcrafted bowls, dishes, and lamps. Call 774–1633.

If you're staying the night, Portland's classiest inn is indisputably the *Pomegranate Inn,* a six-room bed-and-breakfast in the city's tony West End. The inn's Italianate architecture is distinctive in this neighborhood of grand homes, but innkeeper Isabel Smiles has made the interior into a quiet fantasy—part high Victorian, part Red Grooms. Faux finishes, striking furniture, and surprising flourishes embellish the interior, making it at once both exotic and comfortable. Rates during the summer are $135 and up, including a fine breakfast. The inn is at 49 Neal Street; call 772–1006.

Baseball fans should plan to stick around to take in a game with the Portland Sea Dogs, the double-A team affiliated with the 1997 World Series–winning Florida Marlins. The team has been based here since 1994, and its players have included baseball stars catcher Charlie Johnson, who was here one year, and shortstop Edgar Renterria, who played here two summers.

Games are played at the frequently sold-out 6,000-seat *Hadlock Field,* an intimate stadium built between railroad tracks and the brick Portland Expo building. A game here has the nostalgic feel of old-time baseball, and you can actually hear the players talk among themselves on the field. Come early if you have general admission seats so you don't end up way down the left field line.

Hadlock Field is located at 271 Park Avenue, just off I–295. Parking is challenging during games; shuttle buses serve the stadium from downtown Portland and satellite parking lots. Tickets are $4.00 to $6.00. Order tickets by phone at 879–9500.

Cape Elizabeth Area

J ust across the harbor in South Portland you'll find the small but intriguing *Portland Harbor Museum,* located in the brick ordnance repair shop of former Fort Preble (1808–1950). This harborside museum features exhibits on local sea culture and history, and through its rotating exhibits and permanent displays about nineteenth-century shipbuilding it provides some insight into the workings of the waterfront. In particular you'll learn about the Liberty Ship era during World War II, when 236 of the ships were built in South Portland.

The Portland Harbor Museum is open mid-May to mid-December. From mid-May through June and during September the museum is open Friday to Sunday from 1:00 to 4:00 P.M. In July and August it's open Monday to Friday from 1:00 to 4:00 P.M. and Saturday and Sunday from 10:30 A.M. to 4:00 P.M. October to December it's open Saturday and Sunday from 1:00 to 4:00 P.M. Admission is $2.00 for adults; children under 12 are free. The museum is on the campus of the Southern Maine Technical College at the end of Fort Road. Follow Broadway from South

Portland to the marina, then turn right on Pickett Street. Fort Road is about 100 yards on the left. For more information call 799–6337.

Not far from Spring Point is another museum with a maritime theme. The *Museum at Portland Head Light* is located in the former keeper's quarters of a lighthouse commissioned by George Washington. This venerable and handsome structure stands on a rocky promontory at the edge of a grassy park. It was completed in 1791 and occupied continuously until 1989; then the light was automated and the keeper's house decommissioned. The house and grounds have a rich history, including frequent visits by Henry Wadsworth Longfellow, who befriended the keepers and often walked here from Portland.

The museum features displays and interpretive exhibits on the history of lighthouses and navigation through the ages. You'll learn about how mariners found their way along coasts from early Egypt to current times, when satellites have largely taken the place of the traditional visual guides. The museum's six rooms also include displays on regional history and commerce. The light tower itself, one of four nationwide that were commissioned by George Washington and have never been rebuilt, is still owned and operated by the Coast Guard and is not open to the public. Plan to bring a picnic when you visit; stunning views across open ocean and the islands of southern Casco Bay may be had from the grassy fields of surrounding Fort Williams Park, which has several picnic tables and charcoal grills. The grounds are open daily from sunrise to 8:30 P.M.

The museum is operated by the town of Cape Elizabeth and is open on weekends in April and May, then daily June to October 31. Open from 10:00 A.M. to 4:00 P.M. Admission is $2.00 for adults and $1.00 for children ages 6 to 18. For more information call 799–2661.

Northern Casco Bay

The state of Maine has a huge and helpful tourist information center in Yarmouth, just off I–95 at exit 17. Across from the center in the large, corporate, brick building is the *DeLorme Map Store,* a highly recommended stop for map nuts or travelers of any stripe. The DeLorme company began as a supplier of detailed maps to recreational visitors headed to the North Woods. The original *Maine Atlas and Gazetteer* caught on, and atlases for other states soon followed. DeLorme also offers a popular line of CD-ROM maps and databases for computer use. The new corporate headquarters opened in 1997 and

Freeport Trivia

L.L. Bean's famous rubber-and-leather hunting boot had a famous flaw: Wearers often found their socks being sucked downwards. If left unchecked, the sock would end up around one's arch. In a giant step for mankind, the boot was reengineered in 1999 with a narrower heel, which ended the disappearing sock problem.

features a massive, revolving globe (1:1,000,000 scale) in the atrium/entryway. The store sells all DeLorme products (naturally), along with a wide assortment of non-DeLorme maps and books about cartography. You also can try out the CD-ROMs on a slew of computer terminals. For more information call (888) 227–1656.

The town of Freeport is best known as the home of *L. L. Bean,* the famous retailer of outdoor gear and clothing. What started as a small shop specializing in leather-and-rubber boots for hunting has grown to the size of a regional shopping mall, with three levels of tents, hiking shoes, plaid shirts, khaki pants, winter jackets, and, of course, L. L. Bean hunting shoes. The store annually attracts thousands of shoppers, a fact that hasn't gone unnoticed by other retailers. In the last decade Freeport has assumed its place as a certified outlet mecca, offering everything from Dansk dinnerware to Patagonia outerwear. To its credit, the town has retained much of its original architecture and flavor, and shoppers can park once and visit most shops on foot. In recent years, however, outlet mania has started its southward creep along Route 1, and there's been a notable outbreak of massive parking lots and chain motels.

One spot in Freeport that hasn't been afflicted by progress is *Wolfe's Neck Farm,* easily one of the state's most scenic bits of agricultural land, located at the edge of the northwest Casco Bay. Visitors approach on a dirt road with broad views across pastures toward the water and to the islands and peninsulas beyond. This 600-acre alternative farm was founded in 1957 by Mr. and Mrs. L. M. C. Smith, both vigorous advocates of no-pesticide agricultural methods. The Smiths pioneered ecologically sound methods of raising beef, and the farm is currently operated by a foundation as a demonstration alternative farm. The foundation carries on the Smiths' doctrine, abstaining from pesticides and chemically refined fertilizers in raising summer and winter feed.

Visitors can stop by the gray clapboarded farmhouse to purchase their frozen USDA-inspected beef, which is offered in a variety of cuts. The beef contains less fat than most beef (which may translate into a slightly tougher cut) and has a beefier flavor than you're likely used to. The university also manages ninety campsites, including many along the tidal bay, for overnight tenting and motor home use. Camping fees are nominal. Also nearby is *Wolfe's Neck Woods State Park,* a 233-acre woodland park with a picnic area and several trails running through the forest and along the bay's edge. (Look for the osprey.) Open for day use from Memorial Day weekend through Labor Day.

To find the farm, head east on Bow Road from downtown Freeport for 2.4 miles, then make a right on Wolf Neck Road. After 1.7 miles, turn left on the dirt road and continue 0.6 mile to the farmhouse. There's no charge to visit the farm or wander the grounds. The office is open for meat sales from 1:00 to 6:00 P.M. Monday through Saturday from 10:00 A.M. to 4:00 P.M. Call 865–4469.

On the other side of I–95 from the outlets is one of the state's more unusual attractions in *The Desert of Maine.* What started in the eighteenth century as a little patch of sand on a newly cleared farm grew and grew like the plague. It soon spread to encompass around 200 acres, with the blowing, shifting sands engulfing trees and buildings.

Like many unusual natural phenomena, this one attracted plenty of attention in the early days of the automobile, and it became a noted tourist trap in the finest sense of the word. (From a 1920s magazine article: "There are acres and acres of shifting sands which are fast obliterating grasses, bushes, trees and even buildings!") Today, you can still tour the desert and see a building from 1938 that's been all but swallowed up by the sands. The Desert of Maine offers plenty of gee-whiz attractions for the average traveler, but it's especially appealing to those interested in geology. The desert was formed when sand carried by glaciers flowed to the bottom of an ancient lake during the retreat of the last ice age.

The Desert of Maine is privately owned and operated. It's open from mid-May to Columbus Day daily from 8:30 A.M. to 5:00 P.M., with guided tours departing every half hour. Admission is $6.75 for adults, $5.75 for seniors and teens, and $3.75 for children ages 6 to 12. For more information call 865–6962.

One of the more enduring and controversial historical figures in U.S. history is Admiral Robert E. Peary, self-proclaimed discoverer of the North Pole and former resident of Casco Bay. Some hail him as one of America's greatest heroes; others dismiss him as an egomaniacal fraud. Photo analysis and exhaustive studies notwithstanding, no one seems to know for sure if Peary actually made it to the North Pole or perhaps erred in his calculations (or doctored them). No matter where you stand on the debate, however, a couple of local attractions cast light on the explorer's personality and achievements.

Located in the far reaches of Casco Bay, *Eagle Island* was Peary's summer home for years when he was plotting and attempting his conquests of the Pole. As a teenager growing up in Portland, he vowed one day to own the craggy seventeen-acre island. He accomplished this in 1879, purchasing it for $500. In 1904 he built a home here, which he expanded with a pair of imposing circular stone rooms in 1912.

Peary's heirs donated the island to the state, with much of the furniture from the years when the explorer occupied the place prior to his death in 1920. There are few formal exhibits, but enough furniture and household goods are present to convey a sense of Peary's character. Among the items on display are birds Peary collected as a young amateur taxidermist, as well as some of his later possessions. The upstairs bedrooms are creaky, small, and full of the smell of salt air. Be sure to leave time to wander the island; footpaths meander through forest and along rocky bluffs to the southern tip of the island, which has been taken over as a rookery by hundreds of gulls.

Eagle Island is open Memorial Day to Labor Day; admission is $1.50 for adults, 50 cents for children. Five moorings on the northwest side of the island are available to those traveling here on their own. Those without their own boats have two choices: From Freeport's town dock, Atlantic Seal Cruises offers two tours daily (9:30 A.M. and 1:30 P.M.) to the island with an hour's stopover. The fare is $20 for adults, $15 for children under 12; call 865–6112. From Portland's waterfront, Eagle Tours leaves Long Wharf daily (at 10:00 A.M.) and includes an eighty-minute visit to the island. The fare is $15.00 for adults, $9.00 for children under 9. For more information call 774–6498.

Chamberlain the Hero

*O*ne of the great heroes of the Civil War has long ties to Brunswick. General Joshua Chamberlain was a professor of rhetoric at Bowdoin College when the war broke out. He enlisted and was shipped south to fight with the 20th Maine Infantry Regiment. Chamberlain's valor was soon proven in a number of encounters (including the Siege of Petersburg), and he was promoted to general. Chamberlain may be best known for his valiant stand at Gettysburg, which was well depicted in Michael Shaara's bestselling novel The Killer Angels.

After the war Chamberlain returned to Maine, where he served as four-term governor of the state, as well as president of Bowdoin College. Chamberlain's contributions are commemorated in a lovely memorial, the General Joshua L. Chamberlain House, located at 226 Main Street in Brunswick. Admission is $4.00 for adults, $2.00 for children. For more information call 729–6606.

If your curiosity about Peary and his exploits is piqued by Eagle Island, plan to visit the **Peary-MacMillan Arctic Museum,** located on the campus of Bowdoin College in Brunswick, a short drive north of Freeport. Housed on the first floor of distinguished Hubbard Hall, this thoroughly intriguing museum celebrates the Arctic accomplishments of Bowdoin alumni Peary and Donald MacMillan. In three exhibit rooms you'll get a good overview of their lives (MacMillan was on Peary's successful 1909 North Pole assault and subsequently became an able Arctic explorer in his own right) and see a number of the artifacts used during the attempts on the Pole, including dogsleds, snowshoes, and the gear used to make afternoon tea.

Other exhibits include a selection of items from the Arctic, ranging from stuffed birds such as the snowy owl, eider, and puffin to beautifully crafted Inuit snow goggles. Watch for the eerie tupilak carvings the Angmassalik Inuit created as effigies to bring harm to their enemies. On your way out note the Latin inscription carved in the lintel above the doorway: *"Inveniam viam aut faciam."* According to Peary's biographer, the explorer penciled this motto above the bunk in his ship after losing most of his toes to frostbite during his unsuccessful 1899 expedition. From Seneca, it translates, "I shall find a way or make one."

The museum is open year-round Tuesday through Saturday from 10:00 A.M. to 5:00 P.M. and Sunday from 2:00 to 5:00 P.M. Admission is free. For information call 725–3416.

Sebago Lake Region

ebago Lake long has been a popular destination with summer folks, who have ringed this massive lake (the second largest in Maine) with cabins and summer homes. A state park on the north end of the lake features a handsome white sand beach and provides lake access to swimmers and campers throughout the summer (693–6613). From Sebago Lake the Songo Locks connect to Brandy Pond and Long Lake at Naples, the former seat of amusement for the region. (Using a now-defunct canal from the coast, tourists once could travel by boat between Portland and Harrison at the north end of Long Lake.) Today the twenty-seven locks, first built in 1830, are in good working order

and open and close constantly throughout the summer to accommodate the flow of canoes and motorboats and the *Songo River Queen*, a
steamship-inspired excursion boat based in Naples. Two-and-a-half-
hour excursions through the locks are offered twice daily in summer;
the price is $10.00 for adults, $6.00 for children. (One-hour trips up
beautiful Long Lake are $7.00 for adults, $4.00 for children.) Call
693–6861 for more information.

In the rolling hills west of the lake, you may be surprised to come upon
one of Maine's more striking museums. The *Jones Museum of Glass
and Ceramics* is housed in a handsome dark-green farm building dating from 1938 and set amid a hillside cluster of attractive summer
homes. Tall pines and open meadows surround the museum, which contains one of the more extraordinary collections of glass in the nation.
You needn't be a glass connoisseur to enjoy an unhurried walk through
this museum, just have an appreciation for form and color. The collections are as professionally curated and exhibited as at any major urban
museum, with about 6,000 objects on display at any given time.

Rotating exhibits fill much of the first floor of the museum. These
exhibits may feature historical displays, such as recent shows on Sandwich glass and marbles, or may highlight contemporary glassmakers
and ceramicists, who seem constantly to push the boundaries with exuberant colors and fluid forms. The bulk of the museum's collections is
exhibited on the second floor, where you may be surprised by the range
and versatility of glass and ceramics. The collections vary in age from
1400 B.C. (Egyptian glass) to items not long out of the kiln or glass-
blower's shop. You'll also gain insight into the social and economic con-
texts of glassmaking through exhibits that include everything from a
glass mailbox to intricately detailed teapots to attractive embalming-
fluid bottles. Another exhibit area challenges viewers to spot the differ-
ences between reproductions and originals.

The Jones Museum also has a 5,400-book library that is open to the
public for research, as well as an extensive gift shop offering antique
originals (no reproductions) and reference works. Lectures on glassmaking and ceramics are scheduled throughout the year.

The museum is open mid-May through mid-November Monday through
Saturday from 10:00 A.M. to 5:00 P.M. and Sunday from 1:00 to 5:00 P.M.
Admission is $5.00 for adults, $3.00 for students; children under 12 are
free. It is located off Route 107 just south of the town of Sebago. Look for
roadside markers. For more information call 787–3370.

Just up the hill from the Jones Museum is *Douglas Mountain,* a hilltop

Nature Conservancy preserve that makes a fine destination for a short hike on a clear day. This 169-acre parcel features two undemanding trails that run 0.25 mile to the 1,415-foot summit. On the top of the rocky hill is a 16-foot stone tower built in 1925 by the land's former owner, a surgeon who found relaxation in stonework. The top of the tower offers commanding views of the entire region, across Lake Sebago and Casco Bay to the east and westward to the Presidential Range of the White Mountains in New Hampshire. Nearby a sizable boulder has been carved with the phrase *"Non Sibi Sed Omnibus"* ("Not for one but for all"). Visitors in late summer will be rewarded with an ample crop of wild blueberries and blackberries along the trails near the ridge.

New Gloucester Region

The state **Game Farm and Visitors Center** is a sort of wild animal hospital, rehabilitation center, and nursing home for wildlife that couldn't make it on their own in the forests. The animals you'll see at this facility have either suffered from injuries or were orphaned before they could survive on their own. (Some others were raised illegally by humans and are now dependent on handlers to survive.) The center includes a picnic area, a short nature trail, and a mix of animals you might see in the wilds, including lynx, woodchuck, moose, bald eagle, and bobcat. There's also a fish hatchery. The center is operated by the Maine Department of Inland Fisheries and Wildlife, and it's open mid-April to mid-November daily from 9:30 A.M. to 5:30 P.M. (last entry at 4:00 P.M.). Admission is $3.50 for adults, $2.50 for seniors, and $2.00 for children ages 4 to 12. For more information call 657–4977.

Fly Markets

Old fishing stuff never dies. It just keeps getting sold. In the Sebago Lake region, two places should catch the attention of anglers. The aptly named Old Fishing Stuff shop, just west of the causeway in Naples, is filled with old rods made of bamboo and wood (along with graphite and fiberglass), along with lures, flies, reels, creels, and whatever else. It caters to both the serious collector as well as folks rummaging for a bargain. Call 693–5000.

In the nearby town of Raymond, you'll find Bob Lang, proprietor of Lang's Sporting Collectables Inc., which caters to high-end collectors of antique fishing gear. (An auction catalog alone costs $25.) Lang holds three auctions annually in Massachusetts, where some 650 lots of classic fishing gear go under the hammer. To learn how to bid by mail or consign your tackle, contact Lang at 655–4265.

Continuing north on Route 26 you'll pass a handsome assortment of brick and clapboard buildings on a gentle rise amid open meadows and orchards. That's the **Sabbathday Lake Shaker Community,** the last active Shaker community in the nation. Fewer than a dozen Shakers now live in these venerable buildings on 1,900 acres originally settled in 1793 by Shakers carrying on the traditions of Mother Ann Lee and her disciples. These traditions include an emphasis on simplicity in their lives and crafts, a commitment to industry ("Hearts to God and hands to work"), and celibacy. The latter, which seems to get the attention of visitors, raises the question of how the community has managed to propagate itself for nearly 200 years. The answer: For many years the Shakers adopted orphans. One of the older sisters present today was herself adopted. After this practice was disallowed by the state, the community became dependent on converts to carry on their work. Today several of the more committed Shakers are in their thirties.

Waiting room at the Sabbathday
Lake Shaker Community

The Shakers—not to be confused with the Quakers—received their name from the dances they once executed during their religious celebrations. The practice was discontinued around 1900 in deference to the older Shaker members. In addition to their religious ceremonies, the Shakers are best known for their furniture and baskets, which display an unmatched devotion to practicality and simplicity.

A good introduction to the Shaker life and tradition may be had through one of the tours of the village offered daily except Sunday throughout the summer. Nine of the buildings were constructed before 1850, and all are possessed of an unvarnished grace and refinement. Of particular note is the meetinghouse, built in 1794 and still used for Sunday services in summer (the public is invited). The downstairs room is spare and open; the light streaming in through the windows seems part of the design. Examples of fine woodworking are displayed throughout several buildings, representing a variety of Shaker communities. You can identify each chair's provenance by the finials, which were unique for each community. The museum also displays examples of later Shaker craftsmanship and design, some of which display a mild but startling flirtation with Victorian ornamentation. Be sure to stop at the gift shop, where you can buy herbs grown in the community's garden and sold here since 1799.

An introductory tour of the village (about one hour) costs $6.00 for adults and $2.00 for children ages 6 to 12. An extended tour (one hour and forty-five minutes) is offered in July and August only and costs $7.50 for adults, $2.75 for children. It's open Memorial Day to Columbus Day (closed Sundays) from 10:00 A.M. to 4:30 P.M. For more information call 926–4597.

**PLACES TO STAY
IN SOUTHERN MAINE**

CAPE ELIZABETH
Inn by the Sea,
40 Bowery Beach Road,
799-3134

FREEPORT
Coastline Inn, 209 Route 1,
865-3777

Dutch Village, Route 1,
865-6682

Harraseeket Inn, 162 Main
Street, 865-9377

Maine Idyll Motor Court,
325 Route 1, 865-4201

KENNEBUNKPORT
Bufflehead Cove Bed &
Breakfast, P.O. Box 499,
967-3879

The Colony, Ocean Avenue,
(800) 552-2363 or
967-3331

Maine Stay, 34 Maine
Street, (800) 950-2117 or
967-2117

Tides Inn By-the-Sea,
Goose Rocks Beach,
967-3757

Village Cove Inn, 29 South
Maine Street, 967-3993

White Barn Inn, Beach
Street, 967-2321

OGUNQUIT
Beachmere Inn, Marginal
Way, (800) 336-3983

Chestnut Tree Inn, 93 Shore
Road, (800) 362-0757 or
646-4529

Cliff House, Shore Road,
361–1000

Grand Hotel, 102 Shore
Road, 646–1231

Pink Blossoms Family
Resort, 66 Shore Road,
646–7397

OLD ORCHARD BEACH
Grand Beach Inn,
198 East Grand Avenue,
(800) 926–3242 or
934–4621

The Ocean House, 70 West
Surf Street, 934–2847

PORTLAND
The Danforth,
163 Danforth Street,
(800) 991–6557 or
879–8755

Eastland Hotel,
157 High Street, 775–5411

Holiday Inn By the Bay,
88 Spring Street, 775–2311

Inn at Park Spring,
135 Spring Street,
(800) 437–8511

Portland Regency Hotel,
20 Milk Street,
(800) 727–3436 or
774–4200

West End Inn, 146 Pine
Street, (800) 338–1377 or
772–1377

THE YORKS
Anchorage Inn, Route 1A,
York Beach, 365–5112

Stage Neck Inn, York
Harbor, 363–3850

York Harbor Inn, Route 1A,
York Harbor, (800)
343–3869 or 363–5119

**PLACES TO EAT
IN SOUTHERN MAINE**

CAPE ELIZABETH
Two Lights Lobster Shack,
225 Two Lights Road,
799–1677

FREEPORT
Falcon Restaurant, 8 Bow
Street, 865–4031

Harraseeket Lunch
& Lobster Co.,
Main Street
(South Freeport),
865–4888

Helpful Web Sites

Casco Bay Weekly (Portland)—
www.cascobayweekly.com

City of Portland—*www.ci.portland.me.us*

DeLorme Map Store—*www.delorme.com*

Friends of Admiral Peary's Eagle Island—
www.gwi.net/~eagle/

Greater Portland Chamber of Commerce—
www.portlandregion.com/

Kittery–Eliot Chamber of Commerce—
www.kittery–eliot–chamber.org/

Kittery Shopping—*www.thekitteryoutlets.com*

L. L. Bean—*www.llbean.com*

Portland Press Herald—*www.portland.com*

Town of Bath—*www.curtislibrary.com/brunswick.htm*

Town of Ogunquit—*www.communitynetwork.
com/ogunquit/ogunquit.html*

York Chamber of Commerce—*www.yorkme.org*

Selected Chambers of Commerce

Convention and Visitor's Bureau of Greater Portland,
305 Commercial Street, 772–4994

Kittery–Eliot Chamber of Commerce,
P.O. Box 526, 439–2845

Ogunquit Chamber of Commerce,
Route 1, 646–2939

Old Orchard Beach Chamber of Commerce,
First Street, (800) 365–9386 or 934–2500

York Chamber of Commerce,
599 Route 1, 363–4422

Jameson Tavern, 115 Main Street, 865–4196

KENNEBUNKPORT
Federal Jack's Restaurant and Brewpub, Lower Village, 967–4322

Grissini, 27 Western Avenue, 967–2211

Kennebunkport Inn, Dock Square, 967–2621

White Barn Inn, Beach Street, 967–2321

KITTERY
Bob's Clam Hut, Route 1, 439–4233

Chauncey Creek Lobster Pound, Chauncey Creek Road, Kittery Point, 439–1030

Warren's Lobster House, 11 Water Street, 439–1630

OGUNQUIT
Arrows, Berwick Road, 361–1100

Blue Water Inn, Ogunquit Beach, 646–5559

Hurricane, Perkins Cove, (800) 649–6348 or 646–6348

PORTLAND
Bella Cucina, 653 Congress Street, 828–4033

Cafe Uffa!, 190 State Street, 775–3380

Cotton Street Cantina, 10 Cotton Street, 775–3222

Fore Street, 288 Fore Street, 775–2717

Great Lost Bear, 540 Forest Avenue, 772–0300

Street & Co., 33 Wharf Street, 775–0887

Three Dollar Dewey's, 241 Commercial Street, 772–3310

THE YORKS
Cape Neddick Inn, 1233 Route 1, 363–2899

Dockside Restaurant, Harris Island Road, 363–2868

The Goldenrod, Railroad Avenue, 363–2621

Western Mountains

I n their haste to visit the White Mountains of New Hampshire and the Green Mountains of Vermont, many visitors to New England overlook the mountains of western Maine. These rolling, rugged hills haven't developed quite the popular mythology of the other mountains, nor do they offer as broad a range of services for travelers. But the region is well worth visiting for its dramatic landscapes, quiet byways, and vast lakes set amid forested hills. Those with a penchant for outdoor activities will feel at home here with canoe, bike, or hiking shoes. Those whose inclinations take them indoors also will find plenty to do, from historic homes to offbeat museums. Fine inns may be found throughout the area, and there's excellent browsing at unassuming antiques shops (Victorian antiques seem to be the standard in this region, compared to the more common Federal and Empire furniture along the coast).

The Western Mountains aren't defined by a single monolithic mountain range, but rather consist of a series of hills and watersheds. Some 50,000 acres of the White Mountain National Forest slip over the border from New Hampshire into Maine, then unravel into the gentle Oxford Hills. The Mahoosuc Range passes near Bethel and is traversed by the Appalachian Trail; those who've hiked the entire 2,100-mile trail say the Mahoosucs contain some of the most difficult and dramatic segments along the entire route. From the summit of Old Speck Mountain on a clear day you can see Mount Blue, an almost perfectly pyramidal hill 32 miles away in the heart of another range of hills. There's also the Rangeley Lake region, with its network of lakes and mountains, and the impressive Carrabasset Valley, dominated by the Bigelow Range, which offers some of the best Maine hiking opportunities outside of Baxter State Park.

Oxford County

O xford County extends narrowly along Maine's western edge from the village of Porter to the Canadian border, far into timberland territory. The county tends to be rough-hewn in its geography and

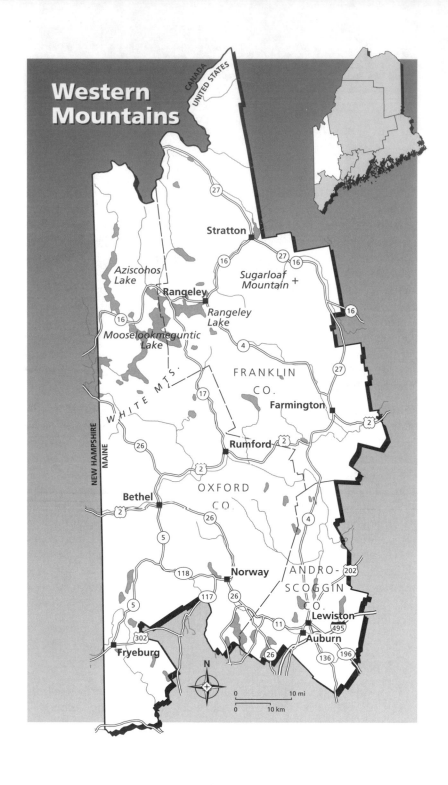

Western Mountains

CANADA
UNITED STATES

Stratton

Aziscohos
Lake

Rangeley

Sugarloaf
Mountain +

Rangeley
Lake

Mooselookmeguntic
Lake

WHITE MTS.

FRANKLIN
CO.

Farmington

Rumford

OXFORD
CO.

NEW HAMPSHIRE
MAINE

Bethel

Norway

ANDRO-
SCOGGIN
CO.

Lewiston

Auburn

Fryeburg

N

0   10 mi

0   10 km

WAYNE'S FAVORITE ATTRACTIONS

1. *Evans Notch*
2. *Grafton Notch State Park,* Bethel area
3. *Paris Hill,* Oxford County
4. *Norlands Living History Center,* Livermore
5. *Orgonon,* Rangeley

culture, with extraordinary gems—both literal and figurative—dispersed throughout.

White Mountains Region

Fryeburg is a modest town of broad streets and open views located on the heavily traveled route between Portland and North Conway, New Hampshire. Best known for the Fryeburg Fair—Maine's largest county fair, held annually at the end of September—Fryeburg also lies on the Saco River, Maine's most popular (and populous) canoeing route. The Saco is distinguished by almost constant sandbars, which invite leisurely excursions with frequent stops. Be forewarned that the river is exceedingly busy on weekends, and some sandbars may offer all the remote wilderness character of New York's Jones Beach.

Several canoe liveries may be found in and around Fryeburg, offering canoe rentals and shuttles up and down the river. Among the busiest and most popular is **Saco Bound**, located just across the state line in Center Conway, New Hampshire. They can help arrange trips ranging from a two-hour, 3-mile introductory paddle to a three-day, 43-mile trip. Canoes rent for $26 per day; the shuttle is an additional $10.50. Call (603) 447–2177.

If you don't feel like hassling with a canoe, there's easy access to a large sandbar on Route 113 north of town. Park in the lot just north of the bridge and walk down to the river.

On Elm Street in Fryeburg, you'll find the **Admiral Peary House**, a pleasant bed-and-breakfast inn. As a recent college graduate, Arctic explorer Robert Peary lived quietly here from 1877 to 1879 while employed as a land surveyor. He had pleasant memories of Fryeburg, where he spent his idle time practicing taxidermy. The exterior of the house retains its nineteenth-century farmhouse charm, but Peary certainly wouldn't recognize the interior if he were to visit it today. The innkeepers maintain six modern and comfortable guest rooms with private baths and have added amenities such as a clay tennis court, a hot tub, air-conditioning, and a spacious country kitchen, where breakfasts are served in inclement weather. A comfortable deck overlooks the well-landscaped yard, and the guests' living room features a fireplace and an antique billiards table. The best room in the house is the "North Pole," located in the former attic, with Palladian windows offering a view out toward Stark Mountain. The guest rooms have more privacy than at many B&Bs, and guests are provided with a filling breakfast in the morning.

Summer and fall rates run between $98 and $138, depending on the room. (Rooms start at $80 in the off-season.) The inn is at 9 Elm Street. For more information call 935–3365.

Peary wasn't the only person of note to call Fryeburg home. Author Clarence E. Mulford (1883–1956) lived here—not on a rugged butte in Utah—while writing his Hopalong Cassidy novels. A collection of his works and a sampling of memorabilia are housed in the *Clarence Mulford Room* at the Fryeburg Public Library. This reading room has a portrait of Mulford as well as displays of historic western guns (including a buffalo gun), model ships and stage coaches, and a case of Mulford's collected works, including editions in Czech, Danish, and Finnish. The library, in the former schoolhouse at 98 Main Street, is sturdily constructed of granite blocks and stays cool even during the dog days of summer. For more information call 935–2731.

Heading northward from Fryeburg, you have a choice of two routes, both appealing. You either can drive north along Route 5 on the east side of Kezar Lake or follow ever-narrowing Route 113 through scenic Evans Notch. The first route gives access to a venerable lakeside resort; the second offers a network of excellent hiking trails to the summits of open mountains.

Kezar Lake, bounded to the west by unspoiled mountains, is regarded by many as the state's most perfect lake. It's also one of its least accessible. (This may be *why* it's considered a nearly perfect lake.) Public roads touch upon the lake only at a crossing called "the Narrows," so the best views are reserved for those owning summer homes hereabouts—author Stephen King among them. Fortunately, there's an alternative for those without the good sense to be born into a family with a Lake Kezar summer home.

Quisisana is a rustic lakeside resort set amid towering white pines. Here you're as liable to hear an aria emanating from the forest as the muffled call of a mourning dove. Since 1945 Quisisana has offered its guests both superb cuisine and a varied musical menu, with selections ranging from opera to popular show tunes. Owner Jane Oran recruits her summer staff from conservatories around the nation, and the students make beds, wait on tables, and perform nightly in the vintage wooden recital hall with dramatic views down the lake. Up to 150 guests reside in cozy white cabins scattered about the grounds and along the lakeshore, occupying their days with swimming, sunning, canoeing, and exploring the surrounding hills. Extra recitals are sometimes also scheduled for rainy-day diversions.

The musical repertory schedule is designed around a weeklong stay, but shorter visits can sometimes be accommodated early in the season. Quisisana is 3.5 miles north of Lovell; look for road signs as you approach. Figure on spending between $260 and $270 per couple per day, including all meals and entertainment. For more information call 925–3500.

If you opt to head north on Route 113, you'll first drive through farmlands with open vistas of distant ridges. But soon enough those ridges start to converge at **Evans Notch**, and the valley becomes pinched and narrow, as does the road itself when you enter the national forest. As you climb, views of the valley open up, with glimpses of the scraggly peaks above you. The forest is dense with birch, beech, and maple trees, which often overarch the road to create a shady canopy.

If you're so inclined, set out on one of the hiking trails to these ridges for sweeping views of western Maine and the taller peaks of the Carter and Presidential ranges. A list of suggested hikes is available from the U.S. Forest Service's office in Bethel. (Write to: Evans Notch Ranger Station, RFD 2, Box 2270, Bethel, ME 04217, or call 603–824–2134.) One hike that may be accomplished in a couple of hours without map or guide is to the summit of **East Royce Mountain**. This 1.3-mile trail ascends steadily through hardwoods and along an attractive brook, ending at open granite ledges with excellent views across rolling hills toward Kezar Lake. The trailhead, with parking for about twenty cars, is on the west side of Route 113 just north of where the road begins its descent toward the town of Gilead. The trail is moderately demanding and is well marked.

TOP ANNUAL EVENTS

1. **Sled Dog Races, Rangeley,** early March, 864–5364

2. **Maine State Parade,** Lewiston-Auburn, early May, 784–0599

3. **Heritage Days,** Norlands Center, late June, Livermore Falls, 897–4366

4. **Sebago–Long Lake Chamber Music Festival,** Harrison, July & August, 583–6747

5. **Old Time Fiddler's Contest,** Rangeley, mid-July, 864–2117

6. **Maine Storytelling Festival,** Harrison, mid-July, 583–6747

7. **Moxie Festival,** Lisbon Falls, mid-July, 783–2249

8. **Founders Day, Paris Hill,** mid-July, 743–2980

9. **Great Falls Balloon Festival,** Lewiston-Auburn, late August, 782–8964

10. **Fryeburg Fair,** Fryeburg, late September–early October, 935–3268

A Quiet Retreat for Campers

If you're equipped for camping, there are several U.S. Forest Service campgrounds in the Evans Notch region, but none as quiet and remote as the Crocker Pond campground located down a dirt road south of Bethel. With only eight campsites, it often fills on weekends but remains out-of-the-way enough that sites are generally available during the week. Several quiet ponds in the area are suitable for fishing, and a couple of hiking trails near the campsite provide access to the backcountry. For more information on this campground or recreational opportunities, contact the Forest Service's Evans Notch Ranger Station in Bethel at 824-2134.

If you'd rather not serve as your own beast of burden, consider signing up for llama trekking at the **Telemark Inn**. This distinguished inn, housed in a summer retreat built by a wealthy businessman in 1900, is located deep in the countryside near Bethel on the eastern edge of the White Mountains. Innkeeper Steve Crone was the first White Mountain entrepreneur to offer this pleasurable way of visiting the mountains. Crone offers day trips as well as overnight excursions, with varied destinations that include open mountaintops and riverside glens. The inn also can arrange canoe expeditions and eco-hikes in search of eagle and wolves. The lodge is comfortable but primitive—all rooms share baths, and there's only electricity when the generator is on. Three-, five-, and seven-day packages are available. For more information contact Steve at 836–2703.

Bethel Area

Heading northeast of the Evans Notch region, you'll soon arrive at the dignified town of Bethel, full of yellow-and-white clapboard houses and abounding with evidence of a comfortable, prosperous history. A number of attractive early homes front the Bethel Common—an elongated greensward with benches and a fountain—as does the venerable Bethel Inn, long a destination for those seeking respite from sultry eastern cities. The inn was built by the famous neurologist Dr. John Gehring, who also opened the nearby Gehring Clinic, a treatment center for nervous disorders. (Bethel once was referred to as "the resting place of Harvard" because of the high proportion of patients from Cambridge's academic community.) Nearby are the tasteful brick buildings of Gould Academy, a respected private secondary school founded in 1836.

Facing the common you'll also see the simple but distinguished **Moses Mason House**, now owned and operated by the Bethel Historical Society. This 1813 Federal-style house with the characteristic fan over the front door was built by Dr. Moses Mason (1789–1866), one of Bethel's early civic leaders. The house is believed to be the first in the district to be painted white and the first built on a stone foundation; locals told Mason the wind would certainly blow it over. Mason served not only as town doctor but as postmaster and justice of the peace. The original contents of the house were auctioned off in the 1970s, but many of these items are finding their way back through local donation. The house and its intricate woodwork are meticulously maintained, with period furniture filling the rooms.

If you're in the least interested in American primitive painting or the history of decorative arts, the front hallway alone is worth the price of admission. The walls of the entryway and the second-floor landing are covered with a sweeping paint-on-plaster mural attributed to well-known primitive painter Rufus Porter. A seascape with boat at anchor graces the first floor; along the stairs and on the second floor is a forest scene, dense with the delicately wrought boughs of white pines. The walls were first painted a century and a half ago, and they have never been papered or painted over, yielding one of the best examples of early decorative painting in the state. Be sure to note also the intriguing chair built by Mason, made of curly maple, crushed velvet, and moosehorn.

The Moses Mason House is open in July and August daily except Mondays from 1:00 to 4:00 P.M. Admission is $2.00 for adults, $1.00 for children. For more information call 824–2908.

Just northwest of Bethel is the booming *Sunday River Ski Resort*. For years Sunday River was a quiet family mountain slowly going out of business, like many small New England ski areas. After it was acquired by entrepreneur Les Otten, the resort grew dramatically, with the ski area expanding along the ridge toward the New Hampshire border. The resort has become nationally famous for its snowmaking capacity—it sometimes produces enough snow to remain open into June. After turning around this humble ski area, Otten has gone on to acquire many other major ski mountains in New England, including Sugarloaf, Mount Snow, Haystack, Pico, Killington, Sugarbush, Attitash, and Bear Peak.

As at most ski areas, the pace slackens considerably in summer, but the resort has developed a mountain-biking center with 60 miles of trails and access to the high, rocky ridge via two chairlifts modified to carry bikes. *The Sunday River Mountain Bike Park* offers various options, from full-day passes to one-time lift rides. Trail passes are $24 per day, with full-day bike rentals (including passes) available at $50 to $60. Helmets are mandatory.

To get to Sunday River, head north of Bethel on Route 2, then look for signs indicating a left turn to the resort at about 2.5 miles. For more information call 824–3000.

You also can rent bikes at **Bethel Outdoor Adventures**, located on Route 2 just north of Bethel. They rent canoes and kayaks, too, and have a campground on the banks of the Androscoggin River. Rates are $17.50 for a kayak, $25.00 for a canoe, and $25.00 for a bike. For more information call (800) 533–3607 or 824–4224.

Head north on Route 2, then turn left on Route 26. You'll be headed toward northern New Hampshire, and into *Grafton Notch State Park*. This is one of western Maine's premier drives—rugged, rounded mountains rise up on either side of the winding road, and they seem to catch wayward clouds on their summits. Clear, rushing streams and waterfalls cascade along the roadside, and the Appalachian Trail passes through here. (Excellent day hikes can be launched along the trail in either direction.) Several roadside attractions feature engaging natural phenomena. At Screw Auger Falls the river corkscrews down through a maze of granite scoured out by torrents during the thaw of the last ice age. Mother Walker's Falls features a tiny waterfall underneath a massive slab of rock that crashed down from the cliffs above. You really have to snoop around to find it.

Oxford Hills

Oxford County is noted in certain circles for its deposits of rare minerals, including fine grades of tourmaline prized by gemologists. To learn more about local minerals, plan a stop at **Perham's of West Paris**, one of the nation's preeminent destinations for rock hounds. Founded by Stanley Perham in 1919, this rock shop has just about everything for the inveterate collector of minerals and gemstones. A wide array of rare crystals and other minerals from around the world are for sale, displayed neatly on glass shelves and in white cardboard boxes. For neophytes, a small museum provides a fine overview of what's what in Maine, including several remarkable samples of the elusive watermelon tourmaline, a delicate crystal of smoky pink ringed with a thin rind of emerald green. For those who prefer the finished product, Perham's also has an extensive jewelry selection.

Perham's owns five quarries within 10 miles of the shop, which are open free of charge to rock collectors. The quarries invariably yield something intriguing and are a popular destination with families looking for an inexpensive and enjoyable way to while away a sunny afternoon. Ask for a quarry map at Perham's front counter.

Perham's is endlessly patient with novices, but it caters to the experienced collector as well, selling prospecting hammers and chisels, detailed field guides, lapidary equipment, metal detectors, and gold-panning dishes. Even if you're not a committed rock hound, browsing is entertaining and provides a glimpse into the intriguing subculture of the rock collector. A poem posted on the back wall may sum up the outsider's view:

> *I think that there shall never be*
> *An ignoramus just like me*
> *Who roams the hills throughout the day,*
> *To pick up rocks that do not pay.*
> *For there's one thing I've been told*
> *I take the rocks and leave the gold.*

Perham's is open from 9:00 A.M. to 5:00 P.M. daily, except Thanksgiving and Christmas. The shop is located on the north side of Route 26 near the village of West Paris. For more information call 674–2341.

In the industrial town of Rumford, where the downtown is located on a river island in the shadow of a Boise Cascade paper mill, you'll find the vestiges of an enlightened experiment in corporate paternalism dating from the early twentieth century. The **Strathglass Park Historic District** consists of fifty-one elegant brick buildings located in a parklike setting amid pines and silver maples on a hillside across from the mill. The neighborhood's character is sort of Birmingham, England, by way of Boston's Beacon Hill.

The homes were built in 1901–1902 by Hugh Chisholm, a principal in

Road to Whimsville

I'd wager that you won't find a more international collection of place names than in western Maine. Perhaps the most famous signpost is in Lynchville (near North Waterford), at the intersection of Route 5 and Route 35. Here you'll see the mileage to nearby Maine towns with names like Denmark, China, Poland, Paris, and Norway. The famous sign has appeared in postcards and countless snapshots. It's also been cut down and stolen dozens of times. Note that it's now mounted on steel I-beams, cleverly planked with wood to preserve the old-fashioned effect.

Another riff on the same theme can be found at a lesser known signpost in the village of Casco, over near Lake Sebago. That signpost offers direction and mileage to these familiar-sounding Maine towns: Washington, Jefferson, Madison, Monroe, Jackson, Van Buren, Harrison, Lincoln, Garfield, and Clinton. It was put up in the mid-1990s by a local Boy Scout troop.

the Oxford Paper Company. Appalled by the living conditions of many company workers and hoping to attract a more qualified workforce, Chisholm commissioned a New York architect to design these spacious duplexes surrounded by broad lawns. Workers nominated by their foremen were given first crack at renting the new homes at reasonable rates, for which all services were provided. The company sold off the buildings in the late 1940s, and today they are all privately owned. For the most part they remain in fair to good condition. To reach Strathglass Park, turn off Route 2 uphill on Main Street, then make the next right between the tall stone columns.

Another intriguing historic setting, albeit from an earlier age, may be found in southern Oxford County, not far from Route 26. *Paris Hill* is notable both for its assortment of handsome Federal-style homes and as the birthplace of Hannibal Hamlin, a Maine political icon and vice president under Abraham Lincoln during his first term. This ridgetop setting, with views toward the White Mountains, serves as a fine backdrop for an uncommonly well-preserved village of nineteenth-century houses. With the highway some distance away, it also has a dignified country feel that in other towns has been compromised by noisy automobile traffic and the relentless widening of roads.

Gilded Hills

*E*ver hear of the Maine gold rush? Didn't think so. But the nation's first gold strike was in Byron, a small town on Route 17 north of Rumford. That find—a legitimate if small one—triggered a whole series of later gold rushes following the 1849 California Gold Rush. The fortunes made out West made it easy to dupe investors into believing that they should act quickly if they didn't want to get left behind. Under such mass delusion, a number of "paper mines" and fraudulent corporations were created to tap Maine's untold gold wealth, subsequently enriching the unscrupulous and impoverishing the gullible.

Like many scams, this one was made all the more believable because gold does exist naturally in parts of Maine. Even today the land around the Swift River in Roxbury and Byron grudgingly yields up gold flakes and the infrequent tiny nugget. You can try your hand at gold panning anywhere along the stream. A good place to begin is at Perham's of West Paris, where you can buy a gold pan and ask for advice on where to go and the best techniques.

At any rate, panning is a good excuse to poke around on quiet streams. You may even run into an old-timer panning along the stream, who may proffer some suggestions and stories.

The *Hamlin Memorial* in Paris Hill is located adjacent to Hannibal Hamlin's grand estate on the village green and is the only building open to the public. This stout granite building served as a local jail between 1822 and 1896. In 1901 it was purchased by one of Hamlin's descendants and converted into a library and museum, which it remains to this day. The museum displays examples of early American primitive art, local minerals, and items related to Hamlin's life. It's open Tuesday through Friday from noon to 5:00 P.M. and Saturday from 10:00 A.M. to 2:00 P.M. For more information call 743–2980.

In nearby South Paris is the *McLaughlin Garden and Horticultural Center,* a popular stop for anyone interested in landscaping and plants. The gardens were started in 1936 by Bernard McLaughlin, an amateur gardener who worked in a local grocery store. When he retired in 1967, he devoted himself full time to his gardens, collecting plants from the world over. After McLaughlin's death, the home and gardens were acquired by a nonprofit foundation, which now maintains the grounds and is striving to restore them to their former grandeur with the help of various other groups, including the Maine State Historic Preservation Commission and the national Garden Conservancy. On the grounds is a gracious tea room, where visitors can enjoy light lunches or a nice cup of tea.

The gardens are located at 97 Main Street in South Paris and are open daily during the growing season; admission is free (donations accepted). For more information call 743–8820.

Androscoggin County

Androscoggin County tends to fall between the cracks. It's not the Casco Bay region, but neither is it the Oxford Hills or the Kennebec Valley. It's included in the Western Mountains section because many people travel through the county en route to the mountains from the coast. Don't rush the trip; this small county can best be appreciated at a slow pace.

Poland Spring Area

Just north of the Sabbathday Lake Shaker Community (see "Southern Maine"/"New Glouster Region") in Cumberland County, you'll cross the county line and come to Poland Spring. Actually, there's a good chance you'll drive through it without noticing it. History is strong here, but a town center is not.

Poland Spring gained worldwide fame in the nineteenth century for its waters. In 1794 Jabez Ricker of Alfred, Maine, purchased this land with its fine spring from the Shakers and established his farm and an inn for travelers. Business was steady if not spectacular for half a century, until Jabez's son, Hiram, became convinced that the waters from the spring had cured him of chronic dyspepsia. The spring soon became well known for its healing abilities, and by 1876 the Rickers advertised their water as "a sure cure for Bright's Disease of the kidneys, stone in the bladder and kidneys, liver complaint, dropsy, salt, rheum, scrofula, humors, and all diseases of the urinary organs." A sprawling grand hotel with sweeping views of the Oxford Hills was built in 1875, with the famous waters pumped into the hotel via a steam pump. At its pinnacle the resort boasted a 200-foot-long dining room and a fireplace that consumed 6-foot logs. The complex also included a number of spacious annexes and outbuildings for guests and staff.

Much of the resort's history may be seen in exhibits in the *State of Maine Building*, located off Route 26 on the grounds of the former Poland Spring Hotel (look for signs). This turreted stone building was constructed for the 1893 Chicago World's Fair, where it was used to display Maine's products. After the exposition the Rickers dismantled the building, shipped it to Maine, and rebuilt it on their grounds as the resort library.

Today the building contains fascinating memorabilia of the Poland Spring Hotel, including a model of the main hotel (which burned to the ground in 1975), early photographs, and examples of dinnerware and other accoutrements of resort life. Detailed cardboard models of architecturally significant buildings of Maine, constructed by Larry Smith, are on the third floor. The building itself is an architectural gem, with an open, courtyard-like interior and a lacy skylight brightening the dark woodwork.

The State of Maine Building is open in July and August daily from 9:00 A.M. to 1:00 P.M. It's also open June and September on weekends only from 9:00 A.M. to 1:00 P.M. Admission is $1.00; children under 15 are free.

Poland Spring bottled water is still sold in shops all along the eastern seaboard and beyond, although the claims for its powers have been tempered somewhat. (It cures thirst, but little else.) You'll find it in virtually all Maine grocery and convenience stores. Perrier, the French mineral water company, now owns the facility and pumps the water up from the aquifer for bottling and reshipping in a modern and hygienic plant. It's not open to the public for tours.

STATE OF MAINE BUILDING, POLAND SPRING

Lewiston-Auburn and Vicinity

Not far from Poland Spring is the unassuming town of Lisbon Falls, dominated by formidable brick factory buildings along the Androscoggin River. In a small storefront in the center of town, you'll find a somewhat peculiar shrine to another beverage that claimed to be a curative elixir.

In 1885 Dr. Augustin Thompson—a native of Union, Maine—patented and began producing something called Moxie Nerve Food. Thompson, a master of marketing, claimed that the secret to the beverage had been obtained by one Lieutenant Moxie. Adventurer Moxie had witnessed South American Indians consuming the juice of a certain plant, which infused them with preternatural strength. The miraculous plant was brought back, or so the story went, and given to Dr. Thompson, who distilled this beverage and named it after its discoverer. Thompson claimed that Moxie would "cure brain and nervous exhaustion, paralysis, loss of manhood, softening of the brain and mental imbecility." So popular was Moxie that its name soon entered the English language, becoming synonymous with pluck and courage. Moxie was the soft drink of choice throughout New England in the early twentieth century until it was eclipsed by Coca-Cola, which now owns the name and manufactures the product.

Where does Lisbon Falls come into this tale? Through the door of Frank Anicetti's Kennebec Fruit Store, otherwise known as the *Moxie Capital of the World*. Anicetti's store, opened by his grandfather in 1914, has become a virtual Moxie museum, housing a wide selection of Moxie paraphernalia (cassettes, T-shirts, and books) and other items of interest to Moxie aficionados. In addition, Anicetti sells his own Moxie ice cream, which he says is not available anywhere else, and is willing to talk about Moxie and its history longer than perhaps any other living human being. The store is also headquarters for the Moxie Festival, held annually in mid-July. Anicetti's store is located at the corner of Route 196 and Main Street in downtown Lisbon Falls. For more information call 783–2249.

The twin cities of Lewiston-Auburn form the commercial center of Androscoggin County, making up Maine's second largest urban area after Portland. The area was widely known in the nineteenth century as one of the shoemaking capitals of New England; during World War I, 75 percent of all canvas shoes in the world were made in Lewiston. Vestiges of Lewiston's boom times are clearly seen in the vast, Dickensian factory buildings lining the river's edge. Between the two cities the Androscoggin tumbles over a series of falls, and during spring runoff it presents a gloriously tumultuous display. West Pitch Park on the Auburn side of the river is a fine place to view both the cataracts and Lewiston's historic skyline of square factories punctuated with soaring spires.

You might find it worthwhile to visit the spires at the *Church of Saints Peter and Paul*, an imposing Gothic edifice that looms over the city and lends it a distinctly European flavor. The church, built during the Great Depression, is a proud testament to Lewiston's fiercely Catholic French-Canadian population, which settled here in great numbers during the city's glory days as an international manufacturing hub. This church is notable for a pair of 168-foot towers made of Maine granite and a magnificent, lofty nave with a lovely rose window. After years of deterioration an extensive $2 million restoration was undertaken in the 1980s, and the church has regained much of its former luster.

Also in Lewiston is the campus of **Bates College**, a distinguished four-year liberal arts school that can claim Edmund Muskie and Bryant Gumbel among its alumni. Bates began more than a century ago as a Baptist seminary; it subsequently expanded both its academic mission and its campus. Many distinctive buildings grace the attractive grounds, which are overarched with an abundance of trees. Worth visiting is the modern Olin Arts Center, where community performances are staged and the college's permanent collection is on display. Paintings in the airy Museum of Art include works from the noted Marsden Hartley Memorial Collection. Hartley was a Lewiston native who went on to international acclaim for his bold, colorful landscapes, many of which portrayed the hills of Maine.

One of the better antiques shops in the state is across the river in Auburn. Don't come to **Orphan Annie's** looking for Empire furniture or moose heads. The focus here is on collectibles you can carry with you, many dating from the art deco and art nouveau period. Look for old toys, hats, Depression glass, cigarette cases, and advertising, along with their superb collection of early stained glass. It's a great place to lapse into nostalgic reveries, and an easy spot to lose track of time. (You can always buy a watch.) It's open daily from 10:00 A.M. to 5:00 P.M. (open at noon on Sundays) at 96 Court Street. For more information call 782–0638.

Livermore Area

Maine's numerous historic homes and buildings—from Kittery to Madawaska—provide good vantage points to view the state's past. But one destination near the town of Livermore offers more than just a view. It offers a chance to travel back in time; more precisely, a chance to experience life on a Maine farm circa 1870.

Norlands Living History Center, with its weekend programs called "adult live-ins," occupies a special niche in the adventure travel market. Between four and fifteen guests arrive on Friday afternoon at the elaborate, Italianate farmhouse, surrounded by 445 acres of forest and farmland, and live another life through Monday afternoon. Guests assume the identity of a historic character associated with the farm; they even have the option of donning vintage farm clothes. Guests don't exactly experience the rose-tinted, bucolic life celebrated by nineteenth-century poets, however. There's little time for reading sonnets beneath an applewood bower. Living in the past means sleeping on a cornhusk and straw mattress atop a rope bed in a room with peeling paint and plaster, pumping water into a basin for morning ablutions, and assisting with the slaughter to put food on the table. Don't look for a restful vacation so much as for a remarkably in-depth education. (There are some concessions to modernity: Modern toilet paper augments the corncobs supplied in the outhouses.)

During the course of the long weekend, guests (both men and women) labor in the fields, tend the horses and oxen, do the cooking on a massive Queen Atlantic woodstove, and work on quilts. They also visit a school, using quills and inkpots in the lessons, and research the history of their characters in early farm documents.

Whether you make an extended visit as a "live-in" or just drop by for a two-hour tour, you'll certainly come to feel you know the Washburn family, who built this farm in the wilds of Maine early in the nineteenth century. In the Gothic library you'll hear stories about the fantastically successful Washburn sons; they built the library as a memorial to their parents. Three of the brothers served in the U.S. Congress simultaneously (representing three different states), a feat that has not been duplicated by any family since.

In July and August Norlands offers frequent tours of the newly restored manor house, which include a lesson at the schoolhouse. Tours are offered daily between 10:00 A.M. and 4:00 P.M. and cost $5.50 for adults and $2.00 for students. Norlands is located on Norlands Road (off Route 108) northeast of Livermore and south of Livermore Falls. For more information on the live-in program or special events, call 897–4366.

Franklin County

Rugged Franklin County includes Mount Blue, Rangeley Lake, the Carrabassett Valley, and a host of remote villages, each with little more than a general store and a video shop. Accommodations range from high luxury to basic necessities, but the landscapes and bountiful wildlife are uniformly enchanting.

Rangeley Lakes Region

Driving northward on Route 17 from the towns of Rumford and Mexico, you'll soon come to a point known locally as *"Height of Land."* You'll know when you've arrived. After following the twisting road as it ascends the rolling hills, you'll suddenly find Mooselookmeguntic Lake at your feet, massive, indomitable, and (most likely) stippled with whitecaps. The view is perhaps the most spectacular in Maine, made all the more so because it comes so unexpectedly.

The far lakeshore and two of the largest islands clearly visible at the southern end of the lake—Toothaker and Students—are part of a private wilderness preserve. Private, but open to the public. The *Stephen Phillips Memorial Preserve* was founded two decades ago by Phillips (since deceased), who feared the twin threats of commercial development and state management. His concerns about development proved well founded: Much of Mooselookmeguntic's shoreline was subdivided and developed for second homes during the real estate frenzy of the 1980s. The dozens of miles of lakeshore and island property in the preserve are maintained in a natural state and offer some of the more scenic and wild landscapes in Maine. A handful of the lakeside campsites are within a short walking distance from a car, but the majority of the sixty maintained campsites are accessible only by boat. Canoes may be rented at the preserve headquarters, which has a canoe launching ramp.

Reservations are accepted by mail or by phone (864 2003). If you don't have a reservation, a wooden board near the preserve headquarters is adorned with color-coded washers indicating available, occupied, and reserved sites.

If you'd rather travel by foot than canoe, a number of excellent hikes are available in the Rangeley region. For starters, you might hike the mile-long trail to the summit of Bald Mountain, located on Mooselookmeguntic's lakeshore near Oquossoc; look for trail signs on the lakeshore road 0.8 mile south of Haines Landing. For the more ambitious, a hike along the Appalachian Trail to the top of *Saddleback Mountain* offers rewarding views and a chance to explore a distinctive alpine ecosystem along the barren, windswept ridge. The rugged hike is just over 10 miles round-trip, starting where the Appalachian Trail crosses Route 4 between Rangeley and Madrid. Be sure to bring warm clothing, since the weather can deteriorate rapidly above timberline with unpleasant consequences for the ill prepared.

The sleepy town of Rangeley, on the east shore of sparkling Rangeley Lake, has been a favorite destination for outdoorspeople for more than a century. The town's elevation is 1,546 feet, and the evening temperature often has a bit of a bite even in the midst of summer. Outdoor activities like hunting, fishing, and canoeing are the main allure during the warmer months, and in the winter both downhill and cross-country skiing, as well as snowmobiling and ice fishing, provide the entertainment.

Travelers find a number of options for lodging and restaurants in the area, from very modern to very rustic. The chamber of commerce (864–5364) has a booth at the lakeside town park and can offer plenty of information on what's available.

One person smitten with the Rangeley region was Wilhelm Reich, a controversial scientist who had worked with Sigmund Freud. While working with Freud in Austria, Reich came to believe that Freud's theories of sexual behavior not only had academic usefulness, but also could be applied clinically. Reich authored *The Function of the Orgasm* and attempted to cure neuroses by releasing sexual energy. This was controversial enough, but his theories about "orgone"—a sort of life force that he claimed could be detected, measured, and manipulated—led to a final break with Freud.

Following Hitler's rise to power, Reich departed Austria and lived in four countries before finally settling at Rangeley in 1942 to further his study of "orgonomy." He designed and built an angular stone house, high upon a hill overlooking the lakes, which he called **Orgonon**. With an array of peculiar-looking devices, he set about furthering his studies but failed to convince many mainstream scientists of orgonomy's validity. He also

Snowmobile Boom

*U*ntil recently, winter was the slow season in Maine, when the residents seemed to slip into a sort of quasi-hibernation along with the bears. With the booming popularity of the snowmobile, that's changed in the last few years, and many mountain communities now are seeing more business on winter weekends than in the summer.

Maine has some 12,000 miles of groomed snowmobile trails lacing the interior, and services aren't hard to find. It's rare to go more than 30 miles between fuel or food stops; look for the informal signs tacked up to trees at intersections pointing you to these outposts of civilization.

If you have your own snowmobile, you probably have a long list of favorite destinations. If you're simply interested in sampling some time on the trail, the offerings are more limited. But a growing number of outfitters are now offering rentals, lowering the threshold to motorized winter adventure.

In the Rangley Lake region, you can try Dockside Sports (864–2424) or Rev-It-Up Sports (864–2452), both of which offer rentals and can provide tips on destinations. Near Sugarloaf try Flagstaff Rentals (246–4276) in Stratton. For more information on laws, trail conditions, events, or clubs, check the Maine Snowmobile Association Web site (www.mesnow.com), or call 622–6983.

constructed something called a "cloud buster," a frightful-looking creation that he claimed removed orgone from the atmosphere, thereby shifting the atmospheric balance and producing rain.

In 1947 the *New Republic* magazine published an article entitled "The Strange Case of Wilhelm Reich," drawing attention to Reich's claims. The article focused the unwelcome spotlight of the Food and Drug Administration on Dr. Reich, and in particular on the "orgone energy accumulators" he built at Orgonon. Patients sat in these boxlike accumulators, which were designed to absorb orgone and infuse the inhabitants with a renewed energy. The FDA accused him of fraud and took him to court. Reich paid no attention to the courts, which he maintained lacked the authority to pass judgment on scientific matters. In 1957 Reich was finally arrested after one of his students crossed state lines with an accumulator. The strange case of Wilhelm Reich ended at a federal penitentiary, where shortly after incarceration he died of heart failure at the age of 60.

Orgonon was bequeathed to a private trust and today is managed as a memorial to Reich and his works. The building and views are visually stunning, and the fifteen-minute slide show about Reich's life offers a fascinating look at a complex mind. Many of Reich's devices are on display inside the house, as are many of the Edvard Munch–like paintings he created after he took up oil painting in 1952. A cloud buster is exhibited near a bust of the scientist a short walk from the house at an overlook with a magnificent view of Rangeley Lake.

Orgonon is open in July and August Tuesday through Sunday from 1:00 to 5:00 P.M. (open in September on Sundays only). The hour-long tour is $4.00 for adults; children under 12 are free. The grounds are 3.5 miles west of the town of Rangeley on Route 4. For more information call 864–3443.

Just a mile east of Rangeley on Route 16 is the **Rangeley Lakes Region Logging Museum,** which was founded in 1979. It took seed about ten years earlier, when longtime woodsman and resident Rodney Richard saw a timber foreman about to dump an antiquated piece of logging equipment down an embankment. "I'll take that," he said, and so the collection began.

The museum is located on eighteen acres and is a good spot to learn more than a little about the history of the timber industry in the region, which was home to the state's last stands of virgin timber (they didn't survive the late-nineteenth-century logging boom). Exhibits include hundreds of burly and rusted artifacts from the golden days of timbering, along with more contemporary chainsaw carvings and the wonderful faux primitive oil paintings of Alden Grant.

The museum is open Saturday and Sunday from 11:00 A.M. to 2:00 P.M. from late June to early September. For more information contact Rodney Richard at 864–5595.

Classic lakeside lodging can be found at **Grant's Kennebago Camps**, located 9 miles up a dirt road west of town. At the end of the nineteenth century, Kennebago Lake was renowned for its king-size brook trout, and eager "sports" ventured here to try their hand. Today the camp features a cluster of updated cabins around a main lodge, many of which have a buttery yellow pine interior and remarkable lake views. Meals are in a dining room whose walls are filled with bits of angling history. For reservations or information call (800) 633–4815 or 864–3608.

About 30 miles from Rangeley on Lake Webb near the town of Weld is another wonderful place to spend a night. The **Kawahnee Lodge** was built in 1929 by a camp shop instructor as a place for parents to stay when visiting their kids at the adjacent summer camp. It's classic Maine, built with yellow birch and a cobblestone fireplace, the whole affair seemingly held together by the creaks of the lustrous pine boards. The guest rooms in the lodge are fairly small, and most share hallway baths. A dozen cabins along the lake also are available for rent, although these are usually reserved by the week. Rates are under $100 for the lodge rooms with shared bathrooms, up to $160 for a three-bedroom cabin. The lodge is open mid-May to mid-October; call 585–2000.

Carrabassett Valley

I f you've developed a hankering to see a moose (most visitors to the state don't go away happy unless they've seen one), the drive from Rangeley to Stratton and onward up to Eustis stands a good chance of delivering. This remote 25-mile trip up Route 16 and continuing on Route 27 passes through prime moose habitat, with low-growing shrubs offering a tasty banquet for these herbivores. Your best bet is to head out shortly before sunset and enjoy the drive, perhaps making your destination the attractive and popular Porter House Restaurant in Eustis. For reservations call 246–7932.

In Eustis look for the roadside historical marker overlooking the Dead River, along the route of Benedict Arnold's 1775 march toward Quebec. (For background, see information on the Arnold Historical Society Museum, Lower Kennebec Valley/Gardiner and Hallowell.) At this bend in the river, the ill-starred expedition faced hurricane-force winds that toppled trees and created yet another obstacle. In the distance you can see Bigelow Mountain, named after Colonel Timothy Bigelow of Arnold's crew, who scaled the 4,150-foot peak in a vain attempt to see the lights of Quebec.

The towns along this part of Route 27 fall within the orbit of **Sugarloaf USA,** a modern, active ski area offering more than 2,800 feet of vertical drop, the largest in Maine. In summer attention shifts to golf and Sugarloaf's well-respected eighteen-hole golf course, designed by Robert Trent Jones II. There's also mountain biking on 50 miles of trails on and around the resort. Stop by the Sugarloaf Outdoor Center, which also offers guidance on hiking and fly-fishing. The resort is concentrated around the base of the mountain and features a seven-story brick hotel, the Sugartree Health Club, and a number of condominium villages, where condos may be rented by the night or the week. For more information call 237–2000 or (800) 843–5623.

Kingfield is the gateway to Sugarloaf and the Carrabasset Valley. Named after William King, Maine's first governor, Kingfield is a handsome and dignified town with a vaguely Old West feel to it, a world apart from the modern chalets of Sugarloaf. Travelers often come here for more than just the skiing: There's also the delightful **One Stanley Avenue,** a highly regarded restaurant in a Victorian house (265–5541), and the 1908 **Herbert Hotel** (800–843–4372), which has been tastefully

Porches for Rocking

*I*n the transitional period between the weeklong vacation at the sprawling summer resort and the overnight stop at a simple motel, visiting Maine more than not meant renting a lakeside cabin for a week or two. (In Maine these are often called "camps," which are not to be confused with the sort of camps where urbanites deport their kids.) Days were spent fishing, canoeing, or biking— gentle exploration where the chief quest was to fill an idle day.

There's still much to be said for this sort of vacation, and Maine is still an excellent destination for this brand of advanced idleness. How to find the perfect place? More and more cottage owners seem to be offering rentals on the Internet, and a little snooping ought to turn up some descriptions, photos, and contact information. Another alternative is to request a copy of the free "Guide to Camp and Cottage Rentals," published by the Maine Tourism Association. Updated annually, this handy brochure offers brief descriptions and black-and-white photos of places available all around the state. For a copy write Maine Tourism Association, P.O. Box 2300, Hallowell, ME 04347, or call 623–0363.

refurbished in recent years right down to the moose heads, baby grand piano, and wine closet in the old walk-in phone booth. It's more funky than polished, and above-average meals are served in the spacious old dining room.

Before leaving Kingfield be sure to visit the **Stanley Museum** on School Street. You've no doubt heard about the Stanley twins, F. O. and F. E., inventors of the Stanley Steamer. The twins and their five brothers and sisters were born and raised in Kingfield, and this intriguing museum is a well-designed memorial to their many talents. Even before the twins launched their automobile enterprise, they had made their fortune with inventions in the dry-plate photographic process, creating a company that was eventually purchased by George Eastman, Kodak's founder.

The museum, housed in a Georgian-style schoolhouse built with Stanley family donations in 1903, includes an informative exhibit on the family's history as well as three restored steamers. These aren't simply static museum pieces; the staff periodically takes them out for parades and other events. (The oil pans on the maple floor beneath the cars attest to their operational capabilities.) These exquisite automobiles, which had more in common with steam locomotives than with today's internal combustion engines, were first constructed as a hobby. When the Stanleys brought their car to the first New England auto show in 1898, they won both the time trials and the hill-climbing contest and received one hundred orders for their car within a week. The autos were manufactured between 1897 and 1925, reaching their pinnacle in 1906, when they set a land speed record of 127 miles per hour.

The museum, founded in 1981, also celebrates the achievements of the other Stanleys, most notably Chansonetta, the twins' younger sister, who proved herself an accomplished photographer. Her haunting portraits of rural and urban New England in the early nineteenth century are exceptional and have of late attracted respect and attention in the fine art world.

The Stanley Museum is open May through October Tuesday through Sunday from 10:00 A.M. to 4:00 P.M. Open November to April by appointment. Admission is $2.00 for adults, $1.00 for children. For more information call 265–2729.

At the northern end of the Sugarloaf universe is the town of Stratton, which offers several low-key hotels and restaurants. Among the more interesting is the **Widow's Walk**, an old, creaky bed-and-breakfast inn in an architecturally distinctive house built in 1892. Oramendal Blanchard, then Stratton's most prominent citizen, owned a timber mill as well as the local power and water companies; his Queen Anne–style home is notable for the curiously proportioned roof on the turret, which looks as if it were designed by a daft hatter. Inside, the six guest rooms are spartan but clean, furnished in flea market antique style. Many Appalachian Trail hikers hitch rides to the inn from the trail crossing 5 miles south to enjoy a shower and a hearty meal before making the final push toward Mount Katahdin. Room rates are $30 for two in summer and $48 in winter, including breakfast. For more information call 246–6901.

Farmington and Vicinity

*A*nother bit of local celebrity may be found on the eastern edge of the county, in the prosperous town of Farmington. A branch of the University of Maine is located here, as is the nearby **Nordica Homestead**, birthplace of one of opera's glamorous stars. Lillian Norton was born at this modest farmhouse in 1857, then at age 7 moved with her family to Boston. In the city she studied at the conservatory under John O'Neil, who rightly marked her as someone with significant talent. Following her studies she changed her name to Nordica, to reflect her northern roots, and was soon off to Europe. There she took the concert halls by storm. She became widely renowned as one of the few sopranos who could sing Wagnerian roles in tune, and she was feted by kings and presidents alike.

Unassuming Wilton

*S*outhwest of Farmington is the unassuming lakeside town of Wilton. There's not much here to attract the attention of tourists, but it is home to some intriguing historical footnotes. In 1823 Sylvia Hardy was born here. At just shy of 8 feet tall and 400 pounds in weight, Hardy became known as the "Maine Giantess." As with many unusually tall and short people of the era, she was recruited by P. T. Barnum, who billed her as the "tallest woman in the world." She died in 1888 and is buried in the Wilton cemetery.

Wilton also was home to Henry Bass, inventor of the loafer and founder of a successful shoe manufacturing empire. A bit of trivia: The famed Bass "Weejun"—a sort of fancy moccasin—gets its name from the last two syllables of "Norwegian." In Wilton you'll also find the Wells family, which runs a venerable cannery that claims to be the last in the nation to can fiddleheads, those springtime delicacies that go so well with scrambled eggs and served as a side dish. You usually can turn up canned fiddleheads in supermarkets around Maine.

Well after her fame blossomed, Nordica's sisters purchased her birthplace as a birthday present to the star. Following the diva's death in 1914 (she succumbed to pneumonia while on a tour of the South Pacific), the 1840 home became a memorial to the legendary singer, and many of her possessions were shipped here. Among the interesting items in the collections are the diva's opera gowns (including a Viking-helmeted Brunhilde outfit) and numerous photos from her career. A number of gifts presented to Nordica by admirers also are displayed, including a lacquered teakwood table from the Empress of China and a garish velvet-and-gilded chair from Diamond Jim Brady.

The Nordica Homestead Museum is located off Routes 4 and 27, 2 miles north of Farmington. Turn right on Holley Road and continue for 0.5 mile; the homestead is on the right. Open June 1 to Labor Day daily except Monday; hours are 10:00 A.M. to noon and 1:00 to 5:00 P.M. (Sundays it's open afternoons only.) Between Labor Day and October 31, the museum is open by advance reservation. Admission is $2.00 for adults, $1.00 for children. For more information call 778–2042.

We can't leave Farmington without mentioning that it was also the home of Chester Greenwood, who in 1872 invented that humble but eminently useful bit of winter outerwear, the earmuff—or ear protector, as he called it. The town celebrates his accomplishment each December during Chester Greenwood Day, when the earmuff-adorned citizenry assembles for considerable mirth and frivolity.

About 18 miles southwest of Farmington look for the **Mainely Critters Museum**, on Route 2 between Dixfield and East Dixfield. The museum is the project of Diane and Vance Child, both taxidermists who have put on display many examples of their work, including a full-size moose, a black bear, deer, coyotes, and bobcats. About 60 percent of their animals are found as roadkill. The museum is free (donations encouraged) and open most days from 9:00 A.M. to 5:00 P.M. (closed Fridays). For more information call 562–8231.

PLACES TO STAY
IN THE WESTERN
MOUNTAINS

BETHEL
Bethel Inn, On the
Common, 824– 2175

Holiday House, Main
Street, 824–3400

Sunday River Ski Resort,
Sunday River Road, Newry,
(800) 543–2754 or
824–3000

CARRABASSET VALLEY
The Herbert, Main Street,
Kingfield, 265–2000

Inn on Winter's Hill, Route
142, Kingfield, 265–5421

Sugarloaf Inn, Sugarloaf
Mountain, (800)
THE–LOAF or 237–2000

CENTER LOVELL
Center Lovell Inn and
Restaurant, Route 5,
(800) 777– 2698 or
925–1575

Pleasant Point Inn and
Restaurant, Box 218,
925–3008

FARMINGTON
Farmington Motel, Falls
Road, (800) 654–1133 or
778–4680

Mount Blue Motel, Wilton
Road, 778–6004

RANGELEY
Country Club Inn, Country
Club Drive, 864–3831

Rangeley Inn and Motor
Lodge, Main Street,
864–3341

WATERFORD
Kedarburn Inn, Route 35,
583–6182

The Waterford Inne,
Box 149, 583–4037

PLACES TO EAT
IN THE WESTERN
MOUNTAINS

BETHEL
Great Grizzly, Sunday River
Road, 824–6271

Sudbury Inn, Main Street,
824–2174

Helpful Web Sites

Bates College Museum of Art—
www.bates.edu/acad/museum/

Ski Maine Association—*www.skimaine.com*

Sugarloaf USA—*www.sugarloaf.com*

Sunday River Ski Resort—*www.sundayriver.com*

Town of Bethel—*www.nxi.com/WWW/bethel/
homepage.html*

Town of Rangeley—*www.rangeleymaine.com*

Selected Chambers of Commerce

Androscoggin County Chamber of Commerce,
179 Lisbon Street, Lewiston, 783–2249

Bethel Area Chamber of Commerce,
Cross Street, (800) 442–5826 or 824–2282

Greater Farmington Chamber of Commerce,
30 Main Street, 778–4215

Oxford Hills Chamber of Commerce,
166 Main Street, South Paris, 743–2281

Rangeley Lakes Region Chamber of Commerce,
*Lakeside Park, Rangeley, (800) MT–LAKES
or 864–5364*

Sugarloaf Area Chamber of Commerce,
Valley Crossing, 235–2100

Sunday River Brewing Co., Sunday River Road, 824–4253

FRYEBURG
Oxford House Inn, 105 Main Street, (800) 261–7206 or 935–3442

KINGFIELD & CARRABASSET VALLEY
Bag & Kettle, Sugarloaf Base Area, 237–2451

The Herbert, Main Street, Kingfield, 265–2000

One Stanley Avenue, 1 Stanley Avenue, Kingfield, 265–5541

Trufulio's, Route 27, 235–2010

RANGELEY
Country Club Inn, Country Club Drive, 864–3831

Doc Grant's Restaurant, 629 Main Street, 864–3449

Rangeley Inn Dining Room, Main Street, 864–3341

WATERFORD
Lake House, Route 35, (800) 223–4182 or 583–4182

Lower Kennebec Valley

The Kennebec River flows from Moosehead Lake in northern Maine some 150 miles to the Atlantic Ocean at Phippsburg. The river is famed for the excellent fishing and challenging white water along its northern stretches (see "North Woods"). As it descends toward the sea, the river slows and broadens, meandering through farm country and past former mill towns, trading posts, forts, and other vestiges of a varied history. The Kennebec was one of the first rivers in Maine to be explored by Europeans, who established trading routes along its length. In fact, Massachusetts' Plymouth Colony built a fur-trading post at the present site of Augusta as early as 1628. Some historians say that business was so profitable that settlers were soon able to pay off the debts incurred by the Mayflower expedition.

Kennebec County

Kennebec County is a rough circle in the midst of the state's southern tier. The county is some distance inland from the coast, but it can trace its history to seafaring days when lumber ships sailed up the broad river valley, providing a vital link to the world beyond. Today this gentle county offers inviting pastoral landscapes and historic riverside communities, including the state capital at Augusta.

Waterville Region

Starting upriver from Waterville, you'll find the **L. C. Bates Museum**, situated on the campus of the Hinckley School just off Route 201 south of the intersection with Route 23. The museum was founded by L. C. Bates, a successful entrepreneur from West Paris, Maine, who financed the conversion of this industrial arts building to a museum in 1924. The conversion produced eight galleries full of exhibits on natural history. The museum was operated until the late 1960s, when it fell into desuetude and was closed and locked up. In 1990 a group of local citizens banded together to reopen the museum, which had been largely

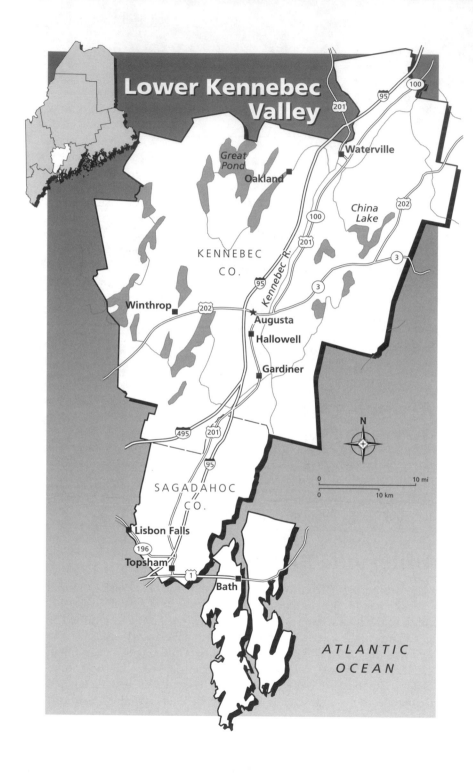

Lower Kennebec Valley

Great Pond

Oakland

Waterville

China Lake

KENNEBEC CO.

Kennebec R.

Winthrop

★ **Augusta**

Hallowell

Gardiner

SAGADAHOC CO.

Lisbon Falls

Topsham

Bath

ATLANTIC OCEAN

N

0   10 mi
0   10 km

undisturbed over the years save for an impressive accumulation of dust and cobwebs.

Thanks to this benign neglect, the museum was preserved in a wonderfully archaic state. The place boasts a copious collection of minerals; baskets by the Penobscot Indians; cases featuring stuffed bear, caribou, and the peculiar calico deer; and no fewer than seven magnificent moose heads. Among the best parts of the collection are the stuffed birds—including exotic birds of paradise and the rare quetzal from Central America—displayed against outstanding impressionistic backgrounds painted by nationally known illustrator Charles D. Hubbard. Be sure also to note the massive stuffed marlin caught off Bimini by the novelist Ernest Hemingway in 1935. No one seems quite sure how it got here. On the school grounds near the museum are several walking trails, which pass several handsome stone edifices and memorials. The trails are open to the public during museum hours; ask for a trail brochure at the front desk.

The Bates Museum is open from May 1 until the middle of November Wednesday through Saturday from 10:00 A.M. to 4:30 P.M. and Sunday from 1:00 to 4:30 P.M. Admission is $2.00 for adults, $1.00 for children 12 and over, 75 cents for children under 12. For more information call 453–4894.

Waterville is home to **Colby College**, just outside town on gentle Mayflower Hill, which offers a sweeping view of the rural countryside. The campus has a staid, brick-and-ivy appearance befitting an institution of higher learning that can trace its ancestry back to 1813, when the school was founded as the Maine Literary and Theological Institution. Following the Civil War it was renamed for Gardiner Colby, a Boston merchant and philanthropist, and in 1871 the college began admitting females. Although the campus has a historic and settled character, that's a bit misleading. The college moved from its original downtown site in the early 1950s, and today's classically styled buildings date from that era.

Worth visiting when you're on campus is the Colby College Museum of Art. The museum, housed in an open, modern wing appended to a more traditional brick structure, contains works by such Maine luminaries as

Bird Trivia

Ospreys (also called fish hawks) are large, handsome silvery-white raptors that all but disappeared from Maine in the 1950s and 1960s due to DDT poisoning. They've bounced back with vigor in the past two decades, and nesting pairs now number more than 2,000 statewide. Look for the unkempt nests on piers and telephone poles. For some reason, the nests are particularly numerous on the power towers along I–95 between Augusta and Bangor.

Winslow Homer, John Marin, and Andrew Wyeth. The gallery also regularly shares masterpieces of the art world with the Portland Museum of Art. Exhibited for one semester every two years are selections from the Payson collection, including works of Van Gogh, Renoir, and Degas. The museum is particularly known for its collection of paintings by contemporary artist Alex Katz. The museum's summer hours are Monday through Saturday from 10:00 A.M. to 4:30 P.M. and Sunday from 2:00 to 4:30 P.M. Admission is free. For more information call 872–3228.

Where the train tracks cross Main Street near downtown Waterville, you'll find the *Railroad Square Cinema.* The owners originally took two good ideas—fine movies and fine foods—and combined them into one with a funky restaurant in the lobby. A fire in 1994 forced the theater into new quarters across the parking lot, and two restaurants— Grand Central Cafe and Kafe Kino—opened adjacent to the movies. The movies and restaurants are located at 17 Railroad Square; for more information call 873–6526. Ask about the annual Maine International Film Festival, held each July.

East of Waterville look for the new home of the lively *Common Ground Fair*. Between 1976 and 1997 the fair was held in Windsor at the community fairgrounds; in 1998 the fair moved to its own 220-acre grounds between Unity and Thorndike. Sponsored by the Maine Organic Farmers and Gardeners Association, the fair features craftspeople, representatives from nonprofit organizations, and organic farmers demonstrating what they do. The fairgrounds bustle and teem like any county fair, but you're more likely to see farmers with ponytails and bandanas than tractor caps. There's the usual trotting out of prize vegetables and livestock as well as demonstrations of traditional New England crafts and activities, such as canoe building and horse-powered logging. Food is available from vendors (no sugar or caffeine), and upwards of 50,000 visitors pass through the gates

Getting Your Two Cents' Worth

*W*aterville is—or was—home to the world's only pedestrian toll bridge. Look for the Ticonic Foot Bridge over the Kennebec River, built in 1903 for workers who had to cross from houses on the far side to the Scott Paper Company. From the time it opened until 1962, every person who crossed it was charged two cents, gaining the bridge the more enduring local name The Two-Cent Bridge. It still stands but has been closed to all since the early 1970s.

WAYNE'S FAVORITE ATTRACTIONS

1. *L. C. Bates Museum,* Waterville region
2. *Maine State Museum,* Augusta
3. *Maine State House,* Augusta
4. *Maine Maritime Museum,* Bath
5. *Reid State Park,* Georgetown Island

during the three-day event, which is held the third weekend after Labor Day.

The new fairgrounds are on Crosby Brook Road off Route 220; look for signs. Daily admission is $6.00 for adults, $2.00 for children and seniors. For more information call 623–5115.

Augusta and Environs

Classic plays are performed throughout July and August by the **Theater at Monmouth,** a professional repertory company founded in 1970 some 13 miles west of Augusta. Several plays are staged each season, and the series usually includes a work or two by Shakespeare. Shows rotate each evening, offering theatergoers the option of coming back a second night for a different show. Reservations are recommended. For more information on performances, call 933–9999 Tuesday through Sunday 10:00 A.M. to 8:30 P.M.

Even if you're not much of a theater aficionado, it's still worth a trip to Monmouth to view **Cumston Hall,** the grandiose building where the plays are staged. Built in 1899–1900, this architectural flight of fancy incorporates minarets from the Middle East, Palladian windows, classical pediments, Romanesque arches and flourishes, and Victorian stained glass. Its interiors are lavishly painted with elaborate murals featuring Renaissance-style draped figures and hovering putti. In addition to the opera house, the building is home to the town hall and library.

The building was designed by Harry H. Cochrane, a Monmouth resident of multiple talents. Cochrane, sometimes called the "Maine Leonardo," was an artist and muralist by training. He lacked formal education in architecture but (he told an interviewer) studied the building arts to aid his career in decorating public spaces. Cochrane went on to paint the murals in the building, design the stained glass, create the plaster ornamentation, compose the music, and conduct the orchestra for the building's opening night. Cochrane afterward designed six other houses scattered about Monmouth, a town that displays an architecturally eclectic style. Monmouth is also home to the **Monmouth Museum**, a small and engaging historical museum open Tuesday through Sunday from 1:00 to 4:00 P.M. Admission is $3.00 for adults, $1.00 for children. For more information call 933–2287.

The **Maine State Museum** in Augusta should by all accounts be on the beaten path. Surprisingly, it isn't. Few Maine residents—and even fewer out-of-staters— seem to be aware of this jewel of a museum. Evidently its administrators have done a far better job in designing this thoroughly modern, informative, and appealing museum than in getting the word out.

Housed in one of those nondescript gray buildings that seem to characterize government complexes everywhere (the museum shares a roof with the Maine State Library and Archives), the collections are aesthetically arranged and neatly presented. There's a sense of discovery and exploration around each corner, from grainy film clips of early loggers working the river drives to a convincing replica of a water-driven woodworking shop. Extensive exhibits provide an overview of both the cultural and the natural history of the state—from the craft of boatbuilding to extinction of the eastern caribou.

One exhibit of particular interest is entitled "12,000 Years in Maine" and covers the broad sweep of Maine's earliest inhabitants. A dozen millennia ago the state's terrain more resembled the open Arctic tundra than the dense woodlands of today, and migratory native tribes passed through the region hunting caribou. Displays of artifacts found near Azichohos Lake (near Rangeley) and a full-scale diorama of a

Cumston Hall, Monmouth

LOWER KENNEBEC VALLEY

prehistoric meat cache are especially engaging. Be sure also to take the time to see the unique artifacts from the so-called Moorehead phase of Native American development (4,800 to 3,800 years ago), which are characterized by long, graceful arrowheads and adzes.

Plan to spend about two hours at the museum, which is located on the grounds of the state house complex on State Street in Augusta. It's open Monday through Friday from 9:00 A.M. to 5:00 P.M., Saturday and most holidays from 10:00 A.M. to 4:00 P.M., and Sunday from 1:00 to 4:00 P.M. Admisson is free. For more information call 287–2301.

Near the east end of the museum building you'll come upon a bronze statue of Samantha Smith, Maine's young "ambassador of goodwill." Samantha gained unexpected national and international fame after she wrote a letter to former Soviet leader Yuri Andropov questioning his commitment to peace. Andropov responded, inviting the Manchester, Maine, girl to Moscow and setting her off on an early career of diplomacy. That promising career was cut short when Samantha died in a local plane crash in 1985 at the age of 13.

While on the statehouse grounds, take the time to wander around a bit to see the government in action. From the museum, walk to the south entrance of the **Maine State House**, an imposing granite edifice originally designed by Charles Bulfinch, the architect of the U.S. Capitol in Washington, D.C. You can learn about the architecture and history of the building during a self-guided tour. Historical markers guide visitors from one station to the next, pointing out various clues to the building's history, such as the 1907 expansion that greatly changed its profile. If you'd like a more personal touch, pick up the marked phone inside the entrance for a free guided tour anytime between 9:00 A.M. and 1:00 P.M. Monday through Friday. The south entrance was also the former site of the state museum, as evidenced by the incongruous display cases filled with moose, deer, fish, and beaver.

Be aware that major renovations to the state house are under way through at least 2003, so some sections will be closed to the public. For more information call 287–2301.

Top Annual Events

1. *Maine Sportsman Show, Augusta,* late March, 882–7032
2. *Annual Mineral Symposium,* Augusta, early May, 657–3732
3. *Great Kennebec Whatever Family Festival,* Augusta to Hallowell, late June–early July, 623–4559
4. *Heritage Days,* Bath, early July, 443–9751
5. *Antique Show and Sale,* Bath, mid-August, 443–4112
6. *Bluefish Tournament,* Bath, mid-August, 443–9751
7. *Common Ground Fair,* Unity, third weekend after Labor Day, 623–5115

From the upper floor of the state house, be sure to step out onto the open veranda, where you may see legislators and lobbyists chatting in cane-seated rockers. From this vantage you get a fine view eastward across the Kennebec River. The complex of buildings across the river is the Augusta Mental Health Institute. Directly below and across State Street is Capitol Park, where you'll find Maine's Vietnam Memorial as well as the tomb of Enoch Lincoln (a relative of Abraham), the Maine governor who moved the capital from Portland to Augusta in 1827, seven years after statehood. The park also was used as an encampment during the Civil War.

Across the Kennebec from downtown Augusta is **Fort Western**, a relic of the days when the river was the state's central trading route. The fort, built in 1754 by the Kennebec Proprietors (a group of major landowners), served as a garrison and supply station to protect traders venturing into the interior. The Arnold expedition passed by in 1775 en route to Quebec, but the structure was never used in combat.

Today the original 100-foot-long garrison house survives in nearly pristine condition, and the grounds have been augmented by a replica stockade fence and two blockhouses. Visitors take a self-guided walking tour, with informative history lessons offered by costumed interpreters. In the garrison house you'll see clues to the various identities the building assumed both during and after its service as a fort. The building at one time or another contained a store, officers' quarters, and other dwellings, even serving as a tenement in the 1920s. Look for intriguing bits of Americana, including an ingenious mousetrap that uses a falling block of wood to capture its prey.

Fort Western is on the east bank of the Kennebec at 16 Cony Street. Open daily Memorial Day to July 4 from 1:00 to 4:00 P.M. Between July 4 and Labor Day it's open from 10:00 A.M. to 4:00 P.M. Monday through Friday and from 1:00 to 4:00 P.M. weekends; all holidays from 1:00 to 4:00 P.M. only. Open weekends only Labor Day though Columbus Day, from 1:00 to 4:00 P.M. Admission is $4.50 for adults, $2.50 for children ages 6 to 16. For more information call 626–2385.

Gardiner and Hallowell

Head 2 miles downstream from Augusta along the Kennebec's west bank (follow Route 27), and you'll pull into the quiet riverside town of **Hallowell**. Many of the younger state employees live and congregate in Hallowell, lending it a more spirited character than many

Maine towns of its size. Water Street, a compact thoroughfare of stout brick buildings, offers surprisingly upscale places to dine and drink, as well as a number of good antiques shops for browsing. Much of the nineteenth-century commercial architecture has been well preserved, and the gentrification has been subtle rather than obnoxious. Among the popular spots along Water Street are *Slates* (622–9575), a watering hole and restaurant where you're liable to run into a state legislator or two, and the Wharf Tavern, which has an adjoining billiard hall with old-fashioned pool tables and low brass fixtures lighting the felts.

In Gardiner, a few miles downstream, head for the *A-1 Diner* at 3 Bridge Street. This 1946 Worcester diner is one of those classics sought by diner fans nationwide. Inside you'll find black-and-white tile floors and age-burnished wooden booths, art decoish stools, and neat wood trim. One aspect that's not so classic is the menu. In addition to comfort food like pot roast and mashed potatoes, you'll find creative and delicious dishes like Greek lemon soup, pad thai, and Siamese chicken curry. Don't overlook the delicious tapioca pudding, served with a righteous heap of whipped cream. The A-1 (582–4804) is open breakfast through dinner every day except Sunday, when it closes at noon.

If you're an architecture buff, plan to spend some time walking off your meal by wandering Gardiner's commercial and residential neighborhoods, which have benefited from renovation. The *Gardiner Historic District*, spread along Water Street, comprises forty-seven buildings of note. Stop by either the city hall or the public library for a flyer entitled "Historic Walking Tour of Gardiner."

Gardiner was the staging point for one of the richer episodes involving the Kennebec River: the Arnold expedition in the fall of 1775. General Benedict Arnold, who was later to donate his name as a synonym for "traitor," led one of the more tragic endeavors in the American Revolution in attempting a surprise attack on Quebec. The expedition, with about 1,150 men, endured horrendous conditions during the approach to Quebec through the Maine wilderness and failed miserably to take the city during an attack in December 1775. Arnold himself was wounded and faced misconduct charges after his return to the United States. An excellent fictional narrative dealing with the Arnold expedition may be found in Kenneth Roberts's novel *Arundel*, which is widely available in both new and used bookshops.

Learn more about the expedition at the *Arnold Historical Society Museum*, downstream from Gardiner on the river's east bank in Pittston. This fine historic home dates to 1765 and is furnished with period antiques. The Colburn family lived in the house for nearly 200 years. Visitors get a quick education in the history of decorative arts and architecture in seeing how the house evolved over the years. The guide also will tell you about Major Reuben Colburn, the original resident, who hosted General Arnold and Aaron Burr for two nights while the final arrangements for the expedition were ironed out. In the barn you'll find two early bateaux (flat-bottomed boats), which may or may not have been used in the expedition, as well as a half-dozen replicas commissioned for a 1975 reenactment.

The museum is off Route 127 in Pittston, south of Randolph and Gardiner. Open July and August weekends from 10:00 A.M. to 5:00 P.M. and by appointment; call 582–7080. Admission is $2.50 per adult; children are free.

Sagadahoc County

With only 250 square miles, Sagadahoc is Maine's smallest county, but it manages to pack in a lion's share of history. Much of the state's early (and present) shipbuilding heritage can be traced here, a heritage reflected in many magnificent homes in towns and villages from Merrymeeting Bay up the Kennebec and along the lower Androscoggin River. The terrain is gentle, with thick forests opening for farmer's fields and the occasional settlement.

Richmond Area

South of Gardiner you'll come to the once-prosperous town of **Richmond**, where many sea captains settled in the years prior to the Civil War. Handsome brick buildings line the commercial streets. Elaborate Greek Revival and Italianate homes are tucked away on the side streets. Richmond has by and large been overlooked by the years; it has a slightly unkempt appearance but lends itself to fruitful explorations.

In wandering through Richmond you may find it strange to pass Saint Alexander Nevsky Church with its onion domes or the Saint Nicholas Orthodox Parish Church. Russians began settling here five decades ago. In the 1940s the town caught the attention of Vladimir Kuhn von Poushental, a Russian emigre (and former count under the czarist rulers) who found Richmond's climate and terrain much like that of Moscow. He bought up dozens of farms and buildings around Richmond, advertising parcels for sale in Russian immigrant newspapers.

Transplanted Russians responded, moving in great numbers in the 1950s and 1960s. At the peak of the Russian influx, nearly 500 immigrants lived in this quiet riverside town, and Russian Richmond boasted its own restaurant, bootmaker, and three churches where Russian dramas were regularly staged. Since its peak around 1970, the community has dwindled to around fifty. Spoken Russian may still be heard here and there from yards and open windows as you walk the peaceful streets.

Just a hundred yards or so from the Richmond town landing is **Swan Island**, a 4-mile-long state-owned island managed as the Steve Powell Wildlife Management Area. The island sits in the northernmost reach of **Merrymeeting Bay**, the largest tidal bay north of the Chesapeake. Six rivers feed into the bay, including the Kennebec and the Androscoggin, and some 1,755 acres of islands and mudflats are managed by the staff for wildlife conservation. Thousands of waterfowl and other birds stop over during their spring and fall migrations along the Atlantic flyway. Species include Canada geese, teal, pintail, and the common goldeneye, among many others. Driving around the bay, keep your eyes to the sky for bald eagles—one of the greatest concentrations of nesting eagles in the state is found along these shores.

This inland bay measures some 4,500 acres, but much of the shoreline is privately owned, making a visit problematic. Swan Island offers the best way to have a glimpse of the bay's wildlife. The state Department of Inland Fisheries and Wildlife offers a motorboat shuttle from Richmond to the island between May 1 and Labor Day, and limited camping is available. Island access is strictly limited to sixty people at one time, and reservations are essential. The day use fee is $8.00 per adult, $6.50 for children (includes boat shuttle). Reservations must be made in writing at least one week prior to arrival. Call 737-4307 or 287-8000 for more information.

Several miles outside the village is the **Richmond Sauna and Bed and Breakfast**, as unusual a bed-and-breakfast as you'll find in Maine. Opened in 1976 by former aerospace engineer Richard Jarvi, this B&B, located on a quiet dirt road, is housed in a fine 1831 home with five guest rooms and a two-room suite. Guests are treated like, well, guests. There's a baby grand piano in the dining room and a well-stocked library, and you're free to use the kitchen to make dinner or lunch or just to sit on the kitchen couch and chat with the other guests, who tend to be young professionals from Portland and Boston.

Although the accommodations are homey and comfortable, what really attracts people is the rustic building next door, where you'll find saunas, a hot tub, and a swimming pool. (Bathing suits are optional, even in the communal hot tub and pool.) Lodging prices include use of all the facilities, or if you're just passing through, you can stop by for a sauna or swim. The six private saunas are wood-fired and sufficiently steamy, with the hot tub and pool just outside the door, making for a short dash in winter. Jarvi, a congenial host, has stocked a refrigerator in the waiting room with a selection of juices. Massages are available at $40 per hour, or $25 per half hour.

Lodging is $65 per night for a couple ($85 for the suite), $50 for a single. There is a $15 per person per hour sauna charge (includes access to pool and hot tub). Sauna hours are from 6:00 to 10:00 P.M. in the summer and from 5:00 to 9:00 P.M. in the winter; closed Mondays. The sauna is 1.1 miles west of I–95 on Route 197. Turn left on Route 138, then make the immediate left on Dingley Road. For more information call 737–4752.

Bath and Environs

Nearing the ocean you'll come to the historic town of Bath. At the small downtown park along the Kennebec, there's a sign greeting visitors arriving by boat: WELCOME TO BATH, MAINE—CITY OF SHIPS—HOME TO THE BEST SHIPBUILDERS IN THE WORLD. If you arrived by boat, you're already aware of the city's main industry, having passed the imposing drydock of Bath Iron Works, where an Aegis class destroyer or other navy ship may be undergoing repairs. In fact even arriving by car you may have figured out Bath's prominence: The towering red-and-white striped crane of the shipyard—the fourth largest in the country—dominates the landscape, providing a navigational landmark for those traveling by road and river alike.

The shipyard isn't open to the public, but you can get a good introduction to Bath's venerable shipbuilding history at the *Maine Maritime Museum* just south of Bath Iron Works. This is one of Maine's most informative museums, with displays ranging from historical oil paintings of clippers and schooners to historic wooden ships moored at the museum's riverside docks. In fact, the museum is located on the former grounds of the Percy and Small Shipyard, which built forty-two schooners between 1894 and 1920. In 1909 the largest wooden ship ever built in America, the 329-foot *Wyoming*, was launched from ways that may be found in the marsh grass at the edge of the river.

The museum is particularly strong in interpretive exhibits—such as the engaging lobstering display—which keep children intrigued and

Lobster Exhibit at Maine Maritime Museum, Bath

enthralled. But it's not a place for kids only. Adults who've harbored quiet fantasies of casting off lines and setting sail for points unknown will enjoy themselves at the Apprenticeshop, where boatbuilders employ traditional techniques in building craft sturdy enough to brave Maine's often tempestuous waters. The builders are happy to entertain any and all questions from visitors.

Museum hours are from 9:30 A.M. to 5:00 P.M. daily (except Thanksgiving, Christmas, and New Year). Admission is $8.50 for adults, $5.75 for children, and $25.00 for families, with discounts for seniors. The museum is at 243 Washington Avenue; look for blue swallowtail pennants directing the way from various points around town. For more information call 443–1316.

Bath's historic brick downtown is worth exploring. This area has much of the charm of Portland's Old Port Exchange, but with a less aggressive quaintness. For lunch there are a number of eateries along Front Street and Elm Street. A walk to the top of Centre Street toward the old Sagadahoc Courthouse will bring you to *Kristina's Restaurant* (442–8577), housed in a pair of nineteenth-century homes connected by a light and airy atrium. Kristina's is well known for its pecan buns, which are about as rich and dense as you'll find anywhere. Expect to wait for seating on weekend mornings, when the brunch attracts folks from Portland and beyond.

Ringing the downtown area are a wonderful assortment of handsome homes, many quite imposing. These reflect both the prosperity of the

A Dismal Winter

*A*bout a half mile west of the fort is the site of the Popham Colony, or what might be called the sister city of Jamestown, Virginia. Both were established in 1607 during the first attempts by Europeans to settle the New World. Jamestown succeeded; Popham failed. About one hundred English settlers under the leadership of George Popham and Raleigh Gilbert landed here in August 1607 and constructed a fort and a storehouse. Called "Northern Virginia Colony" by the English, the settlement never took root. George Popham died during the winter, and Gilbert left for England the following spring. Disenchanted with their prospects, the remaining settlers drifted back to England the following summer, and the colony of Popham was relegated to a historical footnote.

town in the late nineteenth century and the creativity of local architects and builders. Among the most impressive are those lining Washington Street just north of downtown. Check at the local visitor information centers or the town library for a copy of the informative and helpful brochure "Architectural Tours: Walking and Driving in the Bath Area." The guide provides a good overview of the exuberant styles you'll see while touring the town, as well as thumbnail descriptions of specific properties.

A handful of the more impressive structures have been converted to bed-and-breakfasts and open a door to the past for confirmed history buffs. Among the more notable: the handsome 1874 *Galen Moses House,* which has lots of ticking clocks and a mildly eccentric Victorian-Italianate flavor (rooms $69 to $119, 1009 Washington Street, 888–442–8771), and the stern *Kennebec Inn Bed & Breakfast,* housed in a massive bank-like home built in 1860 of bricks imported from England. It was built for a sea captain and shipbuilder and designed by noted New England architect Francis Fassett; it's been recently renovated and now houses seven spacious guest rooms ($100 to $165 per night, 1024 Washington Street, 800–822–9393 or 443–5202).

Mouth of the Kennebec

*W*here the Kennebec River empties into the Atlantic, some 10 miles south of Bath, you'll find *Fort Popham,* a solid granite fortification that watches over the broad river entrance. The fort was constructed during the Civil War, when the North realized how vulnerable Bath's shipbuilding industry was to Confederate attack. The war ended before the massive 500-foot-circumference fort could be completed. Today the 30-foot walls are in good repair, and the structure is notable for its graceful stone staircases. Parking at the fort is limited. Open Memorial Day through September daily from 9:00 A.M. until sunset. Admission during summer months is $2.00 for adults. For more information call 389–1335.

Not far from the fort is 529-acre *Popham Beach State Park*. One of the state's most popular parks, Popham provides access to a broad sweep of beach with glorious views across smaller islands offshore out toward looming Seguin Island and its doleful lighthouse. The beach parking lot fills early on pleasant weekends. A fee of $2.00 per person is charged. For more information call 389–1335.

If you're planning to camp, a spectacular private campground is located not far from Fort Popham at *Hermit Island*. Nick and Dave Sewall have owned and operated the campground since 1953, offering 275 sites (including 63 on the ocean) spread across the open, shrubby bluffs of the mile-and-a-half-long island. Access is by car along a sandy spit, and only tents and pop-up campers are allowed. Although Hermit Island has quite a few campsites, use is kept to a minimum: Only one car and two adults are allowed per site, and day visitors are not permitted. Those lucky enough to obtain a campsite (reservations are essential) have seven beaches to themselves, along with rocky bluffs and tidal pools perfect for exploring.

The island can be reached by car off Route 209 south of Bath. Open from June through mid-October. Rates are $25.75 to $33.75 (add $2.00 on weekends), depending on time of year and location. For more information call 443–2101.

On the east side of the Kennebec River (you need to backtrack to Bath and cross the Carleton Bridge to Woolwich) is Georgetown Island, connected to the mainland by bridge. This area is wooded and quiet, with a handful of low-key attractions to make the detour worthwhile.

At the island's southern tip is *Reid State Park*, located on a former estate. The park has everything from picnic tables set in shady copses, to rocky headlands and a mile-long sandy beach. It's a popular destination on balmy summer days, so head here early to stake your claim to a table or plot of sand. The day-use fee is $2.50.

In driving to the park, you may have noticed the grand shingled mansion on your left near the turn-off to Five Islands. That's *Grey Havens*, a fine summer home that's now one of the region's better bed-and-breakfasts.

A Different Kind of Shell

*D*uring World War II, towers sprouted up all along the Maine coast as the military mobilized to prepare for an invasion from offshore. You can still see the stark, squarish towers along the coast, sprouting inelegantly skyward. Maine's bays were used as anchorages and some of its coastline for target practice.

That history resurfaced in the winter of 1996–1997, when about 100 missiles and rocket motors emerged out of the sand at Reid State Park following the pounding of especially fierce winter storms. None of the armaments were active, but bathers stepped a bit more gingerly during the next summer season.

The place is heavily imbued with the feel of a rambling summer cottage on the coast, with creaky steps, cobblestone fireplaces, and the tang of salt air. Many of the rooms have unrivaled ocean views, and especially grand are the turret rooms, which come complete with binoculars to watch for whales and keep an eye on lobstermen offshore. Continental breakfast is included in the room rate, and guests can use the kitchen to prepare their own lobster feast in the evening. Rooms at Grey Havens start at $100 and climb to $205 for the Oceanfront Suite. For reservations call 371–2616.

A few minutes' drive north of the inn, on Robbinhood Road, is one of Maine's best and most elegant restaurants. Located in a spare and handsome early building that's been renovated to accent the clean lines, the **Robbinhood Free Meetinghouse**'s, menu is huge and far-ranging, with some thirty entrees featuring spices and cooking techniques from around the globe. Dinner here isn't free—figure on $100 or so for two—but it's well worthwhile. Reservations are encouraged; call 371–2188.

PLACES TO STAY
IN THE LOWER KENNEBEC
VALLEY

AUGUSTA
Best Western Senator Inn,
284 Western Avenue,
622–5804

Comfort Inn Civic Center,
281 Civic Center Drive,
623–1000

Holiday Inn—Civic Center,
110 Community Drive,
622–4751

Susse Chalet Guest Lodge,
Whitten Road, 622–3776

BATH
Galen C. Moses House,
1009 Washington Street,
442–8771

Holiday Inn, 139 Western
Avenue, 443–9741

Inn at Bath, 969 Washington Street, 443–4294

GEORGETOWN
The Gray Havens, Seguinland Road, 371–2616

WATERVILLE
Best Western Waterville,
356 Upper Main Street,
873–3335

Budget Host Airport Inn,
400 Kennedy Memorial
Drive, 873–3366

LOWER KENNEBEC VALLEY

PLACES TO EAT IN THE LOWER KENNEBEC VALLEY

AUGUSTA

Burnsie's Homestyle Sandwiches, Hinchborn Street, 622–6425

Hilltop Restaurant, Augusta State Airport, 623–2044

The Senator, 284 Western Avenue, 622–0320

BATH

Beale Street Barbeque and Grill, 215 Water Street, 442–9514

Kennebec Tavern, 119 Commercial Street, 442–9636

Kristina's, 160 Centre Street, 442–8577

GEORGETOWN

Robbinhood Free Meeting-house, Robbinhood Road, 371–2188

HALLOWELL

A–1 Diner, 3 Bridge Street, 582–4804

WATERVILLE

Grand Central Cafe, Railroad Square, 872–9135

John Martin's Manor, 54 College Avenue, 873–5676

Kafe Kino, Railroad Square, 872–9500

Weathervane Restaurant, 470 Kennedy Memorial Drive, 873–4522

Helpful Web Sites

City of Augusta—*www.ci.augusta.me.us/*

Colby College Art Museum—*www.colby.edu/museum*

Hermit Island Campground—*www.hermitisland.com*

Johnny's Seeds—*www.johnnyseed.com*

Railroad Square Cinema—*www.mint.net/movies*

Town of Bath—*www.visitbath.com*

Waterville Online—*www.ci.waterville.me.us*

Selected Chambers of Commerce

Chamber of Commerce of Bath—*Brunswick Region, 59 Pleasant Street, Brunswick, (800) 725–8797 or 725–8797*

Kennebec Valley Chamber of Commerce, *21 University Drive, Augusta, 623–4559*

Kennebec Valley Tourism Council, *179 Main Street, Waterville, (800) 393–8629*

Mid-Maine Chamber of Commerce, *1 Post Office Square, Waterville, 873–3315*

Midcoast

Traveling Midcoast Maine presents a series of logistical challenges. Much of the coastal area between Casco Bay and Penobscot Bay is spread out on long, spindly fingers of land extending southward from Route 1. What's more, many of these fingers are separated from one another by wide rivers—such as the Kennebec, Sheepscot, and Damariscotta—that are spanned by few bridges. The upshot is that after you drive for miles to the tip of a peninsula, you've got to turn right around and head out the way you came in, connecting the points with stints on congested Route 1.

The good news is that because these peninsulas are geographic cul-de-sacs, they maintain a sense of solitude and seclusion rare in other coastal areas. Sometimes surprisingly, old resorts and homes will be found at the tip after a long drive, traces of a time when most people traveled this coastline by water rather than land. There are oceanside farms, leafy hardwood forests, and spruce groves abutting rocky shores. Many of these desultory roads are best wandered at a slower pace than a car provides. Bicyclists almost always return enthusiastic about gently dipping and twisting roads that pass through quiet forests with periodic glimpses of a distant ocean. When the fog moves in from offshore, the views disappear but the pleasant sense of isolation is heightened.

Lincoln County

Lincoln County extends along the coast from Wiscasset to Waldoboro and inland to farm country around Somersville. Two major peninsulas are here: Boothbay Peninsula and Pemaquid Peninsula, both of which are blessed with at least two roads running down and back, allowing a loop tour rather than a return on the original road. The fabled rugged Maine coast may be found in spots (notably at Pemaquid Point), but for the most part, it's a gentle and wooded coastline, ideal for unhurried back-road exploration.

Midcoast

WALDO
CO.

Belfast

KNOX
CO.

Camden

Penobscot Bay

N. Haven I.

Rockland

LINCOLN
CO.

Vinalhaven I.

Wiscasset

ATLANTIC OCEAN

0   10 mi
0   10 km

N

Wiscasset Region

If you're arriving in the region via Route 1, one of the first towns you'll come to is Wiscasset on the western banks of the Sheepscot River.

Just a few blocks off Route 1, at the end of Wiscasset's High Street, you'll come to an imposing building known locally as **Castle Tucker**. This architecturally eccentric brick home was first built in 1807 by Judge Silas Lee, then widely modified around 1860 by Captain Richard H. Tucker, a sea captain who made his fortune in the cotton trade. Tucker added to the front of the Federal-era house a grand three-floor piazza overlooking the river, changing the home's character significantly. Among other alterations inside, he converted a dining hall into a billiards room.

The mansion was owned by Tucker's descendants until 1997, when Jane Tucker donated the property to the Society for the Preservation of New England Antiquities. She still lives on the second floor, but the public is invited to view the first floor of this unique home. The forty-five-minute tour provides an intriguing look at the life of a nineteenth-century sea captain, from the paintings of great ships on the walls to the stiff, medallion-backed Victorian furniture in the parlors. Also noteworthy are architectural flourishes that include an impressive freestanding elliptical staircase, a parquet floor, and plaster trim painstakingly painted to look like oak. A clutter of curios, ranging from an egg collection in the billiard room to unusual utensils in the kitchen, allow for fine browsing.

Castle Tucker stands at the corner of Lee and High Streets. Tours are offered June 1 to October 15 Wednesday to Sunday hourly from 11:00 A.M. to 4:00 P.M. Admission is $4.00. For more information call 882–7364.

A short stroll past the stately homes of High Street will bring you to the extraordinary museum called the **Musical Wonder House**. Here, in a rather stern 1852 house, is a mind-boggling collection of music boxes, gramophones, and player pianos from around the world. It's not the only collection of this sort in existence, but it's certainly one of the best. What's more, owner Danilo Konvalinka delights in playing the music boxes for visitors, unlike curators of other museums where the collections may be seen but not heard.

The museum, which occupies both floors of the building, starts in a grand hallway dominated by a flying staircase. Along the walls are coin-operated music boxes, mostly dating from the nineteenth century. There's no charge to wander in here and try a few boxes, or to browse in the gift shop off the back hallway. But this represents only the tip of the iceberg. Sign up for a tour and you'll have a chance to hear a sampling from among the literally hundreds of music boxes in Konvalinka's collection. The standard tour, which runs about an hour, includes the three downstairs rooms; the deluxe tour, about three hours, also includes four additional rooms upstairs.

The common conception of a music box may be of a small, square box that produces a tinkling, mildly irritating sound when opened. Konvalinka puts that notion to rest. His collection ranges from delicate singing-bird automatons to remarkable orchestral music boxes fully outfitted with snare drums, castanets, chimes, and bells. The musical selections range from Verdi operas to Gilbert and Sullivan tunes, with most everything in between. One of the highlights of the collection is an 1870 Girod music box from Geneva; it is the size of a small coffin and contains, among other things, a miniature reed organ. Konvalinka, an Austrian immigrant who became fascinated with music boxes at age 19, found this exceptional example through a classified ad and spent fifteen years restoring it. Although they represent a wide range of styles, all the music boxes share one thing in common: They produce a rich, wonderful sound that is fully absorbing.

The Musical Wonder House is at 18 High Street. It's open late May to late October (gift shop open until Thanksgiving). Tours are offered daily from 10:00 A.M. to 5:00 P.M. (limited tours after Labor Day). The house is divided into four exhibit areas, with half-hour demonstrations rotating through the four rooms throughout the day. The cost per room is $7.50; there's a $1.00 discount for seniors and children under 12. For more information call 882–7163.

Just north of the village center on Federal Street (on the way to Head Tide), you'll pass the *Lincoln County Museum and Jail*, built in 1811 on a gentle hill overlooking the river. Tours of the jail reveal dim, small cells seemingly carved out of a single block of granite—even the ceilings and floors are made of granite slabs. So it comes as something of a surprise to learn that this jail, based on plans drawn up by John Howard, an early prison reformer, was thought to represent state-of-the-art prison design. Prior to this time, most prisoners were held in large open spaces; the individual cells were thought to be a more humane approach.

The impressive stonework of the three-story jail, which was built with rock slabs ranging from 10 to 41 inches thick, is almost overshadowed by the fascinating graffiti left by early sailors, who, one presumes, were arrested for behaving like sailors. The cells range from a grim isolation cell with a

WAYNE'S FAVORITE ATTRACTIONS

1. *Musical Wonder House, Wiscasset*
2. *Pemaquid Point, Pemaquid Peninsula*
3. *Monhegan Island*
4. *William A. Farnsworth Art Museum, Rockland*
5. *Camden Hills*
6. *Penobscot Marine Museum*

narrow slit for a window to the somewhat more airy rooms on the third floor used for women, debtors, and the insane. The jail was closed in 1913, considered a relic of the past. It did have one more moment of glory before becoming a museum: During Prohibition it was used to store confiscated contraband liquor.

The tour also includes a walk through the adjoining jailer's house, where the warden and his wife lived and meals were prepared. The home features a restored kitchen and a bright exhibit area with examples of the jailer's craft, including early shackles, handcuffs, and photocopies of prison logs through which visitors are free to browse.

The Lincoln County Museum and Jail is open in July and August Tuesday to Saturday from 11:00 A.M. to 4:00 P.M., and Sunday from noon to 4:00 P.M. Admission is $3.00 for adults, $1.00 for children. For more information call 882–6817.

Train buffs flock to the **Maine Coast Railroad**, which offers ninety-minute excursions departing from the waterfront park just off Route 1 in Wiscasset. This is a great way to get away from the traffic and view wonderful scenery while relaxing in comfort in 1930s-era restored railroad cars. The terrain is familiar and comforting—a mix of hardwood forests, river views, and farm fields—as you chug along. One trail runs to Bath, another to Newcastle. Two departures are offered daily from Wiscasset between late June and August. The fare is $10.00 for adults,

Stuck in the Mud

*I*f you look just south of the bridge as you cross the Sheepscot River, you'll notice some moldering hulks in the mudflats off Wiscasset. These are the remains of the **Luther Little** and **Hesper,** two cargo vessels that were abandoned in 1932. They were more famous as wrecks than as active ships, and busloads of photographers once ventured here to capture the picturesque scene of the old boats, their masts and rigging still holding on, easing into oblivion at the water's edge.

Alas, time finally overtook them. A 1978 fire did significant damage, and between 1990 and 1996 the masts fell over, the hulls caved in, and photographers starting passing on by. Today the remains are just indistinct mounds, hardly fitting as memorials to the once-vibrant enterprise of the coastal shipping trade in Maine.

$9.00 for seniors, $5.00 for children, and $25.00 for families. For more information call (800) 795–5404 or 882–8000.

If your appetite's kicked in, swing by the always-popular **Red's Eats** on Water Street just before the bridge in Wiscasset. There's usually a line at this roadside stand, and the reason is this: the lobster rolls. They may be Maine's best. Red's offers take-out only, so pick up your order and then wander down to the waterfront park to enjoy it. Open summers only; call 882–6128.

East of the river and slightly south (turn at the Muddy Rudder Restaurant) you'll come to the **Fort Edgecomb State Historic Site**, which sits on three acres at the south tip of Davis Island. The fort was built following the Embargo Act of 1807, which closed American ports to shipping. Americans were concerned that the act could lead to British attacks, and fortifications were built along the Maine coast. During the War of 1812, the fort was the scene of some skirmishes, which you can learn about while walking the attractive grounds. The site includes an octagonal blockhouse that dates to 1809, and it is generally considered to be one of the best preserved early forts in the country.

The historic site is open daily from Memorial Day to Labor Day; admission is $1.00 for adults; children under 12 are free. For more information call 882–7777.

Inland Lincoln County

Eight miles north of Wiscasset is the village of **Head Tide**. There's nothing in the way of major or minor attractions here, but the fourteen historic buildings wedged in a narrow valley along the Sheepscot make up a virtual museum of early-nineteenth-century architecture. Head Tide was once a major commercial center where millers harnessed the energy from the falls at the head of the tide. Floods in 1896 and 1924 destroyed the mills and doomed the local economy. As a result, Head Tide has the feeling of having been left behind by history. The Old Head Tide Church, dating from 1838, is open to the public on Saturdays from 2:00 to 4:00 P.M. If the weather is warm, a fine swimming hole is located beneath the old milldam next to a small parking area off the road. You can return to Route 1 via Route 194 through Alna, continuing southward on Route 215 after Route 194 ends.

En route to the Augusta area is the **Pownalborough Courthouse**, situated on the Kennebec River in the town of Dresden. This handsome 1761 building in its peaceful bucolic setting is the only remaining pre-

TOP ANNUAL EVENTS

1. *U.S. National Tobog-gan Championship,* Camden, late January, 236–3438
2. *Fishermen's Festival,* Boothbay Harbor, late April, 633–2353
3. *Windjammer Days,* Boothbay Harbor, late June, 633–2353
4. *Strawberry Festival,* Wiscasset, late June, 882–7184
5. *Great Schooner Race,* Rockland, early July, (800) 807–WIND
6. *Lobster Festival,* Rockland, late July, (800) LOB–CLAW
7. *Windjammer Weekend,* Camden, late August, 236–4404
8. *Great Fall Auction,* Owl's Head Transportation Museum, Owl's Head, 594–4418

Revolutionary courthouse in the state and one of only about a dozen nationwide. Built on the parade grounds of 1752 Fort Shirley, the courthouse was constructed by the Kennebec Proprietors shortly after the county was incorporated. During its thirty-two years of service, the courthouse heard cases mostly involving land disputes in this remote part of the state.

After the county seat was moved and the building sold, the old courthouse served a variety of purposes but remained in the same family from 1793 to 1954, when the Lincoln County Historical Society acquired the building and seventy-five acres. Gradual restoration revealed a trove of small treasures: the original paint on the wainscoting in the tavern room; a carving of the sloop *Polly* by a British soldier who was held prisoner here during the Revolutionary War (this was plastered over and thus preserved for 150 years); and the carved initials of James Flagg, the architect's son and the courthouse's builder.

Visitors approach the courthouse down a short dirt road. A magnificent maple tree, thought to be as old as the courthouse itself, stands before this exceptionally well-proportioned building. The tour lasts between an hour and an hour and a half, depending on how many questions you muster, and includes an appealing exhibit on the once-flourishing Kennebec ice trade, when Kennebec River ice was shipped as far away as Calcutta. The courtroom proper is on the second floor and is far more spare and less grandiose than its latter-day equivalent. Perhaps the most subtle indicator of the rich era in which this building was constructed is on the third floor, where you can see a 52-inch-wide pine plank, a sign of the extraordinary bounty of the early forest.

The courthouse is east of Richmond on Route 128, 1.3 miles north of Route 197. Open in July and August Wednesday through Saturday from 10:00 A.M. to 4:00 P.M. and Sunday from noon to 4:00 P.M. Tours cost $3.00 for adults, $2.00 for children under 14. For more information call 882–6817.

Pack rats enjoy snooping around ***Elmer's Barn*** in the tiny village of Coopers Mills, about 21 miles north of Wiscasset on Route 17. You'll have three floors of what might charitably be called "stuff" to poke through. The sign out front does a pretty good job summarizing: FURNITURE, BOOKS, PLUNDER, TOOLS, SOMETHING FOR ALL. Elmer also has a rustic playground for kids to occupy themselves while the parents are rummaging, but as his brochure notes, "Not liable for any accidents or injuries (not a day-care center)." For more information call 549–7671.

Boothbay Peninsula

The Boothbay Peninsula between the Sheepscot and Damariscotta rivers is one of the major stops on the contemporary tourist's pilgrimage along the Maine coast (the others include Camden and Acadia National Park). As such, the town of Boothbay Harbor is often inundated with travelers—and has been since the 1870s, when steamer service to Bath was established. Parking is tight, and the shops tend to reflect the interests of tourists more than of typical Mainers. If time is an issue, I would recommend bypassing the Boothbay Peninsula in favor of the Pemaquid peninsula, farther east, which to my mind has more drama, intrigue, and history.

If you have time for both peninsulas, be sure to sample one of the boat tours out of Boothbay Harbor, with cruises ranging from a short tour of the harbor to day-long trips to Monhegan Island. Whale watches and puffin cruises also are an option, as are deep-sea fishing trips. Tours are plentiful—more than twenty tour boats are berthed in the harbor— and prices range from $5.00 to $35.00. Wander along the waterfront to peruse brochures and discuss options with tour boat captains.

Among the best places for a simple lobster lunch or dinner is the ***Boothbay Region Lobsterman's Co-op***. Cross the footbridge to the harbor's far side and head right on Atlantic Avenue until you see it. This cooperative of local lobstermen serves up lobsters fresh from the sea— you can watch them being unloaded in the afternoons. Order your lobsters at one window, french fries or other extras at another window, then settle in at one of the picnic tables overlooking the harbor. It's open daily from one week before Memorial Day to Columbus Day 11:30 A.M. to 8:30 P.M.; call 633–4900.

Rainy days bring crowds to the classic ***Romar Bowling Lanes***, located in a log cabin just above the footbridge. It's a tiny affair with a handful of candlepin bowling lanes but a perfect spot for diversion on a slow day. The pin resetting machines seem to be getting a bit cranky and idiosyncratic, but that's part of the allure. There's also an adjacent snack bar and pool hall. Call 633–5721.

If you'd like to pilot your own boat in the harbor, try a sea kayak. *Tidal Transit Kayak Company* (633–7140) has a small fleet of rugged, plastic craft at their dock near the Boothbay footbridge. Half- and full-day tours are offered, providing a unique way to view the working lobster boats and pleasure craft that clot the picturesque harbor.

Across the harbor at McKown Point Road is the *Department of Marine Resources Aquarium*, part of the state's ongoing research into marine life. It's a new and attractive pavillion-style building with a variety of lobsters (blue lobsters, a 20-pound lobster), an 850-gallon shark and skate tank, and exhibits about salmon aquaculture. Kids love having a chance to touch the invertebrates in the touch tank, along with petting the live shark. (Don't worry; it's harmless.) The aquarium is open Memorial Day to Columbus Day daily from 10:00 A.M. to 5:00 P.M. Admission is $3.00 for adults, $2.50 for seniors and children.

The Boothbay area is home to a number of comfortable inns and hostelries—some old and refined and others new and cheesy. One of my favorites is the *Albonegon Inn,* a short drive from Boothbay Harbor on quiet Capitol Island, accessible from the mainland via a toy-size bridge. The inn has the motto "Determinedly old-fashioned," and that's more than just a clever gimmick. The creaky old gingerbread home has fifteen guest rooms, many of which face the bay. It's an ideal place to let a day or two unwind slowly, lounging on the oceanside rocks in the sun or reading on fogbound days in the living room. It's like a house owned by the old great aunt you wish you had. Doubles may be had for around $100, including a continental breakfast served in a wonderful seaside breakfast room. Call 633–2521 for more information.

If you're in the mood for a pleasant woodland walk, swing by the *Dodge Point Preserve* on the northeast side of the peninsula just south of Newcastle. This attractive riverside parcel of land is open to the public for quiet recreation. A peaceful lane runs in a loop around the property, past vast stands of red pine, along a pond and marsh, beside stone walls, and beneath towering oaks. The entire loop may be hiked in about an hour; add more time if you stop for a swim at Sand Beach along the tidal river.

The preserve is located slightly over a mile south of the town of Newcastle. Look carefully for a small sign reading FL 30 (fire lane 30) on the east side of the road. The fire road is gated; park alongside River Road.

A crude map is posted near the gate to enable visitors to get their bearings. Open daylight hours. No camping.

Pemaquid Peninsula

The Pemaquid Peninsula is a long wedge driven into the Gulf of Maine between Johns and Muscongus bays. From the attractive river town of Damariscotta to bold Pemaquid Point, the entire peninsula is well worth exploring at a leisurely pace. Stop to enjoy the historic buildings, investigate tide pools, or have a lobster along the ocean's edge. Take the time to explore both arms of this peninsula, Pemaquid Point itself and Christmas Cove.

For background on the marine life of the region and some insight into the marine research that's under way in the state, plan to visit the *Darling Marine Center* in Walpole. Located at the end of a winding drive shaded by pines, this pleasing compound is administered as a research center by the University of Maine. (The somewhat ungainly formal name is Ira C. Darling Center for Research, Teaching and Service.) The campus hosts academic researchers under the guidance of about a dozen faculty members. Most of the buildings are clustered around the upper campus; be sure to wander down about a half mile to the lower campus to see the new flowing seawater facility, which opened in 1991.

The visitor center is open Wednesday and Friday mornings in July and August, when you can sign up for guided tours. For more information call 563–3146. The center is located off Route 129 on the way to Christmas Cove. Turn right after passing the golf course; the center's driveway is 1 mile on the right.

Just north of South Bristol, a pleasantly unadorned fishing village, you'll pass the *Thompson Ice Harvesting Museum* on the east side of the road. An icehouse has been located here for decades; the present icehouse was built in 1990, modeled after one that previously stood at the site. The museum is on land donated by the Thompsons and operated by volunteers who feared that this window on history would be closed forever.

This modest museum isn't merely a historic display; it's an operating icehouse. Each winter, generally in February, community members assemble on the ice pond and use old tools to harvest the ice. First the workers score the pond's surface into blocks of 20 inches by 30 inches. With both machine and handsaws, they then cut out the blocks along the scoring and clear a "canal" the length of the pond. They float the foot-thick ice blocks along using pick poles and ice tongs, load them onto a massive conveyer, and transfer them into the shed, whose walls are packed with 10 inches of sawdust insulation. The 7-foot-high pile of ice is then topped with an insulating layer of hay and sealed up to wait for summer sales.

If you visit in summer, there's little activity but plenty of information. A shed adjoining the storage room displays tools of the trade, and an outdoor display features photos of the ice-harvesting operation. Visitors can scramble up a ladder to look down on the blocks of ice glistening through the hay. The ice is sold throughout the summer to local fishermen, who use it to keep their catch fresh.

The Thompson Ice Harvesting Museum is on Route 129 north of South Bristol. Open in July and August Wednesday, Friday, and Saturday from 1:00 to 4:00 P.M. or by appointment anytime between mid-June and mid-October. Admission is $1.00 for adults, 50 cents for children. For more information or to schedule an appointment, call 644–8551.

The best way to see the Maine coast is by yacht, preferably a very large and expensive one. If such an endeavor is out of your budget, a cheaper way to live out a Walter Mitty–style fantasy is to head to the

Return of the Puffin

The southernmost nesting ground for the common puffin is Eastern Egg Rock, which lies at the outer reaches of Muscongus Bay. Sometimes called the sea parrot, the puffin has a comic-book visual appeal, with stumpy legs, round body, and a truncated, colorful beak. The birds were popularly hunted for their feathers in the nineteenth century and came to the brink of extinction. The Puffin Project was established in Maine to reintroduce the birds to offshore islands, which had been colonized by voracious gulls that destroyed the puffin eggs. The project used various means, including tape recordings of hostile birds, to keep gulls away while the puffins were being resettled. The project has been gloriously successful, and puffins are now breeding on several offshore islands.

These birds rarely venture close to shore; you'll need to hop a boat to view them. From New Harbor you can sail aboard the Hardy III, a 60-foot boat with an enclosed cabin and open top deck. Puffin watches sail daily in the early evening and last ninety minutes. The price is $17 for adults, $10 for children under 12. Check in at the ticket booth near Shaw's restaurant.

More serious birders might consider signing up for Hardy's advanced Windward Bird Expeditions, which is the "enhanced" service focusing on migrating birds. Depending on your interest, you could arrange for trips to Matinicus Rock to see puffins, razorbills, and a variety of terns. Call (800) 278–3346 for further information.

Coveside Bar and Restaurant (644–8282) at Christmas Cove, which was named by explorer John Smith, who is said to have anchored here on Christmas Day in 1614. It's well off the beaten path for those traveling by car but a convenient and well-protected harbor for those cruising by boat. The food at the Coveside isn't all that distinguished, but the atmosphere more than makes up for it. The restaurant overlooks the scenic harbor, and yacht flags from around the world hang from the bar's wall like an unruly shag carpet. Large and impeccably maintained yachts are often moored near the docks, and regular visitors include celebrity yachtsmen.

The fastest and best way to cross from Christmas Cove to Pemaquid Point is by way of Old Harrington Road. Along the way, stop at the spare and handsome *Harrington Meeting House*, one of three meetinghouses built in the area in 1772. (Only one other remains: the Old Walpole Meeting House off Route 129, where services are held at 3:00 P.M. each Sunday throughout the summer.) The Harrington Meeting House, located between two cemeteries with a view to the harbor beyond, was meticulously restored between 1960 and 1967. The interior is austere and elegant, built with massive hand-hewn timbers and an extraordinary eye for proportion and form. An intricately carved pulpit looks out over the box pews. The second-floor galleries were left open to allow for a small museum, which displays arrowheads, portraits of local personalities, and a collection of photographs of early-twentieth-century ships.

The meetinghouse is open July and August Monday, Wednesday, Friday,

Rock of Ages

The Maine Coast is famous for its rugged, rocky shoreline. Be sure to take the time to notice how the shoreline changes and evolves as you travel the coast.

Around Casco Bay the ancient layers of rock strata were folded into an upright position, where the sea then eroded away softer rock, leaving a series of thin, vertical slatelike slabs that flake easily. As a result, the footing can be treacherous, and the conse-

quences of falling on a shoreside scramble can be dire.

Pemaquid Point, in contrast, has broad, horizontal slabs of bedrock washed smooth by the sea. Around Stonington you'll find pillowlike mounds of pink granite that looks as if it would be soft to the touch. Wherever you go, look for the parallel gouges in the coastal rock, carved out by smaller rocks embedded in glaciers as they slowly moved southward during the last ice age.

and Saturday afternoons from 2:00 to 4:30 P.M. No admission is charged, but donations are gratefully accepted.

Farther down the peninsula is *Colonial Pemaquid*, the site of one of Maine's earlier settlements, circa 1625. Since 1965, excavations have been ongoing here, the earth gradually yielding up clues about this village and its settlers, who endured many years of privation as well as attacks from the French and Indians. Today Colonial Pemaquid is maintained by the state. Excavations pock the broad, grassy field overlooking Pemaquid River and Johns Bay, and a small museum on the grounds displays artifacts uncovered during the digs. Abundant historical markers help make sense of the holes, where visitors may view stone foundations of former barracks.

The centerpiece of the park is Fort William Henry, a 1907 replica of a massive stone fort built on the point in 1692. One of many forts built on the site from 1630 onward, Fort Henry was one of the earliest stone forts constructed in the United States and was widely thought to be impregnable. Such assumptions were soon put to rest; the fort was rather easily destroyed by the French led by Baron de Castin, after whom was named the east Penobscot Bay town of Castine. The fort is open to the public and offers fine views across the waters. Next door is a fine old captain's house, built in 1790, which is closed to the public.

Colonial Pemaquid is open from the end of May until Labor Day daily from 9:30 A.M. to 5:30 P.M. Admission is $1.00 for adults, 50 cents for children; this includes both the museum and the fort. The restoration is located west of the town of New Harbor. Turn right off Route 130 just south of the intersection with Route 32. For more information call 677–2423.

Continuing south on Route 130 will bring you to dramatic, windswept *Pemaquid Point*. Near the tip is the scenic Pemaquid Lighthouse, built in 1827 and visible on a clear night 14 miles to sea. Although the point is a popular destination, visitors always sense an air of remoteness and foreboding, even when they share the experience with a number of other people. Pemaquid Point is quintessential Maine coast, particularly when a storm churns the sea and sends waves exploding up the fissures in the rocky point. The town-owned park charges an entrance fee of $1.00 for visitors over 12 and 50 cents for seniors.

Inside the former lightkeeper's house is the *Fisherman's Museum*, filled with all sorts of information and exhibits relating to the sea. There's an informative map showing the sixty-one lighthouses of Maine; displays of netting, traps, and buoys; and a monumental twenty-eight-pound lobster, which, somewhat disappointingly, was caught off Rhode Island. Be sure to take time to wander through the museum and the nearby gallery featuring works of local artists—although the real draw is the smell of the salt air and the surge of the surf. The museum is open daily from 10:00 A.M. to 5:00 P.M. except Sunday, when hours are from 11:00 A.M. to 5:00 P.M. Admission is by donation.

Heading back up the east side of the peninsula on Route 32, you'll pass by the harbor that lends New Harbor its name. One of the better known lobster pounds in the state may be found here at **Shaw's Fish and Lobster Wharf**, where you can enjoy a crustacean while watching the lobster boats come and go through the narrow inlet that provides access to the open sea. From mid-June to Labor Day it's open from 11:00 A.M. until 9:00 P.M. daily; it opens an hour later and closes an hour earlier in spring and fall. For more information call 677–2200.

The **Rachel Carson Salt Pond Preserve** is a short drive north on Route 32. Plan to arrive at low tide, when the seas have receded to leave a quarter-acre tidal salt pond in a broad cobblestoned cove. The pond is perfect for exploring marine life, as author and naturalist Rachel Carson discovered during hours spent here collecting information for her best-selling book *The Edge of the Sea*. The preserve, which is owned and managed by The Nature Conservancy, was dedicated to Carson in 1970. Look for starfish and green sea urchins, and dig through the seaweed for blue mussels, green crabs, and periwinkles. A brochure describing some of the indigenous marine life may be picked up at the registration box. Some seventy wooded acres across the road also are owned by The Nature Conservancy and are open to walking during daylight hours.

If you'd like to be better informed about the wildlife you're seeing, either on land or in the tide pools, consider signing up for one of the weeklong classes at **Hog Island Audubon Camp**, located just off Keene Neck south of Medomak. Six-day sessions focusing on field ornithology and marine biology are offered throughout the summer, with adult "campers" living in rustic housing at the 333-acre island wildlife sanctuary. For more information, contact the Maine Audobon Society, 20 Gilsland Farm Road, Falmouth, ME 04105, or call 781–2330.

Visitors are welcome to walk the trails on the island, but there's a catch: You've got to provide your own transportation across about 150 yards of water from Hockomock Point. The Audubon motorboat shuttle is for program participants only. There's another option: Audubon's mainland headquarters offers a mile-long nature trail with classic Maine views down island-filled Muscongus Bay. Stop by the office and ask for a nature trail guide, then spend an hour or so exploring Hockomock Trail, reading about forest and field ecology as you walk along. To reach the trail, look for Keene's Neck Road off Route 32 about 5 miles north of Round Pond. Drive to the end and follow signs for visitors' parking.

Waldoboro and Vicinity

Back along Route 1 in Waldoboro, lunch at *Moody's Diner* (832–7468) might be in order. If Maine decided to establish an official Maine State Restaurant, Moody's would be a strong contender. It's a scene, although one where tourists are increasingly pushing out the locals, at least in midsummer. The diner has been a popular destination among lobstermen, locals, and truckers for decades and serves heaping portions of basic fare at reasonable prices. Don't gorge too excessively on the main course, since you'll be needing to leave room for some of Moody's famous cream pies. Open daily from 5:00 A.M. to midnight.

Native food of another sort may be found a pleasant drive north of Route 1 in North Waldoboro. *Morse's Kraut House,* which is open only in the off-season, can trace its roots back to 1910, when Virgil Morse began making sauerkraut in his basement for descendants of the German immigrants who had settled in Waldoboro's environs. Old Verge, as he was known, made a tart and tangy kraut that was widely popular and available in local stores. After Virgil's death in 1963, his son and his widow ran the business until finally selling it in 1988. The business has had its ups and downs since then (it went out of business for about a year), but reopened a few years ago and is again offering its tangy kraut made of hand-cut cabbage cultivated in the broad fields across the road from the barn. You can order dogs with kraut along with chips and soda at a snack bar, and enjoy them while admiring the farmland view.

Morse's Kraut House is 7.6 miles north of Route 1 on Route 220. Open September through May Monday through Friday from 8:00 A.M. to 4:00 P.M. and Saturday from 10:00 A.M. to 4:00 P.M. For more information call 832–5569.

Knox County

Named after Revolutionary War officer Henry Knox, one of the area's chief proponents and earliest developers (see Montpelier, this chapter, Thomaston and Environs), Knox County contains some of Maine's highly popular coastal destinations, including Camden and the islands off Rockland. Monhegan Island also is included here, even though Monhegan is actually in Lincoln County, since access is commonly from Port Clyde on the St. George Peninsula. As with much of Maine, the inland townships contain mostly small farms and villages with little in the way of attractions but plenty in the way of peaceableness and charm.

Thomaston and Environs

The hospitable and historic town of Thomaston is dominated at either end by two imposing structures: a cement factory on the east side, and the gray and vaguely sinister Maine State Prison on the west side. One of the more unusual gift shops in the state is adjacent to the prison on Thomaston's main street: the **State Prison Store**. Inside you'll find a variety of items made (or at least assembled) by the inmates. These range from ashtrays crafted from Maine license plates to lobster trap tables, cedar boxes, and simple pine furniture. Not everything is made by the inmates; look for a tag or stamp on the bottom reading "Made by Inmate. Maine State Prison." Items for sale are mostly of wood, but some leatherwork and fabric goods also are represented. The cash register is staffed by uniformed prison officials, who casually mentioned to me that shoplifting was a problem here like everywhere else. Open daily from 9:00 A.M. to 5:00 P.M. except Thanksgiving, Christmas, and New Year's Day. For more information call 354–2535.

The **Maine Watercraft Museum** in Thomaston describes itself succinctly: "an in-the-water hands-on eclectic display of antique and classic smallcraft of unique design and construction and wide array of associated memorabilia."

An even shorter description might be: "boat-buff magnet." This quirky museum features watercraft built before 1960, which range from small-scale recreational watercraft (look for vintage models from Old Town) to doughty saltwater workboats like dories and peapods. The collections also include a great assortment of early and intriguing outboard motors.

The museum is located on two waterfront acres down the hill from Thomaston's main street and on the site of several early boatyards. The best part: Visitors can sign up for excursions on an old launch or a classic ChrisCraft mahogany speedboat. If you're more independent minded, for $10 per hour you can mess around in smaller, paddle-powered boats on your own. With its tiny beach and open grounds, the museum is also a great spot for a picnic. (Bring a lunch from a town deli, or you can buy light snacks here.)

The museum is located at 4 Knox Street Landing. Admission is $4.00 for adults, $2.00 for students and seniors; children under 5 are free. It's open summer and early fall Wednesday through Sunday from 10:00 A.M. to 3:00 P.M. For more information call (800) 923–0444 or 354–0444.

Fans of the art world often make a detour from Thomaston to the *Olson House*, located in the village of Cushing. This stern, hulking house was the subject of countless studies and paintings by revered American painter Andrew Wyeth, most famously in a painting that's become an icon of rural New England life—*Christina's World*, which depicts Christina Olson lying in the fields below her house. The house deteriorated in recent years until it was purchased by John Sculley, the former Apple Computer CEO, who donated it to the Farnsworth Museum, which now administers it.

The house is about 10 miles south of Thomaston at the end of Hawthorn Point Road. It's open Memorial Day weekend through Columbus Day daily from 11:00 A.M. to 4:00 P.M. Admission is $3.00 for adults, $1.00 for children 8 to 18. For more information call 596–6457.

Just east of the Thomaston center, at the intersection of Routes 1 and 131, you'll see a massive Federal home set on a hillside. This is *Montpelier*, home of Henry Knox, Revolutionary War major general, the first secretary of war, and one of Maine's principal landowners during the early days of the republic. (Knox came into his vast landholdings largely through a fortunate marriage.) Seeking to build a country estate not unlike Washington's Mount Vernon or Jefferson's Monticello, Knox set about building Montpelier in 1793. The grand plan ended as a dismal failure. The Maine winters were ill suited to a house of this scale, and Knox proved to be a less-than-shrewd businessman, quickly dissipating his fortune. Montpelier was constructed but never established roots.

The present building is actually a replica, built during the Great Depression, and is not on the original site. The original home overlooked the St. George River and was demolished in 1871 to make way for the railroad. Other than a pair of supporting walls added on the second floor, the present Montpelier is a faithful reproduction of the original. Maintained and operated by the nonprofit Friends of Montpelier, the home is furnished with many items from the original homestead.

Tours run about forty-five minutes and include both floors of this sprawling mansion. Among the architectural elements that distinguish the building are the graceful oval front room, the semiflying double staircase (also referred to as a "butterfly staircase"), and clerestory windows

Montpelier, Thomaston

high above the hallway. Note the detailing throughout, including wallpaper reproduced from scraps of the original and the intricately carved moldings throughout the house.

Montpelier is open Memorial Day through September Tuesday through Sunday from 10:00 A.M. to 4:00 P.M. (Sunday it opens at 1:00 P.M.). Admission is $5.00 for adults, $4.00 for seniors, $3.00 for children 5 to 11, and $12.00 for families. For more information call 354–8062.

St. George Peninsula

Turning south on Route 131, you'll pass a few small fishing towns and soon reach the working waterfront at Port Clyde, the traditional departure point for Monhegan Island. (Island excursions also are available from Boothbay Harbor and New Harbor.) Even if you don't have time to visit the island, Port Clyde is worth the drive. It's a town of weatherbeaten clapboards and worn shingles, clinging to a point seemingly at the edge of the earth. Stop for lunch at the *Port Clyde General Store*, which has a deck out back overlooking the harbor. The general store seems right out of a Sarah Orne Jewett tale, with creaky floorboards and a cracker-barrel atmosphere (although the selection of wine is probably better than Jewett might have expected). A deli counter in the back offers sandwiches and pizza. Scattered around the deck are lumber, propane tanks, and other items destined for the islands hereabouts.

If you're just down for the day, be sure to make a detour to **Marshall Point Light**. The handsome white tower was first built in 1823, then rebuilt in 1858. (If it looks dimly familiar, it may be because this was where the bearded Forrest Gump turned around and headed back west during his long-walk phase.) The lightkeeper's house, with its small museum focusing on local culture, is worth a visit. But the real draw is the view out toward lumpy Monhegan Island on the far southern horizon, along with closer Mosquito Island to the east with its open pasturage for sheep. Bring a picnic.

Access to **Monhegan Island** is via the *Laura B.*, a sturdy boat operated by Captain James Barstow with three departures daily in midsummer (fewer trips the rest of the year). The 12-mile trip takes one hour and ten minutes. The boat passes several inshore islands before making the open-sea crossing to the misty pale blue knob of Monhegan. Reservations (372–8848) are encouraged. The round-trip fare is $25.00 for adults, $12.00 for children, and $2.00 for pets. Parking at Port Clyde is an additional $4.00 per day.

It's clearly more than coincidence that artists have flourished on 700-acre Monhegan Island and have been attracted to its distant shores for decades. Rockwell Kent, Robert Henri, and George Bellows all spent time on Monhegan; noted painter Jamie Wyeth (the current star of the legendary Wyeth family) still summers here and on nearby islands. The island is imbued with a stark natural drama and is often graced with a thin, almost arctic light. The architectural style is also unique, putting its own island twist on the traditional Maine vernacular. In recent years the island has become somewhat inundated with day-trippers who spend an hour or two wandering about before returning to the mainland. The number of overnight accommodations has held steady, however, and seems about the right carrying capacity for the island. To get a real sense of the place, plan to spend at least one night. You'll be doing yourself an injustice otherwise.

Monhegan has several inns and B&Bs, but reservations are essential during the peak months of July and August; write or call for details. Addresses are the same for all: Monhegan Island, ME 04852. The Island Inn (596–0371) is the largest of the bunch, with six of its rooms featuring private baths. The Monhegan House (594–7983) is rambling and picturesque and has the best front porch for idling and watching the quiet comings and goings of island byways. My favorite is the funky, casual Trailing Yew (596–0440), which has rooms spread about a compound of several buildings, most offering views of the ocean. Guests are equipped with kerosene lamps (there's no electricity here), and family-style meals are served in the main building.

A small local history museum is situated at the island's most dramatic point—the rounded hill capped with a lighthouse overlooking the village. You'll find a compact collection of intriguing artifacts related to life at a remote outpost. Also ask about the new art museum. Also ask about the new art museum, which opened in 1998 and features changing exhibits of island art. It's located in the Assistant Lightkeeper's cottage.

Be sure to bring hiking boots or sturdy shoes, since walking is the thing. About two-thirds of the island is undeveloped, ranging from dense, quiet forests to open meadows atop dramatic headlands. If you're spending the night, you'll have time to walk the Cliff Trail around the island's perimeter as well as explore some of the inland trails, such as the peaceful Cathedral Woods Trail.

Rockland Area

ack on the mainland, continue eastward up the coast from Port Clyde. You'll soon make this discovery: You're actually heading more northward than eastward. That's due to Penobscot Bay, a massive indentation in the Maine coast extending about 50 miles from Port Clyde to Bucksport. Three major islands with year-round communities are located in the bay, along with dozens of smaller, uninhabited islands. Following Route 1 along the western edge of the bay affords occasional views, but, as always, you'll get a better sense of the area if you leave the security of the main highway and venture on the smaller byways.

From the attractive and still-bustling seaport town of Rockland, make a detour to the *Owls Head Transportation Museum*, another one of those attractions that at first sounds dreary and dull but turns out to be quite fascinating.

Housed in a series of multicolored hangars at one end of the regional airport, the cavernous, 65,000-square-foot exhibit space is filled with an array of automobiles, planes, bicycles, and motorcycles, many of which show an attention to extravagant aesthetics that has long since been abandoned by designers. The collection ranges from a 1910 Harley Davidson motorcycle ("Does the work of three horses," claimed the advertisement) to a 1929 Rolls Royce Phantom 1 Tourer. There's also a replica of a 1911 Burgess-Wright Model F, the Wright Brothers' first production plane. For the more mechanically inclined, there's a room called the Engineerium, which displays the museum's impressive collection of internal combustion engines.

Most Maine museums are best visited on weekdays, when the crowds are thinnest. That's not the best advice for Owls Head; special events are usually scheduled for Saturdays and Sundays in the summer, during which the fine museum pieces are brought out of the hangar and taken for a ride or flight. The museum's collections often are joined by other privately owned museum-quality pieces that are driven or flown in from around the region.

The museum is 2.8 miles south of Rockland on Route 73. April through October it's open daily from 10:00 A.M. to 5:00 P.M.; November through March it's open from 10:00 A.M. to 4:00 P.M. weekdays, 10:00 A.M. to 3:00 P.M. weekends. Admission is $6.00 for adults, $5.00 for seniors, and $4.00 for children under 12, with a maximum of $16.00 per family. For more information call 594–4418.

When in Rockland visit the **William A. Farnsworth Art Museum**. One of the state's finest museums, the Farnsworth was established in 1935 when the reclusive Lucy Farnsworth died at the age of 96, bequeathing her estate of more than $1 million to endow a museum in her father's memory. The museum contains a superb selection of American impressionists, including Childe Hassam, Maurice Prendergast, and Josephine Miles Lewis (also distinguished as the first woman to graduate from Yale University). Many of the Monhegan artists also are featured here, among them Rockwell Kent, George Bellows, and Robert Henri. In addition, the museum has an extensive collection of works by Rockland native and internationally acclaimed sculptor Louise Nevelson.

In June 1998 the museum opened the new Center for the Wyeth Family, where works are on display from all three generations of Wyeth: N. C., Andrew, and Jamie. Included in the center is Andrew and Betsy Wyeth's personal collection of Maine-related art. Another major expansion into an adjacent storefront is slated for 2000. The museum also operates the Farnsworth Homestead on Elm Street. This is the home where benefactor Lucy Farnsworth lived and died. It's open throughout the summer and has been preserved to show a typical Victorian home. Admission is included in the price of museum admission.

The museum is in downtown Rockland at 352 Main Street. Memorial Day to Columbus Day it's open from 9:00 A.M. to 5:00 P.M. daily; the rest of the year it's open Tuesday through Saturday from 10:00 A.M. to 5:00 P.M. and Sunday from 1:00 to 5:00 P.M. Admission is $9.00 for adults,

$8.00 for seniors, and $5.00 for students. (In winter, discount rates by $1.00.) For more information call 596–6457.

Just a few blocks away is the **Shore Village Museum**, an ample and intriguing collection of lighthouse-related items and nautical gear. Anyone remotely curious about the history of lighthouses should visit, as, for that matter, should those who have never given lighthouses a second thought. This rambling building, which also houses a collection of Civil War memorabilia from Rockland's Old Grand Army building, features several rooms filled with lighthouse artifacts, including the largest collection of lighthouse lenses in the United States. Dominating the collection is a spectacular 9-foot-tall lighthouse lens from Boothbay Harbor dating from 1855. The light amplification is extraordinary, answering the rarely asked question of how lighthouses worked before electricity. Throughout the two floors of exhibits you'll also find early navigational gear, compasses, fog detectors, and myriad other items that helped sailors get from one point to another without running afoul of the rocks.

The museum is located at 104 Limerock Street in Rockland. Open June 1 to October 15 daily from 10:00 A.M. to 4:00 P.M. Admission is free, but donations are encouraged. For more information call 594–0311.

In Rockland you'll also find the terminal of the state ferry line that services the large Penobscot Bay islands of **North Haven** and **Vinalhaven**. Both have year-round communities, but Vinalhaven tends to harbor more fishermen and be a bit more earthy than old-money North Haven. Vinalhaven is also a bit more accommodating to tourists, offering overnight accommodations in several B&Bs and motels. Both islands have paved roads winding through forest and field, affording outstanding views of the ocean and offshore islands. If you're disinclined to bike, mopeds may be rented on Vinalhaven. The ferry schedule varies throughout the year; for current information call 596–2202.

In addition to the ferries, one of the larger **windjammer fleets** in the world is based on Rockland's no-nonsense industrial waterfront, offering trips that range from an afternoon to a week. The wooden ships with their towering masts are an impressive sight tied up at dock, but you need to experience these ships under sail to appreciate them fully. Overnight accommodations aboard vary from the cramped to the moderately luxurious. If asked, most captains are forthright about what they offer—nothing makes for a longer summer than trying to cheer up disgruntled customers.

Rates for a week's worth of windjamming run around $110 per day per person, including all meals. Shorter trips cost a bit more per day. Your best bet for scheduling a windjammer vacation is to contact the Maine Windjammer Association for information well in advance of your arrival (P.O. Box 317, Rockport, ME 04856; 800–624–6380; www.sailmainecoast.com). If you're already in Rockland and would like to see if anything's available, stop by the Rockland Chamber of Commerce office at the public landing, where windjammer brochures are distributed. Windjammer cruises also are available out of Camden and Rockport.

Camden and Rockport

The scenic harbor town of Rockport has a more genteel and arty feel to it than Rockland to the south. The harbor, the former home of André the Seal of book and movie fame, is smaller and more scenic; attractive homes and estates cluster along the flanking hills. (Head down to the Marine Park along the waterfront, where you'll find a statue of André, along with three intriguing early lime kilns.)

Up the hill in the tidy village of Rockport, you'll find good browsing for art at the **Maine Coast Artists Gallery** (236–2875) at 162 Russell Avenue. The spacious gallery occupies a nineteenth-century stable on a hillside and features changing exhibits of Maine's best visual artists. Around the corner at 2 Central Street is **Maine Photographic Workshops** (236–8581), an internationally known school of photography offering classes in still photography, video, film, and computer design taught by top professionals in the field. The school has a well-stocked shop with film, photography equipment, and great books, and there's a small gallery where you can see work by students and others. It's open daily from 9:00 A.M. to 5:00 P.M.

On Route 1 at the western edge of Rockport, watch for **Sweet Sensations,** a bakery that features an extravagant selection of pastries and exotic baked goods. Among the most sought-after snacks, though, are the humble macaroons, which are baked to perfection. Stop by and stock up with a bunch for the road. The shop is at 315 Commercial Street (Route 1); call 230–0955.

When John Smith sailed up this coast in 1605, he noted "the high mountains of the Penobscot, against whose feet the sea doth beat." In later years the town of Camden flourished at this location, attracting fishermen and the wealthy rusticators, both of whom saw the advantages in the well-protected harbor. For a long time Camden was something of a secret, a gem hidden between mountains and sea.

Camden is no longer a secret. It's been discovered by just about every traveler to Maine, including tour bus operators. Change has come over the years, and not always for the better. Camden isn't as kitschy as Boothbay Harbor or Bar Harbor, but it seems to be headed in that direction. Nonetheless, a number of elegant inns dot the hillsides around the harbor, and Camden also boasts some excellent restaurants and shops. A walk around town should include the attractive town park, designed near the turn of the twentieth century by the firm of Frederick Law Olmsted, the designer of Central Park. The park offers an excellent view of the harbor, which throughout the summer is packed tightly with tall-masted sailing ships and all other manner of watercraft.

Two spots come well recommended for libations and snacking when in town. *The Waterfront* is a handsome restaurant whose deck hangs out over the harbor. If the weather's nice, you won't find a better spot to spend a late afternoon watching the comings and goings of yachts, kayaks, and other pleasure boats. Too many places take short cuts on their food while the view distracts their customers; this is not one of them. It's located off Bayview Street and is open for lunch and dinner daily (a bar menu is featured between lunch and dinner). Call 236–3747 for dinner reservations. A short stroll off Main Street is *Sea Dog Brewing Co.* at 43 Mechanic Street. It's housed on the ground floor of an old woolen mill that's since been converted to corporate offices. (Delaware-based credit card company MBNA rehabbed this building and others in the region, where it maintains an extensive back-office operation.) The brewpub offers some excellent beers, along with good pub fare. For information call 236–6863.

An oasis of serenity amid Camden's commotion may be found just off Route 1 south of town. *Merryspring* is a sixty-six-acre floral preserve dedicated to the planting and preservation of Maine flowers and shrubs. Although barely a third of a mile from the highway, it's well off the tourist track; if anyone's here when you visit, it's almost sure to be a local gardener or volunteer. An information kiosk near the parking area has maps for the taking. A couple of miles of trails meander through a variety of terrain, with pleasing views of the surrounding Camden Hills. Don't miss the extensive and exuberant herb garden near the entrance, featuring medicinal, culinary, and medieval herbs. The park is open daily year-round from dawn to dusk, and no admission is charged. From Route 1 on the Camden-Rockport town line, head west on Conway Road. Periodic classes and lectures are held in the Ross Center on the property; contact 236–2239.

Two of the most prominent of the *Camden Hills* are located within 6,500-acre Camden Hills State Park: Mount Battie and Mount Megunticook. Battie's 800-foot summit is accessible by car up a short toll road, as well as by foot trail. On the summit is a plaque commemorating one of Camden's most illustrious residents, the poet Edna St. Vincent Millay. The ledges on the southeast face of Mount Megunticook are accessible via a forty-minute hike up a well-marked but rocky 1-mile trail. From either Battie or Megunticook, outstanding views of Penobscot Bay lie before you, including the island of Vinalhaven and the open ocean beyond. Try to arrive at one of the peaks early in the morning, before the crowds ascend, when you can enjoy the sun glinting through the mist on the ocean's surface. There's a charge of $2.00 to enter the park.

Six miles north of Camden look for **Windsor Chairmakers**, located just past Lincolnville Beach. At this handsome shop you can see classic Windsor chairs being made by hand and shop for wonderfully made chairs, beds, dining room tables, and more. If you don't have room in the car, the shop can ship your purchases. It's open daily in summer from 8:00 A.M. to 5:00 P.M.; call 789–5188.

Also consider a detour to **Kelmscott Farm** in Lincolnville. What makes the place unique is its emphasis on rare breeds of livestock—the place

Camden's Castle

*W*hat's that immodest stone "castle" you see along Route 1 just north of Camden's village center? That's Norumbega, a picturesque pile built in 1886 by Joseph B. Stearns. Born in the Maine mountain town of Weld, Stearns was not a natural business-man—he had managed to accumulate significant debts even before he turned 20. But he went into the telegraph busi-ness, learned the business well, and invented duplex telegraphy, which allowed two messages to be sent along a telegraph wire simultaneously. Royal-ties on the invention rolled in from around the globe, and Stearns was able to retire nicely by the time he was 54.

He headed to Camden to build his mansion, using rough stone and timber to construct a rambling,

Queen Anne–style building overlook-ing a beautiful panorama of Penobscot Bay. The home has been remarkably well preserved (it was owned for a time by newspaperman Hodding Carter III). If you're feeling frisky of wallet, you can follow in the footsteps of millionaires by booking one of thirteen rooms at Norumbega, which is now an inn. It's not cheap. Basement rooms (called the "Garden Level") with walk-out terraces start at $155 during the prime summer season, rising to $450 for the fourth-floor penthouse suite. Call 236–4646 for reservations or more information.

For a view of the inn, head next door to Castleview by the Sea, housed in a more modest Cape Cod–style home dating to 1850. Call (800) 272–8439 or 236–2344 for reservations.

is dedicated to preserving endangered farm animals. You can see Cotswold sheep and Gloucestershire old spots pigs along with horses, goats, poultry, and an heirloom garden. The farm is open to the public daily except Monday; hours from April through October are 11:00 A.M. to 5:00 P.M.; from November through March, 10:00 A.M. to 3:00 P.M. Admission is $5.00 for adults, $3.00 for children; children under 4 are free. To find the farm, head east from Lincolnville Beach on Route 173 and continue to Lincolnville Center; turn north on Route 52 and drive for approximately 2 miles; turn left on Van Cycle Road and follow signs. Call 763–4088 for more information.

Waldo County

ounded in 1827 shortly after statehood, Waldo County includes the northeast part of Penobscot Bay. Renowned as a major poultry region earlier in the twentieth century, the county now relies more on small businesses and tourism. It's also a magnet for artists, who have been migrating in number to its pleasant communities, in particular to the county seat at Belfast.

Belfast and Vicinity

he town of Belfast was first settled by Scotch-Irish settlers in 1770; it then went through a series of economic booms and busts related to shipbuilding and the poultry industry. In recent years it has found a fair degree of prosperity as a haven for artists, who live along the coast and in the nearby hills. Their work may be found in several galleries in downtown Belfast—which consists of two commercial streets, one paralleling the harbor a hundred yards above it and one descending to the water's edge. Many fine Federal and Greek Revival homes line the residential streets nearby, especially the Primrose Hill District along High Street (coming from the south, follow the first Downtown Belfast sign).

Near the waterfront you'll find the terminus of the **Belfast and Moosehead Railroad Company**. Once disparagingly called the "Broken and Mended," the B&M had the distinction of being the oldest city-owned railway in the nation until the town finally gave it up in 1991. The new owner has kept it up nicely, recently adding historic locomotives from Sweden and railcars from elsewhere. The excursions depart from an 1870s freight building in an old waterfront rail yard. Passengers travel in coaches dating from the 1920s through the 1940s, pulled by a diesel engine. The route passes along a river, then through forest and field to Unity, where passengers disembark to explore the restored railroad station. Not to spoil the surprise, but the trip also involves a holdup by some unsavory desperadoes, an event that seems to delight more than frighten most children. The B&M also offers "Rail & Sail" packages that include an excursion on the northern reaches of Penobscot Bay aboard the *Voyageur*, a handsome former Mississippi riverboat.

Rides are offered from mid-May to late October. The fare is $16 for adults, $12 for children under 17 for either the boat or the rail trip; ask about special package fares. The depot is on Front Street, near the town landing. For schedule information call (800) 392–5500 or 948–5500.

Northern Penobscot Bay

P assing through Searsport on Route 1, you'll see an attractive complex of white clapboard and brick buildings on the north side of the highway. Stop here. Inside these buildings are some of the most intriguing nautical items anywhere in the state. The **Penobscot Marine Museum** has been somewhat eclipsed in recent years by the rapid growth of the Maine Maritime Museum in Bath, but this extensive collection still has the power to enchant. Like Bath, Searsport was an important shipping town, launching more than 3,000 vessels between 1770 and 1920 and home to 286 ship captains in the nineteenth century. The ships and captains are long gone, but ample evidence of their existence may be found at the museum. The museum unfolds in room after room, revealing its treasures slowly and pleasurably.

Where There's Smoke, There's Fish

S ample some of the state's finest smoked fish right out of the smoker at Ducktrap River Fish Farm in Belfast. The farm began in the mid-1970s as a trout farm and has since developed a national reputation for its fine, all-natural smoked fish, including salmon, mackerel, and tuna loin. (The salmon is especially delectable.) The retail store is on Little River Drive. Coming from the south on Route 1, turn left on Perkins Street (across from Moss Tents), then right on Lower Congress Street. Look for Little River Drive on your left and continue until you see the store. It's open weekdays from 8:00 A.M. to 4:30 P.M. If you decide you didn't order enough after you've consumed your purchase, you also can order by mail. For a catalog or more information, call (800) 828–3825 or 338–6280, or visit the company's Web site at www.ducktrap.com.

Well-presented exhibits throughout the museum complex inform visitors about trade routes, ship design, and the sailor's life. The Douglas and Margaret Carver Gallery contains one of the finest collection of marine paintings in the state; there's also an extensive display of chinaware and lacquered tables brought back from trading missions to the Far East. A portrait gallery highlights the classic weathered faces of the ship captains who sailed from Searsport. Two unusual exhibits include the whaling room, with its centerpiece four-panel Dutch painting of whaling in the Arctic (formerly in Hearst's San Simeon), and rare scenes by accomplished amateur photographer Ruth Montgomery, who accompanied her father on a sailing trip to Argentina aboard the Portland bark *Carrie Winslow* in 1902. Montgomery deftly captured the joys and hardships of life at sea through her lens.

The Penobscot Marine Museum is open daily Memorial Day to mid-October Monday through Saturday from 10:00 A.M. to 5:00 P.M. and Sunday from noon to 5:00 P.M. (last ticket sold at 4:00 P.M.) Admission is $6.00 for adults, $5.00 for seniors, and $2.00 for children ages 7 to 15. For more information call 548–2529.

While in Searsport, stop by the **Harbor Church** on Route 1 and see if the building is open. Inside is a rare treasure: nine stained glass windows by the noted glass designer Louis Comfort Tiffany. This is one of only ten buildings in the country with all-Tiffany windows, which depict both religious and pastoral tableaux. The congregation of the church, which was built in 1819, has dwindled into the single digits and hasn't been able to keep up maintenance on the rare windows. They've suffered from age, neglect, and the weather over the years, but in 1999 a group of area businesses set out to raise $100,000 to restore and protect the windows and make them more accessible to visitors.

Fort Knox, on the Penobscot River across from the mill town of Bucksport, is not to be confused with the place where government used to horde all its gold bullion. But it is well worth exploring, particularly if you're traveling with children. This massive fort seems a valiant exercise in overkill, even considering the strategic importance of the river. Started in the 1840s, the fort was manned during the Civil War and the Spanish-American War but was never attacked. Perhaps with good reason. Visitors today can marvel at the extensive earthworks and sheer granite walls sited dramatically on a bluff overlooking the Penobscot's narrows at Verona Island. The fort is a sprawling labyrinth, full of dim hallways, irregular courtyards, wondrous angles, and echoes that fascinate children endlessly. Much of the masonry work is exceptional, particularly the graceful spiral staircases of hewn granite. In an inspired marriage of art and architecture, *Macbeth* was staged here for two summers in the 1950s. One can only hope for a revival.

Fort Knox (469–7719) is on Route 174 just west of Route 1 at the Penobscot River. Managed as a state historic park, it is open daily from 9:00 A.M. to sunset. Admission is $2.00 for adults, 50 cents for children ages 5 to 11. A flashlight is helpful for exploring some of the long, dark, and eerie chambers.

Just across the river in the town of Bucksport, plan to swing by **Northeast Historic Film**. Housed in the old Alamo Theatre, which opened in 1916, this group is dedicated to preserving New England's film and video heritage. They collect old films by New Englanders and about New England, show them at periodic screenings, and offer them for sale or rent on videocassettes. In the old lobby of the theater you can peruse exhibits on the history of movies and movie-going in New England. Then look at the assortment of stuff in the store, which includes videos, books, and T-shirts.

In summer the newly renovated theater is open Monday through Saturday from 9:00 A.M. to 4:00 P.M. (same hours but closed Saturdays in the off-season). Admission to the shop and exhibit is free; there's a charge for screenings. For more information call 469–0924.

PLACES TO STAY IN THE MIDCOAST REGION

BELFAST
Comfort Inn Ocean's Edge, Route 1, (800) 228–5150 or 338–2090

Edgecombe-Coles House, 64 High Street, (800) 528–2336 or 236–2336

White House Bed & Breakfast, 19 Church Street, (888) 290–1901 or 338–1901

Yankee Clipper Motel, Route 1, (800) 451–8652 or 338–2220

BOOTHBAY HARBOR
Albonegon Inn, Capitol Island, 633–2521

Anchor Watch B&B, 3 Eames Road, 633–7565

Cap'n Fish's Waterfront Motel, 65 Atlantic Avenue, 633–6605

Five Gables Inn, Murray Hill Road, East Boothbay, (800) 451–5048 or 633–4551

Lawnmeer Inn, Route 27, West Boothbay Harbor, 633–2544

Ocean Point Inn, Shore Road, East Boothbay, (800) 552–5554 or 633–4200

Spruce Point Inn, Grandview Avenue, (800) 553–0289 or 633–4152

Topside Motel, McKown Hill, 633–5404

CAMDEN
Best Western Camden Riverhouse Hotel, 11 Tannery Lane, (800) 755–7483 or 236–0500

Blue Harbor House,
67 Elms Street,
(800) 248–3196 or
236–3196

Highland Mill Inn,
25 Mechanic Street,
(800) 841–5590 or
236–1057

Owl and Turtle Harbor
View Guest Rooms, 8
Bayview Street, 236–9014

Towne Motel,
68 Elm Street,
(800) 656–4999

FRIENDSHIP
Harbor Hill B&B, Town
Landing Road, 832–6646

Outsiders' Inn B&B,
Route 97, 832–5197

MONHEGAN ISLAND
Monhegan House,
1 Main Street,
(800) 599–7983 or
594–7983

Trailing Yew, Main Street,
596–0440

NEWCASTLE
Mill Pond Inn, Route 215
Damariscotta Mills,
563–8014

Newcastle Inn, River Road,
(800) 832–8669 or
563–5685

ROCKLAND
Captain Lindsey House
Inn, 5 Lindsey Street,
(800) 999–7352 or
236–3520

Lime Rock Inn,
96 Limerock Street,
(800) 546–3762 or
594–2357

Samoset Resort,
220 Warrenton Street,
594–2511

Trade Winds Motor Inn, 2
Park Drive, (800) 834–3130
or 596–6661

**PLACES TO EAT
IN THE MIDCOAST REGION**

BELFAST
Darby's, 105 High Street,
338–2339

Young's Lobster Pound,
Mitchell Avenue, East
Belfast, 338–1160

Helpful Web Sites

Belfast Chamber of Commerce—
www.acadia.net/belfast/
Belfast and Moosehead Railroad—
www.belfastrailroad.com
City of Rockland—*www.rocklandmaine.net*
Farnsworth Museum—*www.farnsworthmuseum.org*
Hardy III Boat Tours—*www.hardyboat.com*
Maine Photographic Workshops—
www.meworkshops.com
Monhegan Island Ferry—*www.monheganboat.com*
Northeast Historic Film—*www.oldfilm.com*
Penobscot Marine Museum—
www.penobscotmarinemuseum.org
Rockport–Camden–Lincolnville
Chamber of Commerce—*www.camdenme.org*
Searsport Chamber of Commerce—
www.acadia.net/searsport/

Selected Chambers of Commerce

Boothbay Harbor Region Chamber of Commerce,
Route 27, (800) 266–8422 or 633–2353
Damariscotta–Newcastle Information Bureau,
Route 1, Damariscotta, 563–3175
Rockland/Thomaston Area Chamber of Commerce,
Harbor Park, (800) 562–2529 or 596–0376
Rockport–Camden–Lincolnville
Chamber of Commerce,
Commercial Street, (800) 223–5459

BOOTHBAY HARBOR
Boothbay Region Lobsterman's Co-op,
Atlantic Avenue, 633–4900

Lobsterman's Wharf, Route 96 East Boothbay,
633–3443

Rocktide Restaurant,
45 Atlantic Avenue,
633–4455

Tugboat Inn & Restaurant,
100 Commercial Street,
633–4434

CAMDEN
Belmont Inn & Restaurant,
6 Belmont Avenue,
236–8053

Peter Ott's, 16 Bayview,
236–4032

Seadog Brewing Co.,
43 Mechanic Street,
236–6863

The Waterfront, Bayview Street, 236–3747

ROCKLAND
Cafe Miranda, 15 Oak Street, 594–2034

Second Read Books & Coffee, 328 Main Street, 594–4123

Waterworks, Lindsey Street, 596–7950

TENANT'S HARBOR
Cod End Fish House,
372–6782

East Wind Inn, Mechanic Street, 372–6366

DOWN EAST

Where "Down East" Maine begins is a matter of debate and conjecture. The term dates back to early sailing days, when vessels heading east had the prevailing coastal winds and currents at their stern, making an easy go of it from Portland to Eastport. Heading back the other way was a different matter altogether.

Eighteen-wheelers have long since supplanted cargo ships, but the term lingers. Today it refers almost as much to a notion as a destination. The classic Down East landscape ranges from rocky promontories ceaselessly battered by surf to quiet harborside towns filled with lobster boats in various states of disrepair. The image of Down East Maine may vary, but it's unified by a sense of remoteness and isolation, as well as by the idea that it's populated by a laconic, hard-bitten breed that forges ahead despite considerable adversity. Although pockets of Down East Maine may be found west of Penobscot Bay, for the most part it doesn't appear in earnest until east of the bay. And for real aficionados of rugged Maine, Down East doesn't quite start until you get past Mount Desert and average tides start to exceed 20 feet.

No matter where that imaginary Down East line is drawn, east of Bucksport classic coastal Maine begins in earnest. The farther east you head, the fewer tourist amenities you'll find and the grittier and more ineffably authentic the towns become. And then there's the fog, which seems to cling tenaciously to the coast through much of the year. If you arrive and a muffling fog bank is hugging the coast, make lemonade from lemons. Take the time to note how the fog enhances the richness of the foliage, particularly the forests in the Deer Isle area, the lichen-mottled rocks of Mount Desert, and the heaths near Cutler.

Hancock County

Hancock County contains Maine's crown jewels: Mount Desert and Acadia National Park. But don't be blinded by this dazzling display. Be sure to explore the rest of the county, particularly

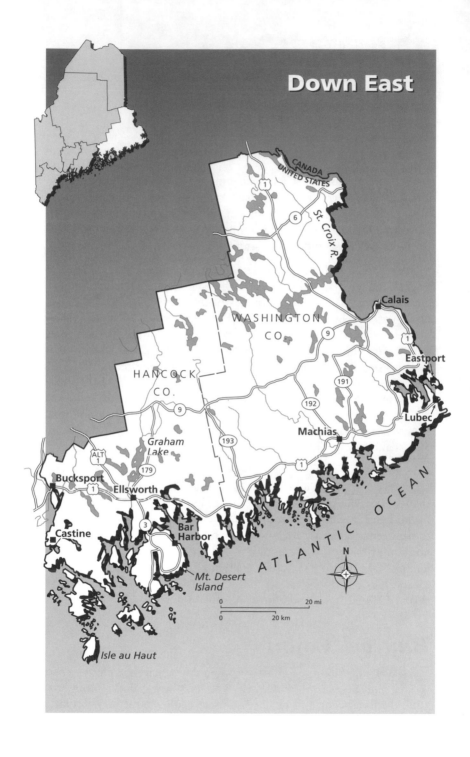

Down East

CANADA
UNITED STATES

St. Croix R.

Calais

WASHINGTON CO.

Eastport

HANCOCK CO.

Lubec

Machias

Graham Lake

Bucksport

Ellsworth

Castine

Bar Harbor

Mt. Desert Island

ATLANTIC OCEAN

N

0   20 mi
0   20 km

Isle au Haut

Deer Isle, which doesn't attract nearly such numbers as its more famous island cousin to the east. The county also extends far inland to the northeast, where you'll find remote lakes, good fishing, and unpretentious small towns.

Castine Area

If you've ever wondered what America looked like before Dutch elm disease, head to the quiet coastal town of **Castine**, about 16 miles south of Route 1. This regal village, where the occasional house that's not of white clapboard stands out like a drunkard at a debutante ball, is overarched throughout by towering, majestic elms. Look closely and you'll see small numbered tags on the trees, indications of the town's tireless efforts to keep the canopy healthy and alive. When signs of disease appear, arborists rush in like a SWAT team. Castine's success rate is admirable, and it's hard not to get a little nostalgic about all the long-gone elms that once graced cities and small towns across the country.

The elms are only part of Castine's allure. There's also the rich and sometimes bizarre military history. In the seventeenth and eighteenth centuries, the town passed back and forth between the French and British at a dizzying rate. Among the luminaries who made appearances in Castine was Miles Standish, who in 1635 was dispatched to aid the British colonists in their resistance against French usurpers. The small band accompanying Standish was unsuccessful, and the French maintained control except for a brief interregnum when the newly aggressive Dutch prevailed. Around 1700 the British once again reclaimed the town and held it, more or less, until the Revolution.

During the Revolutionary War, one of the more ignominious American defeats took place when forty-four American ships failed to capture a thinly defended British fort. A British fleet then forced the Americans to retreat upriver, where the colonists scuttled all ships to avoid capture, returning to Boston on foot. Among those court-martialed for their cowardice in this episode was Paul Revere, the famed silversmith and sentinel; his military career never quite recovered from this ignoble setback. You can learn about these historic episodes at a number of markers throughout the town, as well as at the earthworks marking the sites of Fort George and Fort Madison. On your way into town, look for the remains of the British canal between Hatch's and Wadsworth coves, which was constructed during the War of 1812 (when the British *again* occupied Castine).

The best way to enjoy Castine is to take a walking tour of the quiet, shady streets. Ask for one of the well-written, highly informative walking tour brochures produced by the Castine Merchants' Association, available free at many shops and restaurants.

In addition to the walking tour, several sites lend themselves to brief visits, including *Dyce's Head Light* at the westernmost point of town; follow Battle Avenue to the western end. Although this 1828 lighthouse is closed to the public (it was replaced by an offshore navigational beacon in the 1930s), there are a couple of trails that lead below the lighthouse to rocky bluffs overlooking Penobscot Bay, perfect for an afternoon picnic or an evening sunset walk. Look for the small sign near the lighthouse indicating the way to the public trail.

On Perkins Street stop by the *Wilson Museum* and the adjacent Perkins House. This small brick museum overlooking the water was built in 1921 to house the anthropological collections of local resident John Howard Wilson. Represented are a broad array of crafts and tools from native cultures worldwide, including those of Peru, Ethiopia, Angola, Oceania, and Venezuela. Spears and other weapons from Java and the Philippines fill another case, and the museum houses a display of rifles dating from 1580 to the 1880s. American history buffs will enjoy the replica of the 1805 American kitchen downstairs, as well as the operating blacksmith forge next door. And don't miss the outbuilding featuring the display of winter and summer hearses.

At the *John Perkins House* next door you can tour the oldest home in Castine. Miraculously (or perhaps not so miraculously), the house emerged intact despite British bombardment during the wars. This trim colonial house also was appropriated for British officers' quarters during both the Revolution and the War of 1812. Guided tours of the house in the summer include demonstrations of open-hearth cooking, with guests invited to taste the results.

The museum is open from the end of May to the end of September daily except Monday from 2:00 to 5:00 P.M. Museum admission is free. The Perkins House is open Wednesdays and Sundays in July and August only. House tours are $2.00. For more information call 326–8545.

Castine is an almost perfectly preserved village, but there's one towering anachronism: *The State of Maine*, a hulking, gray, former oceanographic research ship berthed at the docks of the Maine Maritime Academy, one of five academies nationwide training merchant marines. The ship, which rises incongruously over the village, was built in 1990 by the U.S. Navy before it was turned over to the academy as a training vessel in 1997. Cadets spend sixty days at sea during the course of their training, either as "deckies" or as engineers. The ship can house nearly 300 cadets and staff. Midshipmen give guided tours of the ship from mid-July to late August Monday to Friday from 10:00 A.M. to noon and 1:00 to 4:00 P.M. Tours last about a half hour and are free of charge. Call for more information: 326–4311.

A more intimate vessel is the 30-foot *Laurie Ellen,* which so far comprises the entire fleet of the **Castine Steamboat Co.** The captain of the compact tour ship, Randy Flood, claims it's the country's only wood-powered, steam-driven passenger launch inspected and approved by the U.S. Coast Guard. I have no reason to doubt him. It's a handsome boat with a striped canopy and a capacity of eighteen passengers. It's also brand spanking new: It was launched in 1999 after considerable to and fro with the Coast Guard, which wasn't quite sure how to go about certifying a wood-burning tour ship. One-hour tours of the harbor are offered five times daily late June to Labor Day from Dennett's Wharf, near the town landing. The cost is $17.50 for adults, $10.00 for children. For more information call 374–2536 (or contact Randy via his cell phone aboard the boat during the summer: 266–2841). The Web site is www.castinesteamboat.com.

Deer Isle

The drive from Castine to Stonington takes you through rolling countryside with glimpses of Penobscot Bay and beyond. (A driving detour through **Cape Rosier** peninsula, a pastoral cul-de-sac of early homes and rich landscapes, is an appealing if somewhat indirect route south.) Near Sargentville you'll cross a high, narrow suspension bridge across Eggemoggin Reach to Deer Isle. The bridge was built in 1938, but Deer Isle still retains a subdued and islandlike feel in its villages and rural byways. Like so many coastal Maine communities, the villages of Deer Isle look to the sea. The bridge offers access through the back door.

A scenic drive from the village of Deer Isle will take you along Stinson Neck to the nationally known **Haystack Mountain School of Crafts**, certainly one of the most scenic campuses anywhere in the nation. This summer crafts school offers instruction to about eighty students per session. Its campus was designed in the early 1960s by architect Edward Larrabee Barnes, who was faced with a rugged site consisting of a steep, spruce-studded hillside plunging into the waters of Jericho Bay. Instead of building at the top or bottom of the slope, as many presumed he would, Barnes daringly designed a campus hugging the slope, with dramatic water views from virtually every building and walkway. And instead of disrupting the delicate spruce, moss, and granite hillside with intrusive construction, he designed twenty small shingled buildings that were placed on footings above the ground and connected by "floating" wooden staircases and boardwalks. A broad central stairway serves as a main hallway, descending to the Flag Deck with its spectacular vistas of gently domed offshore islands capped with the sharp tips of spruce trees.

When the workshops are in session (between June and August), visitors are welcome to walk to the Flag Deck and visit the college store, Goods in the Woods, which sells art supplies and craft books. During the instructional sessions, the smells of the ocean and the spruce mingle with the sounds of reggae and wood saws. A nature trail near the shop also is open to the public, but the studios may not be visited except during the weekly tour, which is held Wednesday at 1:00 P.M. (donations requested). Incidentally don't look for Haystack Mountain hereabouts. The school was named after a mountain near the campus's former location.

To reach the Haystack Mountain School of Crafts on Stinson Neck, drive south of the village of Deer Isle on Route 15, then turn left on Greenlaw District Road and follow the signs for 7 miles. The campus driveway is well marked. For more information call 348–2306.

Continuing southward on Route 15, you'll soon arrive at the village of Stonington. This southernmost point of Deer Isle can seem remote and desolate, particularly when the fog rolls in and the low, lugubrious moan of the foghorn reverberates along the coast. When the weather is clear, porcupine-back islands clutter the horizon and in the distance the gentle peaks of Isle au Haut rise steely blue above the scene. Stonington is a true fishermen's village. Except for a few crafts and antiques dealers, it retains a salty, gritty feel. One or two inns have upscaled in recent years, but for the most part Stonington offers basic food and accommodations in its restaurants, motels, and bed-and-breakfasts.

It's remote here, but fishing isn't the only industry. There are also the quarries, where much of the fine coastal granite was extensively mined for buildings in New York and beyond at the end of the nineteenth

DOWN EAST

century. One island quarry (on Crotch Island) is still in operation; if you hear the throaty sounds of industry just beyond the harbor's mouth, that's probably it. You can learn a great deal about the town's granite heritage at the **Deer Island Granite Museum**, which opened in 1997. The museum's centerpiece is a large-scale model of the Crotch Island quarry, showing how it would have appeared around 1900. The museum is open from late May through August daily from 10:00 A.M. to 5:00 P.M. (Sunday it opens at 1:00 P.M.). Admission is free; donations are requested.

To really get a feel for the area, plan to abandon your car for a while. Two good alternatives are available: You can travel by sea kayak for anywhere between a few hours and a week among the dozens of islands off Stonington. Or you can venture by mail boat to Isle au Haut to explore Acadia National Park's most remote and wild section.

Sea kayaking has caught on in Maine over the past decade, and anywhere along the coast you're likely to see the graceful, slender craft making their way across open waters to once-remote islands. The sport has been compared to mountain biking on water, and that's an apt analogy. Among Maine sea kayakers the Stonington area is perhaps the most popular. Of the many small islands in the area, a good number are publicly owned and allow camping. The Nature Conservancy also owns several of the islands (day use only), one of which is used to pasture a large flock of sheep. Along Merchant's Row—the local name for the archipelago off Stonington—the islands are rimmed with weathered pink granite that becomes infused with an almost phosphorescent glow at sunset. Exploring one of these miniature wildernesses is an experience like no other in Maine.

With unpredictable wind and fog, the coast's weather conditions are highly volatile. It's best to have some oceangoing experience before renting a kayak and setting out on your own. Failing that, another option is to sign up for a trip with an established guide service. New to Stonington is **Old Quarry Charters,** a kayak rental and guide service located on Route 15 just outside the village (turn left at Ron's Mobil). Entrepreneur Bill Baker offers eighteen kayaks at his waterside compound with two launch sites. He's available for guided tours or lessons

Top Annual Events

1. **Downeast Stampede, Machias,** late June, 255–4402
2. **Eastport Fourth of July,** July 1–4, 853–4644
3. **Bar Harbor Music Festival,** Mount Desert Island, July and August, 288–5744
4. **Lobster Fest,** Castine, late July, 326–4166
5. **Folk Art Festival,** Grand Lake Stream, late July, 796–8199
6. **Claremont Croquet Tournament,** Southwest Harbor, early August, 244–5036
7. **Wild Blueberry Festival,** Machias, mid-August, 255–6665
8. **Blue Hill Fair,** Blue Hill, late August, 374–3701
9. **Wooden Boat Sail-In,** Brooklin, early October, (800) 807–WIND

(he also offers sailboat rentals and lessons), and will rent kayaks to those who can demonstrate some past kayaking experience and paddling proficiency. If you're headed into the area for a few days, ask about campsites, bed-and-breakfast accommodations, and primitive "camping cabins," which share a bathhouse with the tenters. (Some plans for accommodations were still subject to approval by local authorities and not firmed up as of press time.) For more information call 367–8977, or visit Bill's Web site at www.oldquarrycharters.com.

Other outfitters travel from around the state to lead tours among these wondrous islands. Try **Maine Island Kayak Company** on Peaks Island (766–2373) or **Maine Sport Outfitters** in Rockport (236–8797). No experience is necessary, but you'll enjoy yourself more if you're reasonably fit and comfortable on the water. Gliding across the bay, you'll likely discover that there's something very human and peaceful about the pace and scale of kayaking across open waters.

If your outdoor tastes run more to hiking, plan to board one of the mail boats to **Isle au Haut**, so named in 1604 by French navigator Samuel de Champlain. (It means simply "high island.") About half of this big, brawny island is privately owned; the other half, about 2,800 acres, was donated to Acadia National Park.

View with a Room

*W*hat could be more quintessentially Maine than spending the night in a lighthouse? Not much. And there's one inn that offers that experience. The Keeper's House on Isle au Haut occupies a striking 1907 lighthouse station on the island's northwest coast, with panoramic views out toward the Penobscot Bay islands and the Camden Hills. It's a great base from which to explore the island on foot, or just to lounge in Adirondack chairs and watch the shifting light and fog play against the landscape.

The trim black-and-white lighthouse, sitting atop a granite pier, still operates and provides a beacon for fishermen returning to the island. It's not open to the public. But the gambrel-roofed shingled station house next door serves as lodging, with views of the water from nearly every window. It's a rustic experience—there's no telephone or electricity, and light is provided in the evening by gas and kerosene lamps—but one of the best ways to get a sense of the remoteness of a keeper's life. Meals are provided to guests from the original kitchen. There are just six guest rooms (some are in a separate outbuilding), and advance reservations are essential. The price is $255 to $294 per night for a couple, including all meals. Contact innkeepers Jeff and Judi Burke at (207) 367–2261.

Daily mail boat runs take hikers to Duck Harbor, where five Adirondack-style lean-tos are maintained for campers. (Campsites are $25 per night (up to six people); reservations are essential. Call Acadia National Park at 288–3338.) After disembarking, follow Western Head Road—a grassy, wooded lane—to Western Head Trail. This connects to Cliff and Goat trails, which wind their way between spectacular, rocky shoreline and damp, dense forests of fir, spruce, moss, and lichens. From the Goat Trail you can climb to the bald summit of Duck Harbor Mountain, which provides surprisingly open views of the island and eastern Penobscot Bay, including the eastern shore of Vinalhaven Island. From here you can return to the harbor in plenty of time for the return boat. Be sure to pack a picnic lunch to enjoy along one of the many cobblestoned beaches, since no food is available in the park. A water pump for drinking water is located at Duck Harbor; fill up your canteens before you set off. Visitors usually have about six hours to explore the island. A ranger meets incoming boats to provide maps and hiking information.

Round-trip fare is $24.00 for adults, $10.00 for children under 12. Isle au Haut Boat Co. does not take reservations, but they turn away surprisingly few passengers. For a current schedule call 367–6516. Plan to arrive at the dock thirty minutes before departure.

The restaurant selection in Stonington is limited, but recommended is an unvarnished seafood spot called *The Fisherman's Friend,* located on School Street a short drive up the hill from the harbor. The fish is freshly caught and prepared simply and deliciously. The lobster stew is filled with succulent lobster meat and should satisfy the deepest cravings for the crustacean. Prices are moderate; call 367–2442.

Before you depart Deer Isle, take time to visit The Nature Conservancy's *Crocket Cove Woods Preserve*, located a few minutes northwest of Stonington. This hundred-acre preserve contains a fog forest: a rich, quiet, mossy forest of mature spruce, fir, and pine that thrives in the damp, foggy environment prevalent along Deer Isle's south coast. Walking along the short self-guided nature path, you'll hear bird songs filter through the forest and enjoy the contrast of the rough bark of the red spruce against the brilliant green of the soft mosses. Brochures describing some of the natural highlights may be found in the registration box near the entrance. The preserve is open during daylight hours, and no admission is charged. From Stonington, head northwest on the road toward the town of Sunset. Shortly after passing through the village of Burnt Cove, turn left on Whitman Road. Follow along the cove until the pavement ends and a dirt road departs to the right. Drive 150 yards to a small parking area with a registration box.

Blue Hill and Environs

Continuing down east, you'll soon pass through the coastal town of Blue Hill, named after the gently rounded 934-foot hill that dominates the relatively low terrain hereabouts. This aristocratic town, located at the head of Blue Hill Harbor, boasts dozens of historically significant buildings dating from the nineteenth century and earlier. For the last two decades or so, Blue Hill also has served as a magnet for a variety of potters, weavers, and other craftspeople, many of whom sell their wares in shops in the village and outlying areas. Blue Hill is also home to many fine inns and restaurants, and for many decades it has been a popular summer destination for those looking for a somewhat less social season than on Mount Desert Island.

If there's any one historical character who defines Blue Hill, it's Parson Jonathan Fisher, a Harvard-educated cleric who became the village's first settled minister in 1796. Parson Fisher, who lived in Blue Hill for more than half a century, is considered a New England original of the highest order: He was a respected painter, writer, minister, and tinkerer whose energies were indefatigable. His *Morning View of Blue Hill Village* is an enduring primitive American landscape (the painting can be viewed at the Farnsworth Museum in Rockland), and the journal he kept faithfully for fifty-nine years remains a source of interest to scholars and historians.

The **Parson Fisher House**, built in 1814, is open to the public as a

Roost and Roll

*W*hen driving in and around Blue Hill, you can get a taste of the local counterculture character by tuning into WERU-FM (89.9 FM), the community radio station. Originally launched in 1988 in an old henhouse owned by Noel Paul Stookey (of Peter, Paul, and Mary fame), the station began as a collaborative of volunteers, who hosted music and talk shows that reflected local interests and tackled local topics. The station has evolved and become more professional in recent years (it now has six paid staffers), but it's the 150 local volunteers who still provide much of the spirit.

The station has become a leader in the effort to encourage more community broadcasting nationally, an attempt to stem the tide of what it sees as the bland and homogenized content featured at all too many stations. The new headquarters is located on Route 1 in East Orland (between Bucksport and Ellsworth), and you're welcome to stop in and say "hi" during business hours. (If you're traveling around Bangor, it can also be picked up at 102.9 FM.)

memorial to Fisher's many talents. The two-story, four-room house, which Fisher himself built, contains his elegant homemade furniture, copies of books he bound himself, prints and originals of Fisher paintings, maps he surveyed, and examples of the style of shorthand he invented. Of particular interest is a clock with wooden works Fisher made while at Harvard; its painted face represents the five languages he spoke (and used in delivering sermons)—Hebrew, Latin, French, Greek, and Aramaic. About the only thing Fisher wasn't interested in, according to historians, was politics.

The Parson Fisher House is about a half mile south of Blue Hill village on Routes 15 and 176. It is open from July 1 until September 15 daily, except Sunday, from 2:00 to 5:00 P.M. Admission is $2.00; children under 12 are free. For more information call 374–2161.

Also in Blue Hill is the foursquare **Holt House,** home of the Blue Hill Historical Society. Located at the head of the harbor, the home was built in 1815 by one of the first families to settle in Blue Hill. The home was purchased by the Blue Hill Historical Society in 1970 and restored to its earlier appearance. Some of the original stenciling was found beneath the wallpaper and reproduced throughout the home. The collection of local historic artifacts includes furniture, clocks, and kitchenware and continues to grow through donations and purchases. Holt House is open in July and August Tuesday and Friday from 1:00 to 4:00 P.M. Admission is $3.00; children under 12 are free.

Two of Maine's most noted potters are based in Blue Hill and run showrooms where you can peruse and purchase some of their fine works. The bowls, plates, and cups at **Rackliffe Pottery** are marked by concentric rings, and some of the glazes are of a shimmering, rich cobalt blue that seems to mimic the sea. The workshop and showroom on Ellsworth Road (Route 172) is open year-round; call 374–2297 for more information. Potters at **Rowantrees Pottery** have been throwing pots in Blue Hill for more than half a century. Adelaide Pearson started the pottery studio after a conversation with Gandhi in India. (He told her pottery was serious business.) The simple but attractive items produced at the studio are typically crafted with glazes of local materials. The workshop on Union Street is open to the public; call 374–5535.

If the weather's cooperative, you might consider a hike up eponymous **Blue Hill** for a superb view across Blue Hill Bay to the mountains of Mount Desert Island. Drive north on Route 172 and turn left (westward) on the road across from the Blue Hill Fairgrounds. Drive 0.8 mile to the sign marking the start of the trail on the right side of the road.

OFF THE BEATEN PATH

The mile-long hike to the bald, craggy summit (topped with an unmanned fire tower) takes about forty-five minutes.

Ellsworth Area

In the mind of many, the town of Ellsworth is merely a gateway to Mount Desert Island and Acadia National Park. It's become the sprawl capital of Down East Maine, with a handful of outlets, Wal-Marts, and strip malls lining Route 1 east of the town center. Look beyond this, though, and you'll find a couple of sites that are well worth visiting.

The *Colonel Black Mansion*, located just west of town center, is a fine example of a modified Georgian brick residence. Colonel John Black was a land agent for William Bingham, owner of two million acres of Maine; Black constructed this house between 1824 and 1827. Tradition says that the bricks were shipped from Philadelphia and the laborers from Boston. Of note are the triple-hung front windows (note the absence of a front door on the porch—residents entered and departed through the fully opened windows) and the handsome spiral staircase inside. Although the mansion was a full-time residence and office for the colonel, the house was used sparingly by his descendants. In 1930 the home, fully furnished right down to the original family linens, was donated to the county by Black's grandson.

The mansion, set amid 150 wooded acres, is a treasure trove of life in the nineteenth century. The house contains a canopied bed with the original tassels, a rare Aaron Willard clock, and an exceptional collection of blue and white pottery. There are a number of other Victorian flourishes, such as the stuffed peacock (which once roamed the grounds) and a German silver bathing tub.

The mansion is open June 1 to October 15 every day except Sunday from 10:00 A.M. to 5:00 P.M. Forty-five-minute tours are held on the hour and half hour and cost $5.00 for adults and $2.00 for children under 12. Located on Route 172 one-quarter mile south of Route 1. Call 667–8671.

The development of the "revolutionary" Internet is put in perspective at the *New England Museum of Telephony,* which was founded in 1984. The Internet was nothing compared with the arrival of telephone service in rural New England, which ended centuries-long isolation on remote ocean points and in backwoods hamlets. That history is explored here in some depth, showing how telephone service grew and developed between 1876 and 1983.

You'll see plenty of items that would cause only hard-core technical historians to get excited—such as a panel system from Brooklyn, New York, and "a complete #3 Crossbar system from Bradford, Maine." But above all the technical detail rises the scope and scale of the historic enterprise of communication. Each August a telephone fair celebrates the history and technology of those items we now take for granted.

The New England Museum of Telephony is about 10 miles north of downtown Ellsworth off Route 1A, at Lottie Bell Farm, 166 Winkumpaugh Road, North Ellsworth. It's open July, August and September Wednesday

Inside Outlets

*M*aine has two bona fide upscale outlet meccas attracting shoppers from throughout the Northeast—Kittery along Route 1 and the entire village of Freeport.

*So where do native Mainers head when looking for the best bargain? Well, neither of those places—they're too crowded and glitzy. They head to **Marden's** and **Reny's**, two discount chains with a handful of stores statewide that offer salvage and seconds, often at tremendous bargains.*

Marden's is the less conventional of the two. Marden's aficionados know they can never venture into one of its shops in search of something specific. The best tactic is just to go and browse. You'll be amazed at how much stuff you suddenly realize you need. The eclectic stock is often gleaned from disaster areas—places that have been hit by floods, fire, or hurricanes—and you're certain to find imperfections, like smoke smudges or water stains. But there's usually a good if motley assortment of stuff, ranging from hiking boots and casual clothing to furniture and kitchen gadgets.

Marden's stores are located throughout the state. The mother ship is in Waterville at 184 College Avenue (873–6111), and it's sprawling and huge. Other shops are in Portland at the Pine Tree Shopping Center (761–4078), near exit 8 of the Maine Turnpike; at the Northwood Park Shopping Center in Lewiston (786–0313); in Gray at 65 West Gray Road (657–2626), just south of the turnpike exit; and in Brewer (across the river from Bangor) at 564 Wilson Street (989–1750).

Reny's offers a more traditional range of merchandise, with an emphasis on remainders rather than salvage goods. It's sort of like a smaller, discounted Wal-Mart, if you can envision that. You often can find name-brand clothing with the labels snipped out (I've turned up L. L. Bean khakis for less than $10), along with an assortment of foodstuffs, bedding, office supplies, and small appliances.

One of the largest shops in the chain is in Ellsworth (667–5166), just across from the L. L. Bean outlet. Others are in Bath on Front Street (443–6251); Damariscotta on Main Street (563–5757); Camden at the Camden Shopping Center (236–9005); and Belfast at the Belfast Plaza off Route 1, just west of the bridge (338–4588).

through Sunday from 2:00 to 5:00 P.M. Other times may be arranged by calling 667–9491 for an appointment.

On Route 3 about a mile south of Ellsworth (en route to Mount Desert), on the right you'll pass **Stanwood Homestead** and **Birdsacre Sanctuary**. The home was built in 1850 by Captain Leland Stanwood, the father of one of the country's most talented self-trained ornithologists. Cordelia Johnson Stanwood (1865–1958) contributed greatly to the understanding of the natural history and migration patterns of many North American birds, often using the woods behind her simple Cape-style home as an outdoor laboratory.

Today the house and grounds are owned and operated by the Stanwood Wildlife Foundation. The home, with its wide, worn pine board floors, houses numerous mounted birds and an exceptional egg collection, along with period furniture and old photographs. The 130-acre grounds are laced with well-marked nature trails that wind past small ponds and through shady glades. The sanctuary is just yards off the busy highway but has a settled and quiet air. Cages behind the house are used for the rehabilitation of injured birds brought to the sanctuary and may house great horned owls, geese, and red-tailed hawks. There's even a "night deposit" for injured birds found after hours.

Admission to the sanctuary is free. Tours of the homestead (open daily from 10:00 A.M. to 4:00 P.M.) are $2.50 for adults, 50 cents for children. Look closely for the entrance on Route 3; it's on the west side across from the Prompto 10-Minute Oil Change. For more information call 667–8460.

Mount Desert Island

Acadia National Park on Mount Desert Island is the second most popular national park in the United States, eclipsed only by the Great Smoky Mountains. More than five million park visits are recorded annually, and between July 4 and Labor Day weekend, the island can literally fill up, leaving no place to pitch a tent or rent a room. Reservations are strongly encouraged during the peak season.

Getting off the beaten path at Mount Desert (pronounced de-SERT) is a matter more of strategy than of destination. Many visitors display a singular lack of imagination by stopping at Bar Harbor for an hour or two, then heading to the park loop road ($10 per vehicle; pass is good for one week) to drive from one parking lot to another, rarely walking more than a few dozen yards from the road. Admittedly, the coastal loop road is spectacular, with twists and turns and views across Frenchman Bay. But a motor tour provides only a glimpse of the spirit of the place, like viewing the countryside from an interstate highway. Detouring off the loop road and exploring by foot or boat offers a more intimate look at this extraordinary island.

Acadia National Park offers no backcountry camping and only two drive-in campgrounds, both of which can fill up by early morning in midsummer. In addition to the numerous private campgrounds, there is another, little-known option for campers: *Lamoine State Park*, located on the mainland 11 miles from the Acadia visitor center. The fifty-five-acre park is situated on Eastern Bay and has a number of pleasant campsites, including several overlooking the water. There's a boat launch, a pier for fishing, grassy fields, and picnic tables facing across the bay toward Cadillac Mountain and other Acadia peaks. It's a peaceful and quiet place and makes a good spot to unwind after a day in the park. For more information call 667–4778.

Immediately after crossing the Mount Desert Island causeway on Route 3, you'll come to the Thompson Island Information Center. This is a good stop for basic information about island lodging, restaurants, and attractions. It's run by the island's chamber of commerce, but you also can ask questions about Acadia. If you're more interested in park activities, continue on Route 3 toward Bar Harbor to the National Park Service's Hull's Cove Visitor Center. It's open daily mid-April through October, and features exhibits on wildlife, a relief map, a short film introduction to the park, and a bookstore with trail handbooks and field guides. Ask for the free listings of carriage roads and hiking trails. For more information about the park, contact the park head-quarters at 288–3338.

A good introduction to island ecology may be found at the *Natural History Museum* at the College of the Atlantic. This small liberal arts college, founded in 1969, prides itself on its strong environmental focus. The museum is housed in Turrets, a splendid stone mansion built in 1895 for John Josiah Emery. Two rooms on the first floor are filled with exhibits of animals typically found on Mount Desert, ranging from black bear (at least six are thought still to inhabit the west side of the island) to river otter. These fine displays of taxidermy are all prepared by college students, and more than fifty species are represented. On the front porch you'll find sweeping views across the harbor and the Porcupine Islands—the view alone is worth the price of admission—as well as a small "touch tank" for children to experience local marine life.

The museum is on Route 3 just south of the Bluenose Ferry Terminal and is open June 15 to Columbus Day from 9:00 A.M. to 5:00 P.M. daily. Admission is $2.50 for adults, $1.50 for seniors, $1.00 for children under 12. For more information call 288–5015.

It's not hard to imagine **Bar Harbor**, the island's undisputed commercial center, during its heyday, when corporate titans and others maintained magnificent summer "cottages" (read: palaces) along the coastal hills. Think of Bar Harbor in the early 1900s as Newport, Rhode Island, with moosehorns. The Vanderbilts and the Rockefellers were among the families that established summer estates here; in fact, the national park's existence is due in large part to the generosity of these and other wealthy families, who purchased the more spectacular parts of the island and donated them to the U.S. government. (John D. Rockefeller Jr. alone donated 11,000 acres.) Although many fine homes may be viewed at a distance from here and there, the majority were destroyed during an extraordinary conflagration in the

A Fire to Remember

The autumn of 1947 was unusually dry on Mount Desert Island. There had been no rain since May, and the woods were tinder crisp. It was a disaster just waiting to happen. And that disaster finally flared up toward the end of October.

How the fire started, nobody knows. But a small, insignificant wildfire up near Hulls Cove that had attracted some lackadaisical attention early in the week suddenly roared when fierce northwest winds whipped the flames into a frenzy. The fire moved down the east side of the island, destroying many of the extravagant cottages, hotels, and homes around Bar Harbor, then continuing toward Eagle Lake and beyond. The island scene was one of chaos: Islanders were evacuated,

guardsmen were called in to prevent vandalism and theft, and smaller fires flared all around as raccoons fleeing the flames carried their smoldering fur to new territory. Not for two weeks was the fire finally extinguished.

The final toll: 5 Bar Harbor hotels, 67 summer cottages, 170 homes, and 10,000 acres of Acadia National Park were destroyed. Today there's almost no trace of the fire—buildings have been rebuilt, forests have had over a half-century to recover. But when you approach Bar Harbor on Eden Street, notice the stone walls and fancy gates here and there. If they seem a bit excessive for the motels and modern buildings nearby, there's a good reason for it. This used to be the habitat of the grand estates.

summer of 1947, a period of prolonged drought that bred wildfires throughout much of the state. Downtown Bar Harbor was spared, as were some of the year-round homes.

Much of Bar Harbor today caters to the tourist trade, and visitors can select from a wide array of T-shirt shops, restaurants, and bars. One site that retains some of the flavor of the town's past is the **Criterion Theatre**, a magnificent 1932 building that has retained its art deco extravagance. The interior of this 916-seat theater is awash with geometric patterns rendered in soft, earthy colors that seem enhanced in the dim glow of the central lamp. The theater, listed on the National Register of Historic Places, shows first-run films as well as classics. Splurge and pay extra for a seat in the loges, with boxlike seating and privacy partitions. It is located downtown on Cottage Street. For a recorded announcement of the current show, call 288–3441.

Some time around 1905 a rancorous local debate erupted over whether to allow automobiles onto the island. Progress, such as it was, eventually prevailed and horseless carriages were given run of the island, forever disrupting the tranquillity of the place. One of the outraged opponents of cars was John D. Rockefeller Jr. Preferring to get even rather than get mad, he set about designing and building a 57-mile network of quiet, leafy **carriage roads** on the east side of the island, concentrated mostly around Jordan Pond. Rarely has vengeance produced so exquisite a result. The peaceful lanes blend remarkably well with the landscape and include a dozen graceful bridges crafted of local granite. The roads deteriorated following Rockefeller's death in 1960, but a major restoration effort was launched in 1990, and eroded derelict lanes were returned to their former glory.

Carriages today are few, but mountain bikes are plentiful and, it turns out, perfect vehicles for exploring "Mr. Rockefeller's roads." Pack a picnic lunch to enjoy along a stream, or take a side trip on foot for a summit view across the bay. You also might make a detour for outdoor tea and popovers at the Jordan Pond House, a longtime park landmark. The restaurant was opened in the 1870s but burned and was replaced with a more modern structure in 1979. Tea is served daily outdoors on a grassy promenade looking up the lake between 2:30 and 5:30 P.M.; the restaurant also is open for lunch and dinner. You needn't be formally dressed for tea (mountain bikers in spandex are usually well represented), but you should expect a bit of a wait on the warmer days. Call 276–3316.

If you didn't bring a mountain bike, rentals are available in Bar Harbor at **Acadia Bike Rentals** (48 Cottage Street, 288–9605) and **Bar Harbor**

Bicycle Shop (141 Cottage Street, 288–3886). In Southwest Harbor try *Southwest Cycle* (Main Street, 244–5856). Daily and hourly rates are available. Bike shops can provide maps of the carriage roads, and their staff can make suggestions for day trips.

If you're in a horticultural frame of mind, head southward on Route 3 toward Northeast Harbor, where you can visit a pair of extraordinary hidden gardens that are as seldom visited as they are spectacular. The best (but not only) access to the *Asticou Terraces and Thuya Gardens and Lodge* is from a discreet parking lot off Route 3. Look for a small sign reading ASTICOU TERRACES on the left as you wind around Northeast Harbor coming from Seal Harbor. If you pass the grand Asticou Inn, you've gone too far. If you're coming from the north, the lot is 0.5 mile south of the intersection of Routes 198 and 3.

A paved trail leads down to the water and is worth a short stroll. But be sure to cross the highway and begin the climb up the granite steps and through a series of stone terraces overlooking the harbor. The landscaping is remarkable: It seems rugged and wild and ineffably Maine, but it is actually one of the finer bits of outdoor architecture in New England. The hillside was created by Boston landscape architect Joseph Henry Curtis (1841–1928), who summered here for many years and donated the land and his lodge as a "gift for the quiet recreation of the people of this town and their summer guests." At the top of the hill, Curtis's rustic Thuya Lodge (named after the scientific name for white cedar, *Thuya occidentalis*) is open to the public and contains an assortment of antiques and a fine horticultural library.

Behind the lodge, walk through the massive carved wooden gates into the formal Thuya Gardens, with its reflecting pool, gazebo, spectacular flower displays, and lawns trimmed as precisely as putting greens. If the weather's nice, you're certain to find people reading here, talking quietly, or examining the wide variety of common and exotic flowers. The garden was designed by Charles K. Savage, who borrowed elements from famed English designer Gertrude Jekyll and Maine landscape designer Beatrix Farrand.

The terraces and garden are open July 1 to Labor Day from 7:00 A.M. to 7:00 P.M. daily. The lodge is open daily from 10:00 A.M. to 4:30 P.M. A $2.00 donation is requested of visitors to the gardens. The lodge and garden also are accessible by car without ascending the terraces. Head toward Seal Cove from the terraces' parking lot for 0.2 mile, and turn left on the first road. This will bring you to the lodge. For more information call 276–5130.

Just north of the Asticou Inn is the *Asticou Azalea Garden*. These grounds, like the Thuya Gardens, also were designed by Charles Savage but have a vastly different structure and feel. Raked gravel walkways wind through the flower beds, with elements borrowed from both East and West. Benches are tucked into leafy niches here and there, providing for a quiet moment or two. A sand garden, designed after those found in Kyoto, Japan, in the late fifteenth century, invites a pause. The gardens are small—only two and a half acres—but in their design they recall a spacious home, with one private room opening into another. Although lush and inviting throughout the summer, the gardens are at their most spectacular during the last three weeks in June, when many of the fifty varieties of azalea are in bloom.

The garden is located about 100 yards north of the intersection of Routes 3 and 198; look for a parking lot on the east side of the road. Open during daylight hours April 1 to October 31. Admission is free.

From picturesque and snug Northeast Harbor, boats depart regularly for the *Cranberry Islands*, a pleasant archipelago of flat, open islands dotted with summer homes and cranberry bogs. Several options are available to prospective visitors. You can travel with a National Park Service naturalist to outermost Baker Island and spend a couple of hours exploring the delicate, dramatic terrain; or take the scheduled ferry to either Great or Little Cranberry Islands and explore on your own. Neither island boasts much in the way of tourist attractions, and most residents would like to keep it that way. Great Cranberry has a gift shop, grocery store, and small lunch spot open Thursdays through Mondays. Isleford, on Little Cranberry, has about the same with the addition of the Isleford Historical Museum, a small collection focusing on island history and maintained by the National Park Service. It's open daily from 9:45 A.M. to 4:30 P.M.; admission is free.

Beal and Bunker (244–3575) offers six boats daily to the Cranberry Islands. Round-trip cost is $10.00 for adults, $5.00 for children 3 to 12. *Cranberry Cove Boating Co.* (244–5882) departs from Southwest Harbor four times daily to Great Cranberry and Isleford; fares are $12.00 for adults, $6.00 for children under 12. *Isleford Ferry Company* (276–3717) offers a daily two-and-a-half-hour nature cruise, including a brief stop at Isleford, for $12.00 for adults, $6.00 for children under 12. A daily four-and-a-half-hour naturalist cruise to Baker Island costs $17.00 for adults, $9.00 for children. There's also a sunset cruise each evening for $12.00 for adults, $6.00 for children.

In 1930 a Southwest Harbor plumber named Wendell Gilley set off to study a display of taxidermy at the Boston Museum of Natural History. What caught his attention, however, was a display of delicately carved wooden birds. Gilley returned to Maine to take up a new hobby. At the time of his death fifty years later, Gilley was established as one of the nation's foremost carvers of birds. Carvings by Gilley and other master carvers may be seen at the ***Wendell Gilley Museum of Bird Carving*** just north of the town of Southwest Harbor on Route 102.

This modern and airy museum, built in 1981, contains about 250 carvings ranging from miniature birds such as chickadees and mourning doves to massive life-size eagles and turkeys. After looking at some of Gilley's fine handiwork, you can watch a half-hour video about Gilley and his woodcarving, then watch a woodcarver-in-residence at work in the glass-walled studio. One- and four-day wood-carving classes are offered throughout the summer (tuition includes "printed materials, wood, paints, Band-Aids, and other supplies"). A small gift shop sells magnificently carved birds in a wide range of prices.

The Wendell Gilley Museum is open May through December. June through October hours are from 10:00 A.M. to 4:00 P.M. daily except Monday. In May, November, and December hours are Friday through Sunday from 10:00 A.M. to 4:00 P.M. Admission is $3.25 for adults, $1.00 for children under 12. For more information call 244–7555.

The Claremont Hotel in Southwest Harbor is one of the best surviving examples of a grand nineteenth-century island resort. What makes it so extraordinary is that it retains not just the architecture and gracefully simple decor, but much of the quiet, dignified character. Built in 1884 on a low rise overlooking the mouth of Somes Sound, the distinguished four-story wooden hotel once attracted the eastern seaboard's gentry, who summered here for weeks at a time. It's been blessedly unchanged over the years and features nice touches, like rush-seated rockers on the porch and a pianist serenading guests during cocktail hour at the boathouse. The big event is the Claremont Classic, a croquet tournament that ends with a dance on the croquet court.

A room for two in season begins at $140; cottages begin at $170. The hotel is open early June through mid-October. Call (800) 244–5036 or 244–5036.

The west side of Mount Desert is less populated and more forested than the dramatic, congested east side. Acadia National Park maintains a handful of hiking trails here, and gentle, winding roads touch the water at several points. Connoisseurs of country drives will enjoy exploring the roads around Bass Harbor and Seal Cove.

If you're in mind of a classic Maine seafood eatery, make sure you head to **Keenan's** on Route 102A just outside Bass Harbor. It's a popular spot with locals and specializes in no-frills mounds of seafood fresh from the dock. There's no water view, and there are virtually no windows. The atmosphere inside the cramped quarters is created in large part by the banter between tables of hungry customers and the harried servers. Prices are very reasonable for what you get. Open daily in summer; in the off-season it's open weekends only. Call 244–3403.

In the tiny town of Bernard across the inlet from Bass Harbor, look for two intriguing shops of interest to collectors. *E. L. Higgins Antique Wicker* has a good selection of elaborate old wicker, the sort one would expect filled the porches of the grand summer mansions hereabouts eighty or so years ago. It's not bargain priced, but it's a great selection, and much of it has been carefully restored. For information call 244–3983. On Steamboat Wharf Road is *Nancy Neal Typecraft*, which bills itself as "Maine's only printing museum and memorabilia shop." Owners Nancy Neal and Irving Silverman are printing historians and are eager to share their knowledge with their visitors. You can rummage through bins of moveable wooden type, and put together a collage that spells out a cryptic message to yourself. Or buy type to make bookends or key chains. Be creative. The shop is open June to October by chance or appointment; it's best to call ahead: 244–5192.

On the northwest side of the island, stop at Indian Point, site of The Nature Conservancy's *Blagden Preserve*. This 110-acre preserve features about 1,000 feet of shore frontage and a series of meandering, attractive walking trails through mixed hardwood and softwood forest. Bring binoculars and a book to the rocky shore, where the caretakers have scattered a dozen or so red Adirondack-style chairs facing westward across the water toward Blue Hill. Keep an eye out for harbor seals, which commonly haul themselves out to rest on the rocky ledges offshore on sunny days. In the forest near the shores you also might spot (as I did one day) a pileated woodpecker or an osprey.

The preserve is located off Indian Point Road. From the park visitor center at Hulls Cove, head south on Route 198 toward Somesville.

Shortly after passing the Spruce Valley Campground, turn right on Indian Point Road. Proceed 1.7 miles to a fork; bear right for another 200 yards. Look for the preserve entrance on the right amid a row of handsome oaks. Stop at the red caretaker's cottage to sign in and obtain a preserve map.

One of the less-visited parts of Acadia National Park accessible by car is located a 45-mile drive eastward from Mount Desert. But *Schoodic Point*, an isolated, rugged promontory, is well worth the drive. From the town of Winter Harbor, follow the National Park Service sign for Schoodic Peninsula. A winding one-way road soon takes you along the east side of Frenchman Bay; on a clear day magnificent views of Cadillac Mountain open up through the spruce and pine. At the tip a broad expanse of salmon-pink granite angles down to the water's edge, and the ocean tends to be at its most restless here. Bring a picnic; no food is available south of Winter Harbor. Another one-way road leads back along the other side of the spruce-clad peninsula toward the town of Corea. Take it slow and stop at the waysides to enjoy the unfolding show.

Washington County

East of Schoodic Point the coast's character begins to change. You find more shops and restaurants that cater to locals than to travelers. In the harbors lobster boats far outnumber the pleasure craft. Homes are maintained less to impress visitors than to provide sanctuary during the long months of winter. Coastal villages become somewhat more rough-hewn, reflecting a changing ratio of fishermen over summer folk. Down East Maine begins here in earnest.

Heading eastward on Route 1, you'll pass through the towns of Steuben, Millbridge, Cherryfield, and Harrington. Take time to enjoy the architecture along the way, particularly in Millbridge and Cherryfield, where many of the mansions reflect the boom days of the lumber, shipbuilding, and fishing trades. (Some of the finer Millbridge homes have been converted to B&Bs.)

Jonesport and Vicinity

In Columbia Falls the *Ruggles House* is open to the public and offers a direct look into the region's past. This graceful but modest early-nineteenth-century home was constructed for Thomas Ruggles, who moved to town in 1790 aiming to make his fortune in lumber. Ruggles succeeded in his quest and soon became a respected community leader; eventually he was appointed to a judgeship in Machias. In 1818 he commissioned a 22-year-old architect, Aaron S. Sherman, to design his home.

The interior has several elements of architectural distinction, including a magnificent flying staircase in the central hallway, "open Bible" keystones above the Palladian arches, and pine doors handpainted to resemble mahogany. Of particular note is the intricate wood carving throughout the parlor; local lore asserts the carving was executed by a British craftsman who labored three years with a penknife. The home, which was restored from a state of severe dilapidation in 1950, now contains much of Ruggles's original furniture.

The Ruggles House is open June to mid-October Monday to Saturday from 9:30 A.M. to 4:30 P.M. and Sunday from 11:00 A.M. to 4:30 P.M. Tours run about twenty minutes. Admission is $3.50 for adults, $2.50 for children. The house is 0.25 mile off Route 1 in the village of Columbia Falls. For information call 483-4637.

One of the Nature Conservancy's most spectacular Maine holdings is on *Great Wass Island*, located south of Jonesport and accessible by car via bridge and causeway. This 1,579-acre preserve, acquired in 1978, has more than five hundred acres of jack pine—stunted, gnarly trees well suited to the harsh conditions on the island—as well as considerable areas of open heath and bog.

Two trails provide access to the eastern shore from a small parking lot. The trails, which twist over rocky and root-covered ground across relatively flat terrain, may be linked together by a hike along the rocky shoreline, making a loop about 5 miles long. Take some time along the ocean's edge to enjoy the views of the lighthouse on Mistake Island (also a Nature Conservancy holding) and to watch the seals congregating densely on the ledges offshore. Allow about three hours for the entire loop, and be prepared for damp conditions; fog often moves in with little warning.

The preserve parking lot is on the west side of Great Wass Island. From Jonesport cross the bridge to Beals Island and continue onward, bearing right at the fork after you cross the causeway to Great Wass. The pavement soon ends; continue until you pass a lobster pound at Black Duck Cove, then look for the lot on the left side of the road. Maps and a birder's checklist may be obtained at the registration box.

Machias Area

*H*ere's a bit of Revolutionary War lore long buried in the footnotes: The first naval battle of the Revolution took place near the port town of Machias, when ambitious colonists succeeded in capturing the better-equipped British schooner *Margaretta*. The episode unfolded in June 1775, a month after the Battle of Lexington. The *Margaretta* arrived in Machias accompanying a freight ship to procure wood to build barracks for British soldiers in Boston. This action didn't sit well with the citizenry of Machias, who hastily organized an expedition against the British ship. Aboard two smaller ships they successfully attacked the *Margaretta*, mortally wounding the captain and capturing the crew. The story didn't have an entirely happy ending for the colonists. The British vowed retribution, and in subsequent months returned to rout Machias soldiers and burn many buildings.

One place to learn a bit about the battle for the *Margaretta* is **Burnham Tavern**, a pale yellow gambrel-roofed building located on a small rise in the pleasant commercial town of Machias. Constructed in 1770 by Job Burnham, the tavern served as the base from which Jeremiah O'Brien and his townsmen formulated plans for the attack on the

Nothing to Get Bogged Down By

*M*aine has more bogs—and a more diverse variety of bogs—than any other northeastern state. They're especially prevalent in Washington County, where the surface topography and cool, moist air off the ocean conspire to create these floating meadows.

Bogs form where there's little moving water to carry away rotting organic matter, which is often found in kettle holes that were left by retreating glaciers. (A kettle hole is a basin without an outlet created where a massive slab of glacial ice that was buried in the ground later melted, leaving a broad, often circular depression.) Decades of dead leaves, twigs, and mosses accumulate and form a sort of

thick mat that floats on top of the water. This eventually sustains a colony of specialized plants that have evolved to thrive in this hostile environment, which is by and large free of the nutrients typically found in soil.

Especially intriguing is the carnivorous pitcher plant (Sarracenia purpurea). It survives by luring insects into its deep, tubular body, where they're trapped by downward-pointing hairs. Enzymes then digest the insects, providing life-giving nutrients to the plant. Early in the season they're easily spotted by looking for the red, umbrella-like flower that rises on a slender stem above the red-veined pitcher below.

Keep 'em Charged

*T*hose huge antennae you see in a ring between Machias and Cutler are part of the U.S. Naval Computer and Telecommunications Station. It's not likely that you'll miss them—the twenty-six towers soar between 800 and 980 feet into the air, or nearly twice the height of the 555-foot Washington Monument. They're held in place with a web of wires, which can withstand the blustery coastal winters and resultant heavy icing. With this battery the navy keeps in communication with its fleet in the north Atlantic, Europe, and the Arctic. The facility is slated for decommissioning and isn't open to the public.

British schooner. Following the skirmish, it was in the tavern that *Margaretta*'s captain succumbed to his wounds and other British soldiers were nursed back to health.

The tavern was acquired and restored by the Daughters of the American Revolution in 1910 and today appears much as it did during the heady days of the War of Independence. The original tap table is on display, as are a tea set and a chest taken from the captured ship. Up the steep "good morning" stairs are several bedrooms, including one where local Masons first met in 1778. Today the rooms house a collection of tools and other historic objects.

The tavern is open mid-June to Labor Day Monday through Friday from 9:00 A.M. to 5:00 P.M. It is in the center of town just north of the Machias River on Route 192. Tours last about forty-five minutes and cost $2.00 for adults, 25 cents for children. For more information call 255–4432.

A wooden model of the *Margaretta* may be seen at the **Gates House** in the riverside village of Machiasport, several miles south of Machias on Route 92. Built around 1807, this home was in the Gates family for more than a century before it became the headquarters of the Machiasport Historical Society. Located on the tidal river, this classic clapboarded home contains displays related to the marine history of the area and its early life and commerce. A kitchen displays early utensils; local period fashion may be seen upstairs. There's also a telescope offering views down the river toward the open ocean, allowing visitors to duplicate an act that must have been performed dozens of times daily when Machiasport was an active seaside town. The house is open mid-June through early September Tuesday through Saturday from 12:30 to 4:30 P.M. Admission is free. For more information call 255–8461.

If you're continuing eastward toward Lubec, consider the somewhat

longer but more scenic trip via Route 191 through the harbor town of
Cutler. The road offers a fine view of coastal Maine at its most remote and
least developed. Views of the ocean open here and there, and the road tra-
verses broad heaths and blueberry barrens, which blaze a fiery red in fall.

Lubec Region

Maine's easternmost towns, located along Cobscook and Passamaquoddy bays, are known for two major distinctions: the
booming sardine industry that flourished here in the early twentieth
century and the mighty tides that sweep twice daily in and out of the
bays. The difference between high tide and low tide can be as much as
28 feet near Lubec and Eastport, and each tide generates fiercely power-
ful currents that can stymie unwary boat captains attempting to make
headway at the wrong time and in the wrong place.

Not far from the town of Lubec, you'll find the easternmost point in the
United States: **West Quoddy Head**. (East Quoddy Head, if you're wondering, is across the channel in Canada.) This narrow lobe of land
extends off the mainland south of town and is anchored by a distinctive
candy-striped red-and-white lighthouse, one that's appeared on postage
stamps and countless wall calendars. On a clear day you can see from the
lighthouse to the cliffs of Grand Manan, a brawny Canadian island 16
miles out in the Bay of Fundy. The lighthouse, first commissioned in
1807 and rebuilt in 1858, is operated by the Coast Guard and closed to
the public. But visitors may explore the grounds, which are often bloom-
ing with daylilies and wild roses. A short shoreline trail runs southward
along a jagged, 50-foot precipice to Quoddy Head State Park, a 481-acre
ocean-side park with picnicking and limited hiking. During mid-tide
you can witness the remarkable force of the currents as they eddy and
curl around the offshore ledges and rocks.

The lighthouse grounds are open daily from 8:00 A.M. to 7:00 P.M.; the
state park is open daily May 30 to October 15 from 9:00 A.M. to sunset.
The fee to visit the state park is $1.00 for adults, 50 cents for children.

Campobello Island is accessible by bridge across The Narrows from the
town of Lubec. Although the island is in the Canadian province of New
Brunswick (expect a cursory customs check both coming and going), the
United States has a stake in one section of the island: the **Roosevelt Campobello International Park and Natural Area**. This 2,800-acre park,
located about 2 miles from the bridge, is managed by a special international commission with representatives from the U.S. Department of the

Interior and Canada's Department of External Affairs. It claims to be the only park of this kind in the world; at the very least it provides a bit of justification for including a wonderful Canadian destination in a book about Maine.

The park is named for U.S. President Franklin Delano Roosevelt, who summered here almost every year between 1883, when he was 1 year old, and 1921, the summer he was stricken with polio. FDR's father, James Roosevelt, was first lured to the island's beauty and tranquillity when Campobello was being touted as an exclusive resort for the wealthy. He purchased four acres and a partially built home, completing the residence over the next few years. In 1910 the family moved to a significantly larger eighteen-bedroom "cottage" nearby, which was originally built in 1897. The cottage is open to the public.

Lighthouse, West Quoddy Head

Get an overview of the island's history at the visitor center, where you can watch a short film about FDR's long relationship with the island. (He introduced golf to the island; locals approved, since they could graze their sheep on the greens.) The maroon-shingled Roosevelt cottage is a short walk behind the visitor center. A self-guided tour allows a leisurely wander through the spacious homestead, which is an appealing mix of the simple and the grandiose. It's hard to imagine an eighteen-bedroom house feeling like a cozy home, but somehow it does. Helpful guides are on hand to answer any questions you might have. Spend a moment picturing the extended Roosevelt clan gathered in the massive kitchen on the east side of the house during one of the region's infamous foggy mornings.

Nearby is the equally elegant **Hubbard Cottage**, built in 1891 and often open to the public. (If it's closed, it usually means a conference is being held there.) A visit to this classic shingle-style home at the edge of the bay seems a trip to a lost era. The magnificent view across the water to the town of Eastport through the oval window in the dining room alone makes a visit worthwhile. If you'd like to spend more time outdoors, be sure to obtain a map of the park grounds at the visitor center. The park maintains about 8 miles of walking trails through a wide variety of terrain, including a dramatic 2-mile ocean-side hike from Raccoon Beach to Liberty Point. The park is open daily from Memorial Day weekend until mid-October from 10:00 A.M. to 6:00 P.M. eastern time. (Don't forget you're in Atlantic time, one hour later, after you cross the bridge.) Admission is free. For more information call (506) 752–2922.

Eastport and Vicinity

Turning from the ocean and heading toward inland Washington County, you'll wind along beautiful and surprisingly remote Cobscook and Passamaquoddy bays. **Cobscook Bay State Park** is one of the state's finest parks, with many of the secluded campsites located along the water on three peninsulas. A picnic area is near a broad, grassy meadow with fine views down to the water. The park is just off Route 1 (look for the sign) between Whiting and Dennysville. The day-use fee is $2.00 for adults, 50 cents for children.

Another commendable spot for a detour is **Reversing Falls Park**, a scruffy municipal park 6 miles from the town of Pembroke. This 140-acre park is located on Mahar Point, where Dennys and Whiting bays squeeze into Cobscook Bay between the point and Falls Island. Because of the extraordinary tides, water tends to back up here, creating a set of rapids heading one way at one tide and reversing at the next. There's a short walk through mixed forest to the rocky edge of the river; a couple of picnic tables invite a perusal of this natural phenomenon. One day that I visited here, about a dozen seals were playing and leaping in the building current. The best time to visit, I'm told, is about two hours before high tide. One caveat: It's mostly an undeveloped park, and the outhouses here are the nastiest I've seen in travels anywhere, including much of the developing world.

Small signs point you from Pembroke to the park. Sometimes. Other times they're torn down and not replaced for months at a time. Coming from the south, veer right at the Triangle store, then turn east at the IOOF (International Order of Odd Fellows) Hall. Travel 3.4 miles along Leighton Neck to a right turn. Follow this road, which becomes increasingly rugged, to the end and park. There is no charge for visiting the park, which is open during daylight hours.

Those wishing to get out on the water to explore in-depth should contact **Tidal Trails** in Pembroke. Tim and Amy Sheehan, two young Mainers, started the service in 1997, aiming to share their love of Cobscook Bay and its massive tides. Tim works off-season as a biology teacher and knows what's going on both underwater and around the edge of the sea. The Sheehans offer mountain bike, canoe, and sea kayak rentals from their waterfront farmhouse on Pembroke's Leighton Neck, and eco-tours aboard **The Copepod,** a 36-foot lobster boat. Rates are $15 to $35 per person, depending on the tour. They also organize sea kayak

Salmon by the Pen

*T*he towns along Passamaquoddy Bay once thrived on sardines, which were caught and canned here, then shipped worldwide. But tastes changed and demand dried up. The seaport towns suffered. But another fish, now in high demand, is breathing new life into towns: the Atlantic salmon.

Where the roads touch along the bay, scan the waters. You may see what look like floating checkerboards off in the distance. Look closer. You'll see fish leaping, restrained from escape by netting draped over the tops. The pens are especially prevalent in the coves around Eastport, where the nation's largest Atlantic salmon farming operation is located. You can learn more about the new industry, including boat trips out to view the pens, during Eastport's annual Salmon Festival, which is held the second Sunday of September.

tours and offer a unique look at Reversing Falls from an inflatable raft. For more information call 726–4079.

Eastport is a small town with a lot of history. The downtown consists of doughty brick commercial buildings and clapboarded Cape-style homes on a gentle hill above the harbor, which is surprisingly active with freighters and pleasure craft. The town's main street offers several small shops for browsing.

Raye's Mustard Mill, located on the edge of town at Outer Washington Street, produces some of the world's finest mustards. That claim can even be backed up: The Down East Schooner (an American yellow mustard) won first place at a 1996 international mustard competition in San Francisco. The operation is run by Nancy Raye, whose family founded the mill in 1903 to provide mustard for sardine packing. It's now producing upscale, gourmet mustards, and the mill's products have generated legions of devoted fans. You can try samples and pick some up for the road at Raye's Working Museum and Pantry Store, which is open daily from 8:00 A.M. to 5:00 P.M. (opens at 10:00 A.M. on Sunday). For information call 853–4451.

On your way out of town, stop by *Shackford Head* for a stroll to an open bluff with spectacular views of the bay. (Watch for a small sign across from the Irving service station at Country Road and Washington Street; drive 0.7 mile, then turn left on the dirt road and park in the clearing at the road's end.) The walk is about two-thirds of a mile and passes through spruce forest, near a profusion of berry bushes and across a boardwalk. The views from the cliffs are wonderful; from here you'll get a good sense of the extent of salmon farming in the area when you see the acres of floating pens bobbing in remote coves.

Heading north of Eastport toward Calais on Route 1 in Robbinston look for a small festive, yellow shop on the left that overlooks the road and a cove. That's *Katie's On the Cove,* which has developed a committed following for its delicious handmade confections. The owners carefully make small batches using the best ingredients and old Maine recipes. Among the favorites: Needhams (a moist potato, chocolate, and coconut candy not unlike a Mound's bar), Maine Black Bear Paws (maple caramel, pecans, and dark chocolate), and coffee cremes. More traditional offerings include wintergreen and peppermint patties, molasses chews, and candied ginger root. This is a wonderful spot to stock up for sugar-high road tripping. Be sure to pick up a mail-order form, since your friends back home won't believe your descriptions of how good their candies are. For more information call 454–3297.

Continue northward on Route 1. Between Robbinston and Calais there's a small island about a half-mile offshore in the St. Croix River whose appearance is far overshadowed by its historical significance. *St. Croix Island* (so named after two large bays north of the island that appear to form the arms of a cross) was the site of the first attempted permanent European settlement in North America north of Florida.

In 1604 a group of some eighty French colonists under the guidance of Sieur de Monts and his lieutenant, Samuel de Champlain, landed on the island with the intent of establishing a village and trading center. The colonists were so uncertain of what to expect that they brought their own timber for building homes. The island was reasonably secure from surprise attack but lacked a number of amenities, including a ready supply of drinking water. In addition, the island was swept by bitter north winds, prompting Champlain to note that there was "six months of winter in this country." The following summer the colonists abandoned St. Croix Island and resettled at Annapolis Royal in Nova Scotia.

Eastport Trivia
In 1932 a 26-foot great white shark was caught near Eastport. It's still on the record books as the largest shark ever taken in the waters of Maine.

Saint Croix Island is managed as a national monument, but public transportation to the island is not offered—at least not yet. Some plans are in the offing to provide more extensive services for visitors, including a possible information center on the island. A riverside observation area with historical markers is located along Route 1 near the town of Red Beach.

Calais Area

From this eastern corner of Maine, Route 1 heads north to Aroostook County (see "The County"), the road's character changing dramatically. Once you turn and put the sea at your back, few early homes line the road and salt air is replaced by the smell of spruce and fir. Timber companies own and manage a great deal of this land, which is filled with vast lakes and wild lakeshores. The region is highly popular among fishermen, hunters, and canoeists. The village of *Grand Lake Stream*, with its selection of lodges and boat access to numerous remote lakes, has been a favored base among many outdoorspeople for decades. (The bass and landlocked salmon fishing is especially good.) Among the lodges here are Weatherbys (796–5558), Colonial Sportsmen's Lodge (796–2655), and Leen's Lodge (796–5575). All traditionally cater to serious fishermen, but the owners make others feel welcome as well.

You'll learn a lot about the area in a short time if you decide to explore with **Grand Lake Outfitters.** Longtime residents Laura and Steve Schaefer offer canoe and sea kayak excursions up large and often blustery West Grand Lake, as well as trips to some of the quieter lakes and ponds farther afield, where you're likely to spot moose, black bear, or bald eagles. If the water gushing out of the dam is sufficient (it often is in July and August), ask about the white-water rafting trips down Grand Lake Stream. The four-person rafts bump and bounce down the rocky river, and plunge over two small waterfalls on an hour-long trip. It's not the big water of the Kennebec or Penobscot rivers in northern Maine, but it's a fun outing and nonthreatening to younger kids. It's also a great way to see the river and woods from another perspective. Tours are priced from $25. Call 796–5561 for reservations or more information.

If you decide not to head northward from Calais, the quickest way back to the Maine Turnpike and points south is along Route 9, commonly known as the **Airline Road** or simply "the Airline." This straight shot across eastern Maine has roots back to 1857, when Calais citizens established a dirt path to improve mail service from the state's commercial hub at Bangor. In time the route was improved to accommodate stagecoaches, which made the trip daily except Sundays. The eighteen-hour trip was often brutal on passengers, but it was a full day quicker than traveling by steamship. When the steamship companies attempted to curb competition by depicting the route as populated by wolves and bandits, stagecoach ridership surged as adventurers shelled out the fare to claim they had survived the trip. Despite the incongruously modern-sounding name, the Airline is in fact the old name for the route, presumably to distinguish it from the competing Shore Line steamship company.

Today neither wolves nor bandits present much of a problem for motorists, but Route 9 does provide a glimpse at an interesting cross section of Maine. The road passes through thick spruce forests and cutover timberland, across blueberry barrens and open heath. East of the town of Aurora, watch for the road to ascend a glacial esker (a tall ridge of gravel formed by currents running through massive tunnels beneath a melting glacier). The land seems to drop off on either side of the road as if on a man-made embankment; glacial bogs may be seen north of the road from a small rest area. There are few services along the road (an occasional motel or snack bar), but for the most part it's just fast driving. In fact, the Airline seems to be Maine's answer to the autobahn. Even when driving over the speed limit, you're likely to be passed by others evidently in a far greater hurry.

PLACES TO STAY DOWN EAST

BAR HARBOR

Acadia Hotel, 20 Mount Desert Street, 288–5721

Balance Rock Inn, 21 Albert Meadow, (800) 753–0494 or 288–2610

Bar Harbor Hotel–Bluenose Inn, 90 Eden Street, (800) 445–4077 or 288–3348

Bar Harbor Inn, Newport Drive, (800) 248–3351 or 288–3351

Chiltern Inn, 3 Cromwell Harbor Road, 288–2756

Holiday Inn SunSpree Resort, 123 Eden Street, (800) 23–HOTEL or 288–9723

Ivy Manor Inn, 194 Main Street, 288–2138

Villager Motel, 207 Main Street, 288–3211

Wonder View Inn, 50 Eden Street, (800) 341–1553 or 288–3358

BLUE HILL

Blue Hill Heritage Motor Inn, Route 172, 374–5646

Blue Hill Inn, Union Street, 374–2844

John Peters Inn, Route 176 East, 374–2116

CASTINE

Castine Inn, Main Street, 326–4365

Pentagoet, Main Street, (800) 845–1701 or 326–8616

DEER ISLE

Goose Cove Lodge Sunset, 348–2508

Pilgrim's Inn, Deer Isle, 348–6615

EASTPORT

Inn at Eastport, 13 Washington Street, (207) 853–4307

Kilby House Inn, 122 Water Street, (800) 435–4529 or 853–0989

Todd House, 1 Capen Avenue, (207) 853–2328

Weston House, 26 Boynton Street, (207) 853–2907

GRAND LAKE STREAM

Weatherby's Fisherman's Resort, Grand Lake Stream, 796–5558

HULLS COVE

The Colony, Route 3, (800) 524–1159 or 288–3383

MACHIAS

Micmac Farm Guesthouses, Route 92, Machiasport, 255–3008

Riverside Inn, Route 1, East Machias, 255–4234

SOUTHWEST HARBOR

Claremont Inn, Clark Point Road, (800) 244–5036 or 244–5036

The Inn at Southwest, Main Street, 244–3835

Kingsleigh Inn, Main Street, 244–5302

Lindenwood Inn, 118 Clark Point Road, 244–5335

STONINGTON

Inn on the Harbor, Main Street, (800) 942–2420 or 367–2420

PLACES TO EAT DOWN EAST

BAR HARBOR

George's, 7 Stephens Lane, 288–4505

Jordan's Restaurant, 80 Cottage Street, 288–3586

Lompoc Cafe, 32 Rodick Street, 288–9392

Maggie's Classic Scales, 6 Summer Street, 288–9007

Nakorn Thai, 30 Rodick Street, 288–4060

West Street Cafe, West Street, 288–5242

BLUE HILL

Jonathan's, Main Street, 374–5526

Tavern at Firepond, Main Street, 374–9970

EASTPORT
Eastport Lobster and Fish
Company, 167 Water Street,
853–6006

La Sardina Loca, 28 Water
Street, 853–2739

Waco Diner, Bank Square,
853–4046

MANSET
Restaurant XYZ, Shore
Road, 244–5221

Seawall Dining Room,
Route 102A, 244–3020

NORTHEAST HARBOR
Redfield's, Main Street,
276–5283

OTTER CREEK
Burning Tree, Route 3,
288–9331

Jordan Pond House, Loop
Road, 276–3316

PEMBROKE
Crossroads Restaurant,
Route 1, 726–5053

PERRY
The New Friendly
Restaurant, Route 1,
(800) 953- 6610 or
853–6610

SOUTHWEST HARBOR
Keenan's, Route 102A,
Bass Harbor, 244–3403

Preble Grille, 14 Clark Point
Road, 244–3034

STONINGTON
Fisherman's Friend, School
Street, 367–2442

Harbor Cafe, Main Street,
367–5099

Helpful Web Sites

Acadia National Park—*www.nps.gov/acad/*

Bar Harbor Chamber of Commerce—
www.barharborinfo.com

Deer Isle Chamber of Commerce—
www.acadia.net/deerston/

Ellsworth Area Chamber of Commerce—
www.acadia.net/eacc/

E. L. Higgins Antique Wicker—
www.antiquewicker.com

Maine Maritime Academy—
www.mainemaritime.edu

Quoddy Loop—*www.quoddyloop.com*

Southwest Harbor–Tremont
Chamber of Commerce—
www.acadia.net/swhtrcoc/

Tidal Trails—*www.nemaine.com/tidaltrails*

Town of Deer Isle—*www.acadia.net/deerisle/*

Town of Eastport—
www.mainerec.com/eastport.html

Town of Lubec—*www.nemaine.com/lubec_cc*

Selected Chambers of Commerce

Bar Harbor Chamber of Commerce,
93 Cottage Street, (800) 288–5103

Deer Isle–Stonington Chamber of Commerce,
P.O. Box 459, Stonington 04681, 348–6124

Eastport Chamber of Commerce,
Water Street, 853–4644

Machias Bay Area Chamber of Commerce,
23 East Main Street, 255–4402

North Woods

The North Woods consists of millions of acres of forestland, some of it as quiet and removed as when Thoreau traveled through and noted the "general stillness more impressive than any sound." This is the terrain of moose and loon; humans don't so much linger as pass on through.

The North Woods isn't for the garden-variety tourist. Because the region is so wild and undeveloped, car travelers may soon become frustrated at the lack of facilities and access. You can drive only so far on dusty logging roads through commercial timberland before you become a bit weary and start yearning for people and buildings of one sort or another.

The North Woods is best appreciated by those with outdoor inclinations: fishermen, hunters, white-water rafters, and canoeists—especially canoeists. There are hundreds of miles of rivers and streams, as well as thousands of miles of lakeshore, that are best navigated by canoe. Foot-paths exist here and there—notably the Appalachian Trail—but for the most part the North Woods trail network is sketchy at best.

One more brief caveat before you visit the North Woods: This is not a wilderness area but an industrial forest, and there's a big difference between the two. Pockets of undisturbed forest may be found throughout—isolated state landholdings and property owned by The Nature Conservancy—but much of the rest of the North Woods is privately owned by about two dozen timber companies. Virtually the entire forest has been cut at least once, and more likely twice. If you think of the North Woods as agricultural land, like a massive farm with crops on a forty-year rotation, you're on your way to understanding what this region is all about.

Penobscot County

Penobscot County includes Maine's second city, the lumber capital of Bangor. But Bangor is a small urban oasis in country that ranges from rural to wild. The county's borders extend far to the

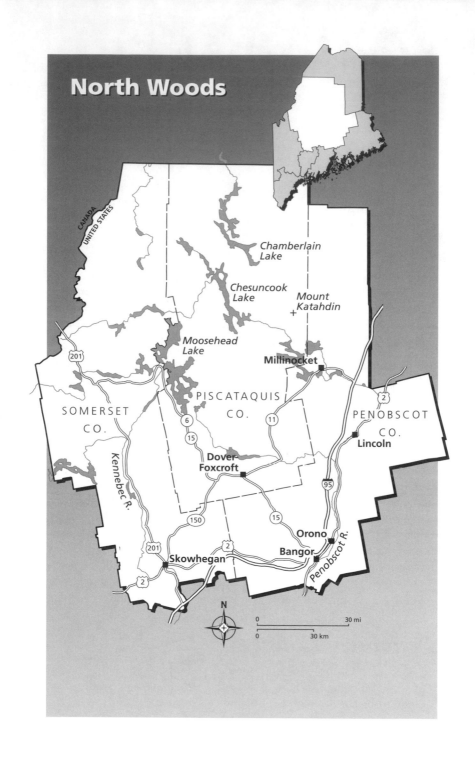

North Woods

Chamberlain
Lake

Chesuncook
Lake

Mount
Katahdin
+

Moosehead
Lake

Millinocket

201

PISCATAQUIS
CO.

SOMERSET
CO.

6

15

11

PENOBSCOT
CO.

2

Lincoln

Dover-
Foxcroft

Kennebec R.

150

15

95

Orono

201

2

Skowhegan

Bangor

Penobscot R.

CANADA

UNITED STATES

N

0   30 mi

0   30 km

north, striking deep into the heart of the timberlands north of the mill town of Millinocket.

Bangor Area

Maine's North Woods begins at the city of Bangor, both geographically and historically. Between 1820 and 1860, Bangor prospered like no other town in Maine as timber merchants employed hundreds of men to cut pine and spruce along the Penobscot and its tributaries, then float the logs down the river during great spring lumber drives. Once at the mills the logs were cut and exported throughout the nation and abroad. In fact, Bangor was the largest lumber port in the world during the 1850s, and with that honor came tremendous prosperity. More than a few fortunes were made. Bangor began a decline in the 1880s as readily accessible trees were depleted and the timber industry moved west. Adding to the decline, a fire leveled much of the city in 1911. Nevertheless, Bangor retains much of historical interest, and it's not hard to imagine the place during its golden days more than a century ago. Bangor's proud woodland heritage may be best captured by the city's de facto symbol: the vaguely menacing 31-foot fiberglass *Paul Bunyan statue* on Main Street between Buck and Dutton Streets. Bangor claims the legendary lumberman was born here in 1834. Other towns, especially those in timber regions of the upper Midwest, naturally dispute the claim.

A good place to get an overview of Bangor history is at the *Bangor Historical Society* at 159 Union Street (at the intersection of High Street).

Bangor Firsts

Among inventors, tinkerers, and the trivia-obsessed, Bangor holds a special place. In the nineteenth century, the city claimed several "firsts," beginning in 1850 when a young man developed the nation's first batch of chewing gum on his kitchen stove. He boiled spruce sap, added sugar, dusted the strips with cornstarch, and started peddling his new chewy concoction in the big cities. It caught on. Eventually he developed a business that employed 200 people producing gum for shipment nationwide.

Bangor was also the first city to erect a Civil War memorial, building it at Mount Hope Cemetery a month *before* the Battle of Gettysburg. It's the birthplace of the canvas-covered canoe and where the extension ladder was invented. It also was the first city in Maine to have an electric trolley system, which was inaugurated in 1889.

The collections are housed in an uncommonly graceful brick home constructed in 1836 for a prominent Bangor businessman. The first floor is furnished much like a typical Victorian home, with medallion-backed chairs, soaring gilded mirrors, and intricate Oriental carpets. Be sure to note the exceptional craftsmanship of the carved frieze and the Corinthian columns in the airy double parlor. Upstairs are galleries featuring exhibits related to Bangor's history. One-hour tours are offered April through December Tuesday through Friday between noon and 4:00 P.M. and on Saturdays from June through September. Tours are $5.00; children under 12 are free. For more information call 942–5766.

I can't precisely explain why, but the **Thomas Hill Standpipe**, built in 1898, is among my favorite architectural eccentricities in the state. Sited atop one of Bangor's gentle hills, the standpipe is essentially a water tank with an observation deck built around it. If nothing else, this 110-foot-high wooden structure attests to the pervasive influence of the shingle style in the late nineteenth century. With its clean lines, white shingles, and colonnaded overlook circling the top, the standpipe also provides a heartening glimpse into a world where even something as utilitarian as a water tank benefited from an architect's eye. The 1.75-million-gallon tank is still used today to provide water to the people of Bangor and is managed by the Bangor Water District. The standpipe observatory may be appreciated from the outside anytime but is open to the public only once a year, usually during the first week in October, for fall foliage viewing. Call the Bangor Historical Society (942–5766) for the exact date.

Fans of architecture and students of the information age might enjoy a stop by the **Bangor Public Library**. The original beaux arts structure, a handsome domed affair, was built in 1912 as the city was pulling itself

America's Boogeyman

*F*orget about the glories of the timber baron days. Bangor today may be best known as the home of horror novelist Stephen King. As befits a writer of novels in the modern Gothic tradition, King lives on a pleasant street of large, handsome homes in an oversized Victorian house reminiscent of the Addams family house, only without the cobwebs and shutters all askew. By all accounts, King is a regular guy around town, involved in various civic and local affairs. He's got a bit more financial clout than most, however. He and his wife, Tabitha, also a novelist, have donated millions to various causes, including the construction of a world-class Little League field and the renovation of the public library.

Thomas Hill Standpipe, Bangor

up by its bootstraps following the devastating fire of 1911. By the 1990s, the library was feeling its age and was crumbling and leaky. A massive campaign was launched to restore and expand the building, and one of the nation's most prominent architects—Robert A. M. Stern—was hired to design a three-story addition. The new library, which opened in 1998, also features some 220 new computer terminals, reflecting the growing shift of libraries from repositories of books to information gateways. The library is at 145 Harlow Street; for more information call 947–8336.

Outside downtown near exit 45 off I–95 is the *Cole Land Transportation Museum*. It's more than your run-of-the-mill vehicle museum—it's an eclectic collection of nineteenth- and twentieth-century vehicles that extends back to the covered wagon days. You can view some 200 vehicles, from tractors to buckboards to sleds, housed in a modern and airy warehouse building. The museum is at 405 Perry Road and is open daily from May to mid-November from 9:00 A.M. to 5:00 P.M.; admission is $3.00 for adults, $2.00 for seniors; children under 19 are free. For more information call 990–3600.

Orono and Old Town

About 8 miles north of Bangor in Orono is the principal campus of the *University of Maine*, which has about 11,000 students. The university began in 1868 as the Maine State College of Agriculture and

Mechanic Arts but broadened its curriculum over the years to encompass liberal arts as well as forestry, business, and engineering. The campus was originally designed by noted landscape architect Frederick Law Olmsted, but the plan was modified somewhat and later additions have obscured Olmsted's original vision. With its attractive buildings and leafy trees, the campus still offers a pleasant place to stroll.

WAYNE'S FAVORITE ATTRACTIONS

1. **Old Town Canoe Company,** Old Town
2. **Mattawamkeag Wilderness Park**
3. **Baxter State Park**
4. **Gulf Hagas,** Baxter State Park area
5. **SS Katahdin,** Greenville

Here you'll find the **Hudson Museum**, a respected and well-designed museum of anthropology and native culture. Occupying three levels in a modern building with an open floor plan, the collections include gold and jade jewelry from the Aztec and Maya cultures of Central America and an exceptional selection of masks and carvings from the native cultures of the Pacific Northwest, including a towering and dramatic Haida house post. Other geographic areas represented include Oceania, the Arctic, and Africa, and there is a special emphasis on the native Penobscot Indians. Local crafts include cornhusk dolls, snowshoes, a birch-bark canoe, ceremonial beadwork, and split-ash basketry.

The museum is open Tuesday through Friday from 9:00 A.M. to 4:00 P.M., and Saturday and Sunday from 11:00 A.M. to 4:00 P.M.; it's closed Mondays and holidays. Admission is free. For more information call 581–1901.

Also on campus is the **Page Farm and Home Museum**. This small museum features a collection of everyday items one might have found on a Maine farm a century ago. The museum is in the last original agricultural building on the university campus, which was built in 1865, before the university was established. You'll find exhibits on dairy and poultry farming, as well as a blacksmith shop and a one-room schoolhouse. The collections are a virtual compendium of life in Maine before 1940. The museum has never bought a thing—every bowl, beam, and breadboard was donated, and everything was made and used in Maine. The museum is open May 15 to September 15 daily from 9:00 A.M. to 4:00 P.M., and the rest of the year it's open Tuesday through Saturday. For more information call 581–4100.

Latter-day Penobscot and Passamaquoddy Indians still inhabit reservations around the state, remnants of early and inequitable land transactions between natives and settlers. One of the more prominent

NORTH WOODS

TOP ANNUAL EVENTS

1. *Sled Dog Races,*
   Greenville, late January,
   539–4324
2. *Garden Show,* Bangor,
   early April, 990–1201
3. *Moosemania,*
   Greenville & Rock-
   wood, late May/early
   June, 695–2702
4. *World's Largest
   Garage Sale,* Bangor,
   late June, 942–4821
5. *Bangor State Fair,*
   late July/early August,
   942–9000
6. *International
   Seaplane Fly-In,*
   Greenville, early
   October, 695–2821

reservations is located just north of Old Town. *Indian Island* was part of a 1786 treaty that deeded most of Maine to the European settlers; the Penobscots retained ownership of more than one hundred islands in the Penobscot River, Indian Island among them. The island, which is home to the Penobscot Nation, is connected via a bridge to the west bank. Visitors are welcome with the understanding that the island is an active community and not a tourist attraction.

New prosperity arrived at the island in recent years following an $80 million settlement for outstanding land claims unearthed in early documents. The windfall has resulted in a handsome new school and the Sockalexis Memorial Ice Arena, named after the Sockalexis brothers, Andrew and Lewis, who went on to prominence in the Olympics and professional baseball in the early twentieth century. Indian Island is also the site of high-stakes bingo games that aren't governed by the state (Indian Island is considered a sovereign nation) and consequently offer jackpots up to $25,000. The reservation usually holds seven games per year; for a current schedule call (800) 255–1293.

Indian Island also has the gravesite of Joseph (Joe) Polis, the Penobscot Indian who served as Thoreau's guide and tutor during his travels through the forests of northern Maine. Polis taught Thoreau the Indian names for various flora and fauna, as well as the lore of the woods. As Thoreau noted, however, Joe wasn't entirely comfortable living off the land. "By George!" Thoreau quoted him as saying, "I shan't go into the woods without provision—hard bread, pork, etc." Their relationship is one of the more intriguing of the nineteenth-century literary world.

To find Polis's grave, cross the bridge and drive a short distance to where the road forks at a cemetery. Park and look for a granite stone topped with a small carved urn in the section of the cemetery closest to the bridge.

Old Town has become synonymous with canoes, thanks to the highly popular line of canoes manufactured by *Old Town Canoe Company*. The well-known company, founded by George Gray in his hardware store in 1900, is now the world's largest canoe manufacturer, selling about 25,000 canoes a year—one of every four canoes sold in America. As a point of fact, Old Town wasn't the first canoe maker hereabouts.

That honor belongs to the White Canoe Company, founded in 1889, which was purchased by Old Town in 1984. Old Town phased out the White line in 1990.

Old Town still makes canoes the old-fashioned way, with wood strips and brass nails; but these canoes cost $2,500 and more, a far cry from the $40 they cost a century ago. The more commonly purchased Old Town canoes these days are made of stuff called Polylink 3, Kevlar, and complex laminates, and they are made using high-tech processes that would certainly confound Mr. Gray.

Despite the modern techniques employed, the factory is still located in a rambling brick and wood factory in downtown Old Town, with wide wooden floors and a healthy measure of timeworn corporate character. In the showroom next door, Old Town sells bruised new canoes at savings over list price and runs a video depicting the manufacturing process. A variety of other canoe accessories also is available here, from life jackets and repair parts to delicate Old Town ash paddles. The factory is an excellent stop for those truly intent on getting the most out of what Maine's North Woods has to offer.

The Old Town factory and shop are at 58 Middle Street, just up the hill from the municipal park. Open Monday through Saturday from 9:00 A.M. to 5:00 P.M.; also open Sundays in summer. For more information call 827–5513.

Northern Penobscot County

From the Bangor–Old Town area, the county narrows and extends far northward. Settlements become more sparse, the lakes bigger and wilder. Many of the smaller roads turn to gravel with little warning.

Downstream, with Paddle

What to do if you're coming from afar and want to spend a few days in a canoe, but don't want to lug all that camping gear and a canoe on your vacation? Contact Allagash Canoe Trips in Greenville. Experience? They've got plenty. They've been running guided canoe trips on Maine rivers since 1953. You can select from a variety of rivers including the Allagash, Moose, Penobscot, and St. John rivers. They provide all equipment, meals, and transportation. For a five-day canoe trip, the cost is $475 per adult, $350 per child. Call (207) 695–3668 for more information, or e-mail alcanoe@moosehead.net.

Summer communities thrive along some of the lakes, but for the most part the widely scattered residents are year-round, and many find their livelihood in the forest as lumber workers or guides.

One of the lesser-known destinations for campers in the North Woods is the **Mattawamkeag Wilderness Park** just outside the small town of Mattawamkeag, north of Enfield on Route 2. The park isn't sparsely attended for lack of beauty; the place has a character that makes it seem like Baxter State Park's younger sibling. Relatively small at just over a thousand acres, this gem of a park sits alongside the wild Mattawamkeag River, a favored destination for serious white-water kayakers and fishermen. Small-mouth bass fishing is good in the spring, with Atlantic salmon arriving later. White-water enthusiasts are challenged by threatening rapids called The Heater and Upper Gordon Falls, both approaching Class V and portaged by all but the most experienced boaters. Those with less experience can enjoy some of the gentler white water above the falls. The park also features a network of hiking trails for exploring the riverside and flanking hills.

Mattawamkeag Park, owned and operated by the town, has nearly fifty drive-in campsites and eleven Adirondack-style shelters. Although it's called a wilderness park (some claim the forest has never been cut here), there are a fair number of amenities—hot showers, Ping-Pong tables, and horseshoes—that challenge even the most liberal definition of wilderness.

The park is an 8-mile dirt-road drive east of Mattawamkeag, which consists of a couple of general stores, a laundromat, and a restaurant. The park is open May 15 to October 15, and a day-use fee of $1.00 per person is charged. Camping fees are $13 to $17. For more information call 736–4881.

It's hard to get a grasp of what life was like in the North Woods before the lumber roads changed the daily routine of loggers and lumber workers. The job is now much like any other: Workers commute to the woods from towns nearby, then return home at night. Before the roads—and especially before the internal combustion engine—an entire subculture thrived in the forest as woodsmen spent weeks at their labors before venturing back to the civilized world.

One place to get a glimpse of that lost world is the **Lumberman's Museum** just west of the town of Patten. Extensive collections fill ten buildings, including one log cabin reconstructed from original 1860s loggers' cabins. This fine museum, housing thousands of North Woods artifacts, was founded in 1962 when the decline of the lumberman's culture was in the offing. Among the displays are early log haulers, a working sawmill, dioramas of the various types of logging camps that appeared in Maine, and literally hundreds of tools used by the loggers, millwrights, coopers, and others who depended on the forest for their livelihood. The reception center, housed in an old Maine Forest Service building, features evocative logging murals painted by local artists.

Open in summer from 10:00 A.M. to 4:00 P.M. Tuesday through Sunday (open Friday to Sunday in spring and fall). Admission is $3.50 for adults, $1.00 for children 6 to 11; children under 6 are free. Located on Route 159 just west of Route 11 in Patten. Call 528–2650.

Continuing westward toward the mountains on Route 159, you'll cross the county line and come to the less-used northeast entrance to Baxter State Park, arguably Maine's most noteworthy outdoor destination.

Piscataquis County

Piscataquis (pronounced Pis-CAT-a-kwiss) is the heart of Maine's timberland region and its least populated county. Even including the relatively populous towns of Dover-Foxcroft and Greenville, the county can muster only 18,000 residents, resulting in a population density of fewer than five people per square mile. Densely forested, the county is marked by attractive hills and beautiful lakes.

Baxter State Park and Vicinity

If you visited the state house in Augusta, you may have noticed in the rotunda the bronze bust of one of Maine's former governors. That was Percival Baxter, who served between 1920 and 1925. The reason he's been granted this place of honor is immediately evident when you're traveling in north-central Maine. Scan the horizon on a clear day and you're likely to see the distinctive sloping ridgeline of Mount Katahdin set amid the lesser peaks of **Baxter State Park**, Percival Baxter's gift to Maine.

Baxter, both as state legislator and as governor, attempted to have the state acquire the land surrounding Mount Katahdin. Displaying the traditional New England animosity to public land ownership, the state legislature rebuffed his efforts. Stymied but not defeated, Baxter set about purchasing the land on his own, using the considerable fortune acquired in part from his father, James Phinney Baxter, one of the pioneers in the Maine canning industry. Between 1930 and 1962 Percival Baxter bought bits and pieces and donated them to the state until he had assembled a block of land totaling slightly more than 200,000 acres. Baxter's central stipulation in handing the property over to the state was that it remain "forever wild."

The state has done an excellent job carrying out Baxter's directive. The roads through the park are of dirt and often in rough condition. The number of campers allowed in at any one time is capped at 700. And the 180 miles of foot trail throughout the park are maintained sparingly, making a hiking trip an adventure rather than a stroll. There have been some threats to the park's wildness: Literally hundreds of hikers now scale Mount Katahdin's 5,267-foot peak on a cloudless summer's day, overburdening the trails and compromising the wilderness experience on the summit. But dozens of other park destinations still offer visitors a place to be alone with the impressive silence of the woods.

Unlike most North Woods locations, Baxter State Park is a hiker's park first and foremost and a canoeist's park second. Day hikers will find a number of excellent destinations that are less daunting—and less crowded—than the Katahdin summit. Try the 2.5-mile round-trip hike to Big and Little Niagara Falls from Daicy Pond, or the 6-mile climb of Mount O-J-I west of Katahdin. The day-use fee is $8.00 per vehicle per day (no charge for Maine residents). If you plan to camp at the park, reservations are virtually essential in the peak summer months. Baxter employs a pleasantly anachronistic method of accepting reservations: You must write in advance, requesting specific dates, and include payment with your request. Phone reservations are not accepted. Write for information on campsites and the reservation process: Baxter State Park Authority, 64 Balsam Drive, Millinocket 04462. The most commonly used access point is the south gate, which may be reached from Millinocket along signed roads.

West and north of Baxter State Park are timberlands under the oversight of *North Maine Woods, Inc.*, a consortium of twenty-one landowners who banded together to manage recreational access. These companies and families jointly own and manage 2.8 million acres of woodlands, which are open to the public for a fee. Don't expect pristine forest, even though your road map may not show any roads hereabouts. As mentioned earlier, this is an industrial forest, managed for the production of fiber to supply paper mills. Recreational uses are secondary.

These woods hold few "destinations" for those who like their attractions neatly packaged. Access to the woods is on often dusty, unpaved logging roads, and you won't find much in the way of picnic areas or scenic turnouts. Along the way, drivers will see clear-cuts, regenerated forests, muskeg (a type of boggy ecosystem common in the northern woods), an occasional lakeshore, probably a roadside moose or two, and periodic glimpses of distant mountain ranges. Most recreation involves fishing, hunting, and canoeing. Because of state cutting regulations and the cooperation of the timber companies, most lake and river shores have remained unharvested for many years and offer a dense backdrop of mixed and softwood forests. When traveling by canoe, expect to see loon, beaver, and plenty of moose. North Maine Woods maintains about 400 campsites, many of them accessible only by water.

The Mighty and Majestic—If Dim—Moose

*M*aine has by far the largest population of moose in New England, numbering more than 25,000. These are big animals—they can weigh upwards of 800 pounds with antlers weighing 50 pounds or more—and are well designed for foraging for grasses and sedges, which they find so appealing. With high, spindly legs and dense bodies, they're also perfectly designed for fatal collisions with cars. The front of the car knocks the legs out, and the body crashes through the windshield, often with grave results. Moose X-ing signs you'll see throughout the state weren't placed there to entertain tourists. They're for real.

The moose is majestic, but few observers accord them much nimbleness of mind. The state issues 3,000 moose hunting permits each year, and all but a handful of those permit holders get their moose. The question everyone then asks is, "What happened

to those hunters who failed to find a moose? Were they sleeping the whole time?" It doesn't take much to outwit a moose.

One example: One late summer day I was walking along an overgrown logging road near Chesuncook Lake when I rounded a bend and came face to face with a moose grazing in the swamp grass along the road. Startled, her head went up, her ears went up, and her eyes went huge and wide as if she had never seen the likes of me before. She quickly turned and twitchily lumbered down the road. Two minutes later, I rounded another bend and came upon the same moose. Head up. Ears up. Eyes wide. And she ran down the trail. This happened four more times, and each time it seemed our encounter shocked her equally anew.

Majestic, yes. Bright, no.

Access fees are collected at various checkpoints around the perimeter. Maine residents pay $4.00 per day per person plus an additional $5.00 per person for camping. Out-of-state residents pay $7.00 per day plus $5.00 for camping. For a map and information, send $3.00 to North Maine Woods, P.O. Box 425, Ashland 04732. The organization's Web site (www.northmainewoods.org) includes information on regulations, checkpoint locations and hours, and more. For more information call 435–6213.

The region's early economic history isn't just a story of producing lumber. Well south of Baxter State Park is **Katahdin Iron Works**, a state historic site that provides some insight into how iron was made during the mid-nineteenth century. Iron ore was first discovered by geographer Moses Greenleaf on Ore Mountain in 1843; within two years, Katahdin Iron Works was built near the site. At its peak in the 1870s and 1880s, the works manufactured some 2,000 tons of raw iron a year, consuming upwards of 10,000 cords of wood to fire the blast furnace. A small village thrived here, with many of the 200 residents involved in hauling logs and producing charcoal in beehive kilns.

There's little trace of a village today at this remote site deep in the woods, but historical markers provide information about the iron

Along the Knife Edge

*I*f you're physically fit and aren't afflicted with a fear of heights, one of the state's premier hiking pathways follows what's aptly called the Knife Edge, which links Mount Katahdin's two peaks. Those who've survived the trail like to boast that it is only a couple of feet wide in some sections, with drops of a 1,000 feet or more on either side.

Technically I suppose that's true, but it's not quite that daunting. The Knife Edge follows a boulder field that's been shaped to a narrow ridge by glaciers and the weather. At certain critical junctures, you need to scramble atop massive boulders and inch your way across. And from atop these boulders, you don't see much below except for the distant glinting of lakes and a dull mass of green that resolves itself into spruce spires only with the aid of binoculars. Acrophobia kicks in while scrambling over these boulders. Knees start to shake; breath becomes short.

In fact, if you peer over the edge, you might find yourself just 6 or 8 feet above other boulders that angle down sharply. It's not the sheer drop to eternity that it appears. But it's hard to convince yourself of that. Two of the three times I've hiked the Knife Edge, I've come upon hikers who simply seized up and couldn't move forward or back—their companions had to talk them through it. Venture here at your own peril.

making process. Take time to marvel at two restored structures: the towering stone blast furnace with graceful arches at its base, and the massive brick beehive kiln (one of fourteen originally situated here) with its domed roof. The Iron Works are open May 20 to Labor Day. To find the iron works, drive 5 miles north of Brownville on Route 11, then turn left on a well-maintained dirt logging road, continuing on for 7 miles to a North Maine Woods gatehouse. The historic site is across from the gatehouse. Admission is free.

Ask directions at the gatehouse and pay the timberland access fee, then continue to **Gulf Hagas**, which has been billed as the "Grand Canyon of the East." That's a bit overly grand, but the 3-mile ravine is an impressive site. You'll find five waterfalls, a slew of rushing cascades, and sheer canyon walls topped with an austere northern forest. A trail follows the rim of the gorge, and side trails offer access down to the river, where you can take a cool dip on a summer's day. The land around the canyon is one of the few Maine parcels outside of Acadia owned by the National Park Service, which acquired it as part of its protection of the Appalachian Trail corridor.

Running the Rapids

*O*ne of the more adrenaline-pumping ways to enjoy Maine's wilds is to sign up for a one-day rafting trip on the Penobscot or the Kennebec River. The West Branch of the Penobscot runs south of Baxter State Park and features one of Maine's most spectacular and demanding stretches of white water: a turbulent, rocky canyon called the Cribworks. After you maneuver through here, the remainder of the trip alternates between open river and quick, exciting plunges over short waterfalls and through narrow gorges. Exceptional views of Mount Katahdin open up along the way.

The upper stretches of the Kennebec River (near The Forks in Somerset County) offer larger waves similar to those found in the canyons of the West,

and they're big enough to invoke genuine terror. The excitement runs its course fairly quickly, however, and you spend the rest of the day floating out of scenic Kennebec Gorge.

Around twenty firms are licensed to run guided rafting trips on the two rivers. Their base camps tend to be concentrated near Millinocket and The Forks, and prices generally range from $85 to $100 per person for a one-day trip, which includes a riverside lunch. Many outfitters also offer lodging options ranging from modern inns to campgrounds. The state's rafting companies are members of a group called Raft Maine, which will refer you to one of the member rafting companies with a single toll-free phone call: (800) RAFT–MEE.

Near Gulf Hagas (ask at the gatehouse) is a thirty-five-acre Nature Conservancy sanctuary called *The Hermitage*. While not a virgin forest, it does include pines up to 120 feet high with diameters reaching 3 feet. The Appalachian Trail passes through the stand, and a few other short trails offer access to these quiet, stately pines. Let your imagination go a bit, and you'll see how the whole northern forest once looked before it became a plantation.

Eastern Moosehead Lake Area

The former frontier town of Greenville is located at the southern tip of Moosehead Lake, Maine's largest body of water. Lying at an elevation of just over 1,000 feet, Moosehead is some 32 miles long and ranges from 1 to 5 miles wide. With numerous bays and coves, the shoreline twists and turns for some 350 miles, serving as home to osprey, eagles, deer, and moose. There are a few vantage points here and there for those traveling by car, but for the most part you'll be required to travel by means other than automobile to get a good sense of the lake's beauty and drama.

One enjoyable option is to take a cruise on the **SS *Katahdin***, a restored steamship (converted to diesel) that's been plying the waters of Moosehead since 1914. The *Kate*, as she's called locally, was built at Bath Iron Works and shipped in parts to Moosehead Lake, where she was assembled and launched by Coburn Steamboat Company. After a twenty-four-year career as a passenger ship, the 115-foot *Katahdin* was retired when the rise of the automobile made her obsolete. She was then outfitted as a boom boat and used by lumber companies for hauling logs (towing logs encircled with a massive wooden boom) down the lake to the mills. The *Katahdin* participated in the state's last log drive, which took place in 1975.

To get a sense of *Kate*'s history, plan a visit to exhibits at the ship's parent organization, the ***Moosehead Marine Museum***. The museum is located next to the dock in what passes for downtown Greenville. There's a small but fine collection of historical artifacts relating to Moosehead's history, including fascinating photos of the last log drive. Leave enough time to browse through the piles of scrapbooks, where you'll find insightful articles and mementos relating to the history of the lake, including pictures of the early fleet and menus from the original Kineo Mountain House.

The museum offers daily trips aboard the *Kate* throughout the summer. A two-and-a-half-hour cruise takes passengers up the lake past

SS *Katahdin*, Moosehead Lake

Moose Island and Burnt Jacket Point to the narrow pass between Sugar Island and Deer Island. This provides a good introduction to the size and wildness of the lake. A longer trip, offered twice a week, will take you halfway up the lake to Kineo Mountain, where you can disembark and explore the grounds of a once-venerable hotel. And for those who have an insatiable thirst for long boat trips, once a month the *Katahdin* cruises to the head of the lake at Seboomook, an eight-hour journey that provides a cormorant's-eye view of the lake's entire shoreline.

The *Katahdin* runs daily July through September and weekends Memorial Day through June. Prices range from $17.00 to $25.00 for adults, $10.00 for seniors, and $9.00 to $14.00 for children 6 and over; children under 6 are free. For more information call 695–2716.

The ***Moosehead Historical Society*** is located on Routes 6 and 15 in Greenville Junction (just west of Greenville proper). The late-nineteenth-century house is an interesting artifact for those curious about the history of decorative arts and architecture. (The carriage house also has displays of Native American artifacts upstairs and a lumberman's display in the basement that includes a collection of early outboard motors.) But more fascinating is the odd, melancholy story of the family, which you'll learn on a one-hour guided tour and which offers some insight into the social relations of the time.

In the early twentieth century, Arthur and Rebecca Crafts, a prosperous couple with numerous local businesses, had two children, Oliver and Julia. Their son died tragically at age 16, after falling through the ice. The parents never really recovered from the death of the heir apparent; they kept his richly appointed room as it was when he died, and his mother delivered presents to the room each year on his birthday. She had a portrait of him commissioned and hung in an elaborately wrought gilded frame; a table beneath it was kept set with fresh flowers.

That left Julia, an attractive young woman whose bedroom was considerably less elaborate, to run the family enterprises. But society being what it was, she needed a man. Not content to let her find her own husband, the parents contracted with a pleasant young fellow named Philip Sheridan, who worked at one of the family's hotels, to be husband. The contract stipulated that he needed to spend a minimum of three months each year with Julia at the home, for which he would be paid a salary.

Julia loved Philip quite a bit; her affections evidently were not returned. Philip kept to the contract's terms to continue to receive his pay, but spent much of the rest of the year traveling and living the high life while Julia kept the family business going. ("He was quite the playboy," reported my tour guide.) Even though Julia divorced him shortly before her death in 1967, the contract remained in force until Philip's death in 1992, and he continued to pocket his salary. He bequeathed the house to the historical society, which has adorned it with period furniture and objet d'art, some of it original to the Crafts.

Tours are offered June through early September Wednesday through Friday between 1:00 and 4:00 P.M. Admission is $2.00 for adults, $1.00 for children. For more information call 695–2716.

Afterwards, stop by the *Village Deli* (Main Street, 695–0771) in Greenville for a sandwich and beverage to go, then head 0.4 mile north on Lily Bay Road; turn left at Preo Street, an easy-to-miss dirt lane. There's a small, unmarked lakeside park at the end of the street with a couple of picnic tables. If it's sultry, this is also a good place for a dip.

For an eagle's-eye view of the Moosehead, several air services offer *float plane trips* from bases near Greenville. The planes fly high enough so you can appreciate the lake's size, but low enough to let you spot an occasional moose browsing in a marsh or along a river's edge. The oldest and largest is Folsom's Air Service (695–2821), which has been serving the North Woods since 1946. Although many of the once-remote lakes are now accessible by logging road, Folsom's offers quicker (and more comfortable) access to the entire region. Sightseeing flights may easily be arranged, ranging from a fifteen-minute tour of the southern end of the lake ($20 per person) to an hour-long tour ($60). You also might want to consider Folsom's fly-and-canoe package. They'll drop you and a canoe off at Penobscot Farm on the West Branch of the Penobscot River in the morning. After you spend the day paddling down the Penobscot and up gentle Lobster Stream, a pilot returns to pick you up at Lobster Lake late in the afternoon ($85 per person).

Even if you're not interested in a flight, it's worth stopping by the hangar at the edge of the lake, just north of town on Lily Bay Road, to soak up the atmosphere and watch the planes take off and land. For more information contact Folsom's at 695–2821. Other float plane charters serving the Moosehead Lake region include Currier's Flying Service (695–2778) and Jack's Flying Service (695–3020).

A range of accommodations is available in the Moosehead area, from motels to B&Bs, but three inns, all rather expensive, deserve special mention. The *Greenville Inn* (695–2206) is located on a hillside overlooking the village and the southern tip of the lake. Housed in an 1895 mansion built by lumber baron William Shaw, this fine inn is a virtual catalog of turn-of-the-century luxuries, ranging from marble showers to exceptional carved interiors of mahogany with cherry trim. The dining room serves excellent meals with popovers the size of footballs. The inn also has a comfortable front porch offering a view across the lake to the hills beyond. A room for two ranges from $135 to $155 ($225 for a suite), including a continental breakfast buffet.

Continuing north on Lily Bay Road you'll come to two other impressive homes. *The Blair Hill Inn* sits regally on a hill with vertigo-inspiring views of the lake from many of the eight guest rooms and the wrap-around porch. The elaborate Queen Anne–style home was built in 1891 and is lovingly and quirkily appointed with Persian carpets and deer-antler lamps. This is a place where you'll instantly feel as if you're living large. The restaurant on the premises just opened in 1999, but is already regarded as among the best in northern Maine. Rooms are $175 to $265 for two. For more information call 695–0224, or visit the Web site at www.blairhill.com.

Nearby is the whimsical *Lodge at Moosehead Lake.* The innkeepers have taken the North Woods theme and run with it, featuring beds suspended from the ceiling on old boom chains (used in logging operations), stick furniture, and rustic headboards carved by a local craftsman. Rates are $175 to $395 per night. For more information call 695–4400, or check the Web site at www.innatmooseheadlake.com.

Somerset County

The west side of Moosehead Lake falls within Somerset County, which extends westward to the Canadian border. Like many of the northern counties, Somerset is long and narrow, encompassing a variety of terrain. This is also timber country: In every Somerset township from Bingham northward, timber companies own five thousand acres or more.

Western Moosehead Lake Area

The west side of Moosehead Lake between Greenville and Rockwood can be quickly covered on Route 15. The road is wide and fast, but it offers few glimpses of the lake until you approach the village of Rockwood. Here you'll be rewarded with a full view of what amounts to the lake's trademark: the sheer, flinty cliffs of Mount Kineo.

Mount Kineo has long been a landmark in the region. Indians traveled from afar to the cliff's base to gather its fine flint for weapons, and one Indian legend claims that the mountain is the remnants of a petrified moose sent by the Great Spirit as retribution for their sins. In the late nineteenth century, the broad peninsula at the base was the site of the Kineo Mountain House, at its heyday perhaps the grandest of the Maine resorts. The stately gabled building boasted more than 500 guest rooms, and the dining room could seat 400 at a time. An immense annex was built to house the staff, some of whom tended a forty-acre garden to provide food for the table.

Alas, the Mountain House closed in 1934 and was demolished in 1938, after the automobile and the Great Depression sounded the death knell for the era of the grand resort. Various attempts to breathe life back into some of the remaining buildings foundered on an uncooperative economy and thin financing. The annex was demolished in 1996, leaving just a golf course (still operating) and an array of handsome, turn-of-the-century homes along the lake's edge.

Water shuttles across the lake are available from Rockwood (look for signs to town landing), allowing visitors to snoop and explore. Once at Kineo you can wander the grounds of the venerable resort and enjoy the extraordinary views down the lake. Be sure to leave two to three hours for the round-trip hike to Kineo's 1,800-foot summit. To find the trail, walk along the golf course, then cut across the eighth fairway to the old carriage road that runs along the west side of the mountain. Follow this about 0.5 mile to a rock with a white arrow pointing uphill. The steep ascent will take you along the cliff's face to a series of ledges looking southward toward Greenville. For a more expansive view, continue along the trail about another 0.3 mile to an abandoned fire tower, which may be ascended for a not-soon-forgotten view of the entire lake. (Not recommended for those afflicted with vertigo.)

One of the more popular activities in the Moosehead Lake region is to sign up for a *moose safari.* You can spot moose on your own, of course, but your odds are better if you head out with the experts. You can travel by pontoon boat, airplane, canoe, foot, or four-wheel-drive vehicle in search of the lanky beasts. The chamber of commerce in Greenville can point you to any one of a half-dozen or more guide services offering moose-spotting trips. Among the better known tours: the Moose Cruise, which is run on comfortable pontoon boats (think: floating living rooms) of The Birches Resort just north of Rockwood ($25 per person; call for reservations, 534–7304).

Other area moose outfitters include the Maine Guide Fly Shop on Main Street in Greenville (695–2266), which runs four-hour excursions by canoe or kayak; Moosehead Safaris, which offers excursions via pontoon boat (contact the Evergreen Lodge, 888–624–3993 or 695–3241), and Ed Mathieu, who leads five-hour backwoods explorations in his handsome wooden canoe (876–4907).

One of my favorite spots for overnighting and dining in the North Woods is *Maynard's in Maine,* a sporting lodge that's been unchanged for nearly a century. The town of Rockwood has grown up around it somewhat (logging trucks rumble by on the road across the river), but it still feels like a trip back in time. The cabins ring a lawn with horseshoe pit and tetherball, and are simple and furnished with flea market vintage stuff. The meals in the Smithsonian-quality dining room are filling, basic, and very cheap—under $13 for soup to nuts. Even if you're not spending the night ($50 per person, including all meals), it's worth calling ahead for dinner reservations (mandatory) and swinging by for a meal, which includes a choice of two entrees nightly. For more information call 534–7703, or visit the Web site at www.maynardsinmaine.com.

The northern end of the lake and the tiny settlement of *Seboomook* can be reached by logging roads in about an hour. The roads are maintained by Georgia-Pacific, which charges a day-use fee at a gatehouse. Like Kineo, Seboomook during its glory days was the site of a fine resort, now long since forgotten. Remaining at Seboomook are a handful of summer cabins, a campground, and a small general store.

Head into the store for an interesting sight: a photograph of a World War II prisoner-of-war camp constructed here in the early 1940s to hold German prisoners captured in the African campaigns. Some 250 prisoners were kept busy here cutting trees and hauling them with horses to the lake for the spring trip to the mills. Evidently the POWs, who were paid for their labor, also were treated well; many returned after the war to take jobs with timber companies. Today, only the pictures remain. The buildings, including sentry towers and the icehouse, have since been reclaimed by the forest, and only an overgrown foundation or two may be found.

Nearby, where the north and south branches of the Penobscot River flow together, you'll find **Pittston Farm**, a longtime North Woods institution. This farm complex stuck deep in the woods was built in the nineteenth century to provide the grain for the horses used in logging. Today it's a rough backwoods lodge and campground favored by anglers and canoeists. Parts of the carriage houses have been converted to rooms with private baths, but most guests still stay in the old farmhouse, where they share hallway baths. Room rates include all your meals, and lunch and dinner are served all-you-can-eat buffet style, and seem to feature lots of dishes that include macaroni. The meals are bargain priced at less than $10, and dining here amid the visiting sports is usually an experience not easily forgotten. Pittston Farm is far enough off the grid that it doesn't have a phone (electricity is provided by a generator), but you can make reservations by calling Folsom's Air Service (695–2821), which will radio your message to the farm.

Route 201

A pleasant drive on Routes 6 and 15 will bring you to scenic Route 201 and the town of Jackman, the starting point of the **Moose River canoe trip**. This 34-mile trip attracts a number of eager canoeists throughout the year not only because of its scenic merits, but because of sheer convenience: Canoeists start and finish at the same point, linking the loop with a 1.25-mile-long portage between Attean and Holeb ponds. A couple of smaller portages around waterfalls are involved; otherwise the river is gentle and forgiving, with only mildly challenging rapids. A number of riverside campsites are located along the way. Trip maps produced by the state are available at the several canoe rental shops in Jackman.

Heading south from Jackman along Route 201 will soon bring you to The Forks, where many of the rafting outfitters serving the Kennebec Gorge and the Penobscot maintain offices (see the sidebar, this chapter, Baxter State Park and Vicinity, for more information on rafting). While you're at The Forks, a short side trip to dramatic **Moxie Falls** will prove rewarding. This beautiful cataract tumbles some 90 feet into a narrow slate gorge. There's a fine mix of forest trees hereabouts, with cedars and other softwoods mingling with birch. A trail skirts the gorge and offers good views of the falls. The brave and the foolish work their way down to swim in the turbulent, clear waters at the base of the cascades.

To find Moxie Falls, turn off Route 201 on the road along the east bank of the Kennebec River. (If you're coming from the south, that means turning right before crossing the bridge over the Kennebec.) Travel 2.7 miles and park near the sign indicating Moxie Falls. A trail of slightly less than 2 miles will take you to the falls.

Finally, before leaving the area, make a stop at the *Floodproof Wire Bridge* in the town of New Portland in the southwest corner of the county. This remarkable suspension bridge, built in 1841, has the aplomb and elegance of a miniature Brooklyn Bridge dropped in a wild, forested setting. The bridge's wooden deck is held aloft over the Carrabasset River on two thick cables—made in Sheffield, England—rigged between two handsome shingled pylons. The bridge was designed by F. B. Morse for the people of New Portland, who were weary of having their bridge wash out in the spring freshets. The fact that it still stands more than a century and a half later would suggest that Morse's design was successful. To find this remarkable structure, turn from Route 127 onto Route 146 in the village of New Portland, then turn left at the sign indicating the way to the bridge. You can drive across through the polygonal openings, but really to appreciate the bridge, park at one end or the other and walk across. If you visit on a sultry day, there's a fine place to swim in the river just downstream.

Heading south from the bridge toward Farmington, look for *Nowetah's American Indian Museum,* located off Route 27 in New Portland. It's a privately run affair owned and operated by Mrs. Nowetah Timmerman, an Abenaki Indian who opened her museum and shop in 1969. She has on display native crafts from North and South America, including stone tools, petroglyph rubbings, a birch-bark canoe, old photos showing some of the ancient crafts techniques, and a collection of 300 Indian baskets. This isn't a stuffy spot with everything enshrined away from visitors—kids are encouraged to touch a number of the displays, and to try crushing corn with mortar and pestle, or play drums and flutes. The museum's gift shop sells a number of items made on the premises, including porcupine quill and bead jewelry, corn husk dolls, and hand-woven rugs. ("We also make such things as deerskin doll clothes to fit the famous Barbie dolls," Timmerman notes.)

The museum is open year-round from 10:00 A.M. to 5:00 P.M. daily, and admission is free (donations are encouraged). For more information call 628–4981.

**PLACES TO STAY
IN THE NORTH WOODS**

BANGOR
Fairfield Inn, 300 Odlin
Road, 990–0001

Holiday Inn, 500 Main
Street, (800) 799–8651 or
947–8651

The Phenix Inn, 20 Broad
Street, 947–0411

THE FORKS
Magic Rivers B&B, West
Forks, 663–2220

Northern Outdoors, Route
201, (800) 765–RAFT or
663–4466

GREENVILLE
Blair Hill Inn,
Lily Bay Road, 695–0224

Greenville Inn, Norris
Street, (888) 695–6000 or
695–2206

Greenwood Motel,
Route 15, (800) 477–4386
or 695–3321

Lodge at Moosehead Lake,
Upper Lily Bay Road,
695–4400

Medawisla Sporting
Camps, Second Roach
Pond, 695–2690

MILLINOCKET
Big Moose Inn Cabins,
723–8391

Nahmankanta Lake Camps,
746–7356

MOOSE RIVER
Sky Lodge, Route 201, (800)
307–0098 or 668–2171

PATTEN
Shin Pond Village,
Route 159, 528–2900

ROCKWOOD
The Birches, Rockwood,
534–7305

Maynard's in Maine, Moose
River, 534–7703

**PLACES TO EAT
IN THE NORTH WOODS**

BANGOR
Dysart's Truck Stop, exit 44
off I–95, 942–4878

Pilot's Grill, 1528 Hammond Street, 942–6325

Sea Dog Brewing Co., 26
Front Street, 947–8004

Helpful Web Sites

Allagash Canoe Trips—
www.mainerec.com/alcanoe.html
Bangor Region Chamber of Commerce—
www.bangorregion.com/
Birches Resort—*www.webcom.com/birches*
City of Bangor—
www.maineguide.com/bangor/index.html
Cole Museum of Land Transportation—
www.colemuseum.com
Hudson Museum of Anthropology—
www.umaine.edu/hudsonmuseum
Moosehead Lake Chamber of Commerce—
www.mooseheadlake.org
Raft Maine—*www.raftmaine.com*
Town of Greenville—*www.ctel.net/~greenvil*
University of Maine—*www.maine.edu*

Selected Chambers of Commerce

Baxter State Park,
64 Balsam Drive, Millinocket, 723–5140
Jackman/Moose River Chamber of Commerce,
Route 201, 668–4171
Katahdin Area Chamber of Commerce,
1029 Central Street, Millinocket, 723–4443
Moosehead Lake Region Chamber of Commerce,
Main Street, Greenville, 695–2702

THE FORKS
Marshall Hotel, Route 201,
(800) 766–7238

GREENVILLE
Auntie M's, Main Street,
695–2238

Blair Hill Inn, Lily Bay
Road, 695–0224

Greenville Inn, Norris
Street, (888) 695–6000 or
695–2206

JACKMAN
Four Seasons Restaurant,
232 North Main Street,
668–7778

Moose Point Tavern
Restaurant, Henderson
Road, 668–4012

KOKADJO
Northern Pride Lodge,
Lily Bay Road, 695–2890

MILLINOCKET
Appalachian Trail Cafe,
210 Penobscot Avenue,
723–6720

River Driver's Restaurant
(at New England Outdoor
Center), Old Midway Road,
(800) 766–7238

PITTSTON FARM
Pittston Farm, Penobscot
River, no phone

ROCKWOOD
The Birches, Rockwood,
534–7305

The County

"The County"—as Aroostook County is referred to throughout the state—has an uncommonly broad sweep and size for New England. Connecticut and Rhode Island together could fit inside it.

Altogether, Aroostook County doesn't square with many preconceptions about Maine. The gentle hills, broad vistas, and sprawling farmlands share little with either Maine's sparkling coast or its dense North Woods. In fact, travelers would be forgiven for thinking they missed a turn somewhere and ended up in Wisconsin. They also would be excused for believing they've wandered into another era: Aroostook often seems to have more in common with the slow pace of the 1950s than the more hectic present.

Most travel guides tend to ignore The County or gloss over the region in a page or two. Not only does it fail to resemble the Maine many travelers seek, but there are few tourist-oriented inns or restaurants. Don't let that deter you. The County has a subtle grandeur and fascinating immigrant history that reveals itself only to those who aren't too hurried to notice. In short, Aroostook County is about as off the beaten path as Maine gets.

Houlton Area

Houlton, the county seat and oldest community in Aroostook, is a good jumping-off point for a ramble. Here the Maine Turnpike and Route 2 both come to an abrupt end and Route 1 passes directly through, suggesting Houlton's geographic importance. Despite its regional stature, this center of commerce has maintained a pleasantly drowsy character through the years.

Take some time to enjoy Houlton's *Market Street Historic District*, a tiny block-long downtown area showcasing a variety of commercial architectural styles from 1885 to 1910. Many of the fine brick buildings have happily avoided the depredations that befell other commercial districts around the nation in the name of modernization. Not that any of these buildings have been preserved as historical monuments. Houlton's

The County

Madawaska

Fort
Kent

Dickey
161

Square
Lake

CANADA
UNITED STATES

11

Caribou

Allagash
Falls

Allagash R.

Presque
Isle

163

Saint John R.

AROOSTOOK
CO.

Ashland

UNITED STATES
CANADA

Long
Lake

N

0   20 mi

0   20km

95   Houlton

1

downtown is strictly business as usual. There's a J. C. Penney, a movie theater, and a video store mixed in among the other shops. Look high along the rooflines at the intricate brickwork. Also be sure to note the elegant First National Bank building on the north side of the square, sandwiched between the theater and another bank. This small columned building dates from 1907 and is almost a caricature of the imposing banks that flourished at the turn of the century in many eastern seaboard cities.

A short walk from Market Square is the White Memorial Building. This impressive 1903 Colonial Revival house, which lords over Main Street like a stern uncle, houses the chamber of commerce as well as the collections of the *Southern Aroostook Historical and Art Museum*. Items and artifacts of local industry and commerce are displayed in eight upstairs rooms, as well as in a downstairs room documenting Houlton's ill-fated Ricker College, which opened in 1848 and was auctioned after bankruptcy in 1979. Various historical items on display upstairs pique the imagination, including a dog mill to power a butter churn, badges from early Republican conventions, and a hand-carved wooden box filled with spruce gum (a typical gift of early woodsmen to their wives or sweethearts).

Keep an eye out for the elaborately detailed diorama of a man sitting near his canoe at a lakeside log cabin. Spruce trees line the forest behind him, and a moose browses along the shoreline. What make this notable is its construction entirely of matchsticks. In 1924 Leon Goodwin entered this work in a contest sponsored by a match company but was disqualified, since the contest rules required that whole matches be used. (Leon glued his into solid blocks, then carved them.) Contest judges were sufficiently impressed, however, to award Leon a special $50 second prize.

The museum (532–4216) is located at 109 Main Street and is open by appointment throughout the year. If you don't get a chance to call ahead, stop by and see if someone from the chamber office downstairs is available to let you in and show you around. Admission is free.

The *Watson Settlement Covered Bridge* is a short detour off Route 1 in Littleton, 5 miles north of Houlton. This bridge boasts two superlatives: It was the last covered bridge built in Maine (1911), and it's the state's northernmost covered bridge. Neither of these claims may seem particularly noteworthy, but the drive to the bridge through lush, rolling farmlands is a nice change of pace from the higher-speed travel on Route 1.

The 150-foot bridge isn't in use today (a more modern concrete bridge runs parallel to it), but visitors can cross by foot and sit along the banks of the Meduxnekeag River. A farmhouse and elms stand on the crest of a hill above, and songbirds proliferate along the banks, making for an inviting picnic spot. The bridge also has the local distinction as a place for teens to express their affections for one another in ink and spray paint; there are some endearing sentiments emblazoned inside the bridge, and some not-so-endearing sentiments.

To find the bridge, turn east from Route 1 at Carson Road. There's a small blue sign indicating a covered bridge, but it's easy to miss. Drive 2 miles, then bear right down the hill where the road splits. The bridge is a few hundred yards beyond the fork.

Presque Isle and Vicinity

For a high-altitude view of the region (or what passes for high-altitude hereabouts), head to **Aroostook State Park**, located south of the city of Presque Isle. The park—Maine's first state park—contains 577 forested acres situated between Echo Lake and Quaggy Joe Mountain. There's swimming and picnicking at the lake (which is ringed with summer homes) and camping at thirty sites managed by the state at the base of 1,213-foot Quaggy Joe. Hiking trails ascend both the north and south peaks, which are connected by a ridge trail, making for a 3-mile loop that can be hiked in a couple of hours. The north summit ledges offer fine views east into Canada as well as west across a seemingly uninterrupted blanket of forest extending to the craggy profile of Mount

The View from Mars (Hill)

Heading north through The County on Route 1, you can't miss Mars Hill on the right, one of the few topographical landmarks of any distinction in the area. This 1,660-foot-high mound played a cameo role early in the extended dispute between the British and the Americans over the border between the United States and Canada. Britain claimed this mound marked the highlands dividing the watersheds between the

Gulf of Maine and the Gulf of St. Lawrence, the agreed-upon boundary in the Treaty of 1782. The United States disagreed and eventually prevailed on the issue of Mars Hill. The U.S. negotiators did, however, later concede extensive territory farther to the north in reaching a final settlement. Today Mars Hill is the site of a modest ski area on its west side and can be hiked for a bird's-eye view of the disputed terrain.

THE COUNTY

WAYNE'S FAVORITE ATTRACTIONS

1. *Nylander Museum,* Caribou
2. *Salmon Brook Museum,* Washburn
3. *New Sweden Historical Society Museum*
4. *Southern Aroostook Historical and Art Museum,* Houlton
5. *Museum of Vintage Fashion,* Island Falls

Katahdin. If time is short, bypass the south peak, which has limited views and an unattractive cluster of radio towers on the summit.

If you're wondering who Joe was and what made him so quaggy, you may be disappointed to learn that the name is merely a corruption of Quaquajo, the Indian name for the mountain. The commonly accepted translation is "Twin Peaked."

Aroostook State Park is open May 15 to October 15. Admission is $1.00 for adults, 50 cents for children ages 5 to 11; children under 5 are free. Follow park signs from Spragueville Road 4 miles south of Presque Isle on Route 1. For more information call 768–8341.

Just beyond the state park on Spragueville Road is *Maxie Anderson Memorial Park*, marking the launch point of the *Double Eagle II*, the first helium balloon to cross the Atlantic Ocean. One evening in August 1978, Maxie Anderson, Ben Abruzzo, and Larry Newman lifted off in the glare of television lights from this farmer's field. Five days and 3,100 miles later, they landed unceremoniously in another farmer's field, in Miserey, France.

Their accomplishment was for balloonists the equivalent of locating the Holy Grail. Over the years dozens of people had attempted the crossing without success, and several had died in the process. To commemorate the historic event, a committee of Presque Isle citizens and businesses created a small park in the field with some modest landscaping, a pair of flagpoles, and a row of benches. The centerpiece is a 15-foot-high tin model of the *Double Eagle II* balloon and gondola mounted atop a brick and concrete pedestal. The park is dedicated to Maxie Anderson, who died in 1983.

Just outside downtown Presque Isle at 79 Parsons Street is the classically nondescript *Winnie's Restaurant and Dairy Bar.* It's the type of place that once proliferated across the United States—before fast-food chains and microwaves put them out of business. Winnie's has managed to thrive in large part because of one item: its fabulous lobster stew. The lobster is rich and succulent, and if you didn't get your fill of Maine's noted crustacean while traveling along the coast, this is the place to indulge. The stew is frozen and sold nationwide via overnight shipping (and periodically on the Home Shopping Network) under the name LeBlanc's Gourmet Lobster Stew. It contains no preservatives or artificial ingredients, and has developed an almost cult following. Many say it's best fresh from the source here in Presque Isle. Check it out when you're in town. The restaurant is open year-round, with extended hours in summer; call (800) 552–0142 or 768–5539.

A typical blockhouse dating from the Aroostook War may be viewed in the town of Fort Fairfield, just a musket shot from the present Canadian border. This replica was built in 1976 based on plans provided to the Maine militia by Captain William P. Parrott. The **Fort Fairfield Blockhouse**, with its heavy timbers and overhanging second floor, was designed to withstand a formidable siege. Narrow windows, barely more than slits, allowed the militia to shoot out of but weren't wide enough for bullets to enter by skill—only occasionally by chance. The overhang was created to allow the occupants to defend the main doorway and first floor by firing through openings in the floor. In the case of Aroostook's blockhouses, of course, all the planning was theoretical since no shots were fired.

Today the blockhouse is maintained by the Frontier Heritage Historical Society, which has filled the blockhouse with various and sundry items of local historical merit. These include a massive early wooden canoe, an old pedal organ, a wooden sheep catcher, and a "potato wheel" used to haul potatoes up from the cellar. The museum, located on Main Street across from the post office, is open irregularly but can be visited by appointment through the chamber of commerce (472–3802).

If you're near Fort Fairfield in mid-July, plan to swing by for the week-long Potato Blossom Festival, which Fort Fairfield has celebrated annually since 1947. The festival lauds Aroostook's principal cash crop and includes road, river, and bike races; fireworks; a parade; and the crowning of the Maine Potato Blossom Queen. The festival is always

A Quiet War

*I*n your travels through The County, you're bound to come across periodic references to the "Aroostook War" of 1839, certainly one of the more obscure and unremembered conflicts in American history. Hostilities—such as they were—were provoked by Canadian lumbermen venturing into territory that both the United States and England claimed as their own.

The American government responded to this encroachment by sending thousands of troops to construct and man blockhouses in the Saint John and Aroostook river valleys. Emotions ran high, but reason prevailed before blood was spilled. After many tense months, the Webster-Ashburton Treaty of 1842 settled the boundary matter between the two nations once and for all.

Top Annual Events

1. *Can-Am Sled Dog Races,* Fort Kent, early March, 834–5354
2. *Midsommar Festival,* New Sweden, weekend closest to June 21, 896–3018
3. *Acadian Festival, Madawaska,* late June, 728–7000
4. *Maine Potato Blossom Festival,* Fort Fairfield, mid-July, 472–3802
5. *Black Fly Festival, Eagle Lake,* early August, 444–5168
6. *Northern Maine Fair,* Presque Isle, early August, 762–0071
7. *Bigrock Octoberfest,* Mars Hill, early October, 429–9743
8. *Scarecrow Festival,* Fort Kent, early November, 834–5354

held the third week in July and attracts upward of 20,000 visitors from around the region. For more information contact the chamber of commerce at 472–3802.

Caribou and Environs

Driving on Route 161 from Fort Fairfield to Caribou, you'll pass by a rambling complex of farm buildings at **Goughan's Strawberry Farm**. This family farm is open to the public between May 1 and Christmas, with pick-your-own opportunities emerging as each season unfolds. The farm is perhaps best known for its twenty acres of strawberries, which are open for picking for several weeks commencing at the end of June. There's also asparagus and rhubarb early in the spring, raspberries in July, and corn, pumpkins, squash, and gourds later in the fall. For visiting children the Goughans also maintain an animal barn with mountain sheep, turkeys, geese, pigs, and ponies. When in the hundred-year-old barn, be sure to notice the "ship's knees" construction—brackets hand carved from massive tree roots and used to hold the rafters in place. A small snack shop on the premises offers hot dogs, hamburgers, ice cream, and—what else?—strawberry sundaes and shortcake when berries are in season.

Goughan's is 4 miles east of Caribou on Route 161. Call for more information: 496–1731.

Anyone with an interest in natural history will enjoy the **Nylander Museum** in Caribou. This small city-owned museum houses the collections of Olaf Nylander, a Swedish-born amateur naturalist who was an inveterate collector of just about everything, but especially shells. (The curator says that he was "really big on mollusks.") Nylander came to Maine in 1880 at age 16. He earned his living as a housepainter and spent his free time amassing vast collections of rocks, plants, and fossils from the local hills and forests, exchanging many specimens with scientists around the world. Much of what is known about the Devonian geologic period in Maine is due to Nylander. The museum, housed in a low building resembling a schoolhouse, was built to display Nylander's collections by WPA laborers in 1938–1939. Nylander served as curator until his death in 1943.

The museum today still has an old-world feel to it, its extensive collections labeled in a tight cramped hand and displayed in old glass cases. Stuffed birds and mounted butterflies fill several cases (there's a wonderful display of tropical birds that borders on the garish), and Nylander's beloved mollusks are amply represented. A small gift shop offers field guides and other natural history items for sale; more serious naturalists can inquire about using the reference collection in the basement. Also take time to poke around the herb garden in the back, where you'll find eighty different species of medicinal and culinary herbs.

The Nylander Museum is at 393 Main Street in Caribou. Open Memorial Day to Labor Day Wednesday through Sunday from 1:00 to 5:00 P.M. Open by appointment the rest of the year. Admission is free. For more information call 493–4209.

If there's any one product that defines Aroostook County, it's the potato. The humble tuber has long been cultivated in Aroostook, and after World War I the industry boomed wildly. With prodding from Maine's Department of Agriculture, the production of certified seed potatoes grew from a mere hundred bushels in 1920 to more than five million bushels in 1942. Although the region's potato industry has been in decline since those golden days, about 90 percent of Maine's potato crop still comes from The County.

Given the central role of the potato, it's a bit disheartening to discover there's no potato museum anywhere in the state. But don't despair. One place that serves as a commendable substitute (until some visionary fills the gap) is the *Salmon Brook Museum* in Washburn, southwest of Caribou on Route 164. This sleepy town, home to a handful of general stores and cafes, can itself claim a place in the history of the potato: The frozen french fry was invented in Washburn and first manufactured by Taterstate Frozen Foods.

The Salmon Brook Museum is housed in an 1852 farmhouse in the center of the village, just off the town green. The simple but graceful home was purchased by the Salmon Brook Historical Society in 1985 and carefully restored to its earlier appearance. The ten rooms inside display nearly 3,000 items of historical interest, from a foot-powered dentist's drill to the town's original postmaster's desk. The displays are well presented and neatly organized, making Salmon Brook one of the better community museums in the state.

For exhibits related to the history of the potato, head upstairs at the agricultural museum in the barn behind the farmstead. You'll find a selection of turn-of-the-century potato harvesters and early potato planters, as well as several different versions of potato seed cutters and other agricultural implements. There's also a beautiful carpenter's chest from 1870 with a set of antique tools and a circa 1950 chainsaw that appears as unwieldy as it does menacing.

The museum is open weekends only from the end of June to Labor Day from 1:00 to 4:00 P.M. and by appointment. Admission is free, but donations are encouraged. For more information call 455–4339.

New Sweden and Vicinity

Northwest of Caribou along Route 161, signs of Swedish infiltration start to appear. You don't need to be an ethnologist to notice it: Towns like Jemtland, Stockholm, and New Sweden crop up along the way, and the mailboxes sport names like Sandstrom, Wedberg, and Johannson. On some homes you'll even notice painted detailing on shutters reflecting the owners' Scandinavian heritage.

To learn more about how the Swedes came to settle in the region, stop by the **New Sweden Historical Society Museum** in New Sweden. The museum is housed in a convincing replica of the community's early Kapitoleum, or meetinghouse (the original burned in 1971). Dominating the entranceway is a bronze bust of William W. Thomas of Portland, who established the community in 1870. An American diplomat in Sweden under Abraham Lincoln, Thomas watched as thousands of Swedes packed off to the Great Plains and other points west to establish communities and build lives. Convinced that hardworking Swedes would contribute much to the state of Maine, Thomas persuaded the Maine state legislature to grant each willing Swedish immigrant one hundred acres of "rich and fertile soil." The first group, numbering fifty-one men, women, and children, arrived in New Sweden in July 1871.

The historical society's three-floor museum is filled with items from the settlement's early days, along with portraits of stern Swedish men and their dour wives. Among the more evocative items are an early bicycle with wooden rims, wooden skis (including one pair more than 9 feet long), a wreath made of human hair intricately woven and tied to resemble flowers, and a handsome tuba. Behind the Kapitoleum is the Lindsten Stuga, a typical early settler's cabin. This was moved from nearby Westmanland in 1982 and contains many of the original furnishings from the Lindsten family. Next door is a schoolhouse that the historical society plans to restore eventually, and beyond that the town cemetery where the local history is preserved in stone.

On the weekend closest to June 21, New Sweden celebrates the summer solstice with its annual **Midsommar Festival**. Each year hundreds attend this two-day pageant, which features costumed dancers, a maypole decorated with local wildflowers, and a festive procession to W. W. Thomas Memorial Park, located on a hilltop with endless views across rich, undulating countryside. At the park a distinctive wooden bandstand in a stately grove of trees is the focus of activities. The celebration ends with a folk dance in which the audience participates.

The Historical Society Museum is on Station Road just east of Route 161 and is open Memorial Day to Labor Day Monday through Saturday from noon to 4:00 P.M. and Sunday from 2:00 to 5:00 P.M. No admission is charged. For more information about the museum or pageant, call 896–3018.

Acadian Maine

As you head toward the Canadian border, the Scandinavian influence fades and the Acadian presence grows. And grows. By the time you reach northernmost Maine between Van Buren and Madawaska, you're as likely to hear French spoken as English when you stop at a store or restaurant.

Maine's Acadians are descended from the early French settlers who made their home in French-ruled Nova Scotia in the seventeenth century. The British drove the French rulers out in 1710, but allowed most Acadian settlers to remain for the time being. The two cultures got along on fairly good terms until the French and Indian Wars heated up in the mid-1700s. Fearing that the French-speaking settlers would support the enemy, the British dispersed the Acadians to far-flung destinations including Louisiana ("Cajun" is a shortened slang version of "Acadian"), New Brunswick, and other locales. New Brunswick initially welcomed the immigrants but eventually turned hostile and drove them inland to the Saint John River valley around 1785. The trials and tribulations of the Acadians were captured in verse by Maine poet Henry Wadsworth Longfellow in his epic poem *Evangeline*.

A good place for a crash course on Acadian culture is in Van Buren, home of the **Acadian Village**, or Village Acadien. This privately run museum consists of a dozen or so buildings, most of which were moved from other locations in the valley or are replicas of historic structures. Representative buildings span a broad time period, from the earliest days to the late nineteenth century. The structures are arranged in a field off Route 1 and include a shoe repair shop, an iron shop, a small railroad station, and a barber shop. (A visit to the barber shop might suggest that times have not really changed all that much.) The most interesting edifice is the Notre Dame de l'Assumption, a log-cabin chapel complete with a bell tower and a cross. Also on the grounds are a collection of baby carriages, an early post office, and the Emma LeVasseur Dubay Art Museum. Guided tours help explain the intriguing history behind the buildings.

The Acadian Village is open from noon to 5:00 P.M. daily mid-June through mid-September. Admission is $3.50 for adults, $1.50 for children. For more information call the chamber of commerce at 868–5059.

Continuing north on Route 1, you'll soon hit the *St. David Church* and *Tante Blanche Museum* in the scarcely noticeable town of St. David (it's almost a suburb of Madawaska, a major mill town to the north). The Romanesque-style church dominates the countryside with its ornate brick facade and handsome stained glass windows, suggesting the strong presence of the Catholic church. The church building was begun in 1911, with the first Mass held in 1913. Next door is the Tante Blanche Museum (open irregularly), housed in a small log cabin and named after an early Acadian heroine. The collections include an assortment of articles of early commerce, industry, and entertainment. Behind the house are an early schoolhouse and a nineteenth-century home representative of an Acadian settlement.

Follow the dirt road down the hill from the museum and toward the river. Shortly after you cross the railroad tracks, you'll arrive at the *Acadian Cross*. Erected in 1985 for the bicentennial of the arrival of the Acadians in the Saint John Valley, the cross is believed to mark the spot where the first settlers landed after descending the river by canoe. Also present are a series of seventeen memorial markers commemorating the original Saint John's Acadians.

Fort Kent Region

*A*nother remnant of the Aroostook War (see "The County"/Presque Isle and Vicinity) may be found in Fort Kent, at the confluence of the Saint John and Fish rivers. The *Fort Kent Blockhouse* may look familiar; in fact, it's the same size and shape as the one described earlier

Northern Maine Trivia

Students at the University of Maine at Fort Kent get an orientation seminar in "Franglais," the English-French hybrid that's often used around the region. Among the best words: gadang-gadang, which translates roughly as "a bit too fancy."

in Fort Fairfield. But this isn't a replica. It's the real McCoy, constructed in 1839 by the Maine militia dispatched to defend the frontier against British encroachments. Some 10,000 troops were stationed in the region for four years before the matter was finally resolved. The blockhouse, which is managed jointly by the state and a local Boy Scout troop, has a scattering of local artifacts and articles about the Aroostook War. A picnic area and tenting sites are located along the Fish River adjacent to the blockhouse. Travel information is available in a nearby building.

The blockhouse is open daily from 9:00 A.M. to dusk Memorial Day through Labor Day. Admission is free. For more information call 834–3866.

Near the international bridge crossing from Fort Kent to the Canadian town of Edmunston, look for the sign marking the end of *U.S. Route 1*. This meager sign seems a bit anticlimactic for the ending of one of America's more notable highways. On the other hand, you can walk around and view the notice from the other side, which seems suitably humble and hopeful: THIS MARKS THE BEGINNING OF U.S. ROUTE 1 ENDING IN KEY WEST, FLORIDA, 2,209 MILES SOUTH.

An Acadian delicacy—well, delicacy isn't exactly the right word—is *poutine,* which you can find in various restaurants on either side of the border along the St. John Valley. Poutine is the very food your doctor has instructed you not to eat. It consists of french fried potatoes slathered with melted cheese and gravy. (Call them North Woods nachos.) In Fort

Read All About It

*F*rench descendants predominate in the river valley near Allagash as they do to the east. But within this sea of French influence also exist islands of descendants of Scottish settlers. There's little evidence of these contrasting cultures to the outside observer, but a series of recent novels by author Cathie Pelletier (an Allagash native) chronicle the picaresque adventures and misadventures of the Catholic and Protestant characters in the fictional town of "Mattagash." The tales—included in The Funeral Makers, Once Upon a Time on the Banks, and The Weight of Winter—span four decades from the 1950s to the present. Pelletier's entertaining accounts are available in a number of Maine bookstores.

Blockhouse, Fort Kent

Kent, you can order up regular fries or have them deliciously "poutinized" at popular Pierrette's Kitchen on East Main Street, 834 6888.

Following Route 161 westward from Fort Kent provides access to the northernmost timberlands managed by the companies of the North Maine Woods consortium. Through-routes to other parts of Maine or into Canada are available only by way of roads that cross these private lands, and a sturdy, high-clearance vehicle is recommended. Those inclined to explore this interesting cul-de-sac can drive the 29 miles to **Allagash** and back on the gently dipping and curving paved road. In midsummer you're likely to see vehicles with canoes on top along the way. Allagash is the northern terminus of a popular 100-mile canoe route from Telos Lake in Piscataquis County. The drive is pleasant and pastoral, following a gentle river valley framed with fields that terminate abruptly at a forested edge. You'll pass several small villages along the way, each with a general store or two and little else.

Route 11

South of Fort Kent Route 11 unspools endlessly through farmlands and dense forest. The road follows the route originally blazed hastily through woodlands in 1839 during the U.S. military buildup to defend the frontier at Fort Kent. The road's relatively ancient lineage is reflected in the surprisingly sheer climbs up hillsides that today would be leveled, blasted, and contoured by road engineers. The northern 37 miles between Fort Kent and Portage are designated as a Maine scenic highway, but the entire 98 miles between Fort Kent and Patten are about as picturesque as you'll find anywhere in the state.

In Ashland make time to stop at one of the two restaurants—Lil's or the Four Seasons—for a slice of *homemade pie*. Both eateries quietly compete with one another for the loyalty of their patrons in a community that seems as if it could barely support one restaurant. As a result the pies are remarkably tasty. The strawberry-rhubarb pie at Lil's, with its thick, crumbly crust and tangy filling, would almost be worth the drive from Kittery.

Few associate The County with fashion, but the exception is Francis Webb Stratton, founder and owner of the *Museum of Vintage Fashion* in Island Falls, about 10 miles east of Route 11. The fourteen rooms in this rambling old house contain some 6,000 articles of clothing amassed over the years by Stratton, who's often on hand to lead tours through the museum herself. The collections are drawn primarily from the 1880s to the 1940s and include a 1907 mourning outfit, a 1927 Girl Scout outfit, and a 1940s leopard fur coat. Stratton has collected clothing more for love than for profit (she plans eventually to donate the building and her collections to the town) and is more than happy to reveal stories about each of the pieces displayed, such as a garnet velvet bodice worn to Teddy Roosevelt's inauguration.

On the third floor, be sure to ask about the 18-inch-high dolls made several years ago by a local artisan. The meticulously crafted doll clothing is intriguing, but even more interesting are the lifelike hands and faces. According to Stratton, they're made from slices of Wonder bread soaked in Elmer's glue, then kneaded and sculpted. As they say in the real estate trade, must be seen.

Tours of the museum last about an hour and a half, with a suggested donation of $3.00 for adults, $2.00 for senior citizens, and $1.00 for children under 11. From June through the first week of October, the museum is open Monday through Thursday from 10:00 A.M. to 4:00 P.M. and by appointment Friday through Sunday. For more information call 862–3797.

PLACES TO STAY IN THE COUNTY

ASHLAND
Four Seasons Inn,
Presque Isle Road,
435–8255

CARIBOU
Caribou Inn and
Convention Center, Route 1,
498–3733

Old Iron Inn, 155 High
Street, 492–4766

FORT KENT
Daigle Bed & Breakfast,
96 East Main Street,
834–5803

HOULTON
Ivey's Motor Lodge, Route
1, (800) 244–4206 or
532–4206

Scottish Inns, Route 2A,
532–2236

Shiretown Motor Inn,
North Road,
(800) 441–9421 or
532–9421

OAKFIELD
Yellow House Bed &
Breakfast, 1040 Ridge
Road, 757–8797

PRESQUE ISLE
Arndt's Aroostook River
Lodge, Parkhurst Siding
Road, 764–8677

VAN BUREN
Colonial Motor Inn,
193 Main Street, 868–5271

Farrell-Michaud House,
231 Main Street, 868–7729

PLACES TO EAT IN THE COUNTY

ASHLAND
Four Seasons Inn, Presque
Isle Road, 435–8255

Helpful Web Sites

Acadian Village—
www.themainelink.com/acadianvillage

Aroostook County—*www.thecounty.com*

Fort Fairfield Chamber of Commerce—
www.fortfairfield.net

Houlton Online—houlton.com

Madawaska Chamber of Commerce—
www.madawaska.net

Maine Acadian Culture Project—
www.nps.gov/maac

Presque Isle Chamber of Commerce—
www.pichamber.com

Town of Fort Kent—
www.sjv.com/virtual/virtual.htm

Selected Chambers of Commerce

Caribou Chamber of Commerce,
111 High Street, (800) 722–7648 or 498–6156

Fort Fairfield Chamber of Commerce,
121 Main Street, 472–3802

Greater Fort Kent Chamber of Commerce,
54 West Main Street, (800) 733–3563 or 834–5354

Greater Houlton Chamber of Commerce,
109 Main Street, 532–4216

Presque Isle Area Chamber of Commerce,
3 Houlton Road, (800) 764–7420 or 764–6561

Lil's Diner, 52 Main Street, 435–6471

CARIBOU
Burger Boy, 344 Sweden Street, 498–2329

Caribou Bowl-O-Drome & Sports Inn, 97 Bennett Drive, 498–3386

FORT KENT
Pierrette's Kitchen, East Main Street, 834–6888

Rock's Motel & Diner, 91 West Main Street, 834–6194

HOULTON
Elm Tree Diner, Bangor Road, 532–3181

York's Dairy Bar, North Road, 532–6079

PRESQUE ISLE
Riverside Inn Restaurant, 399 Main Street, 764–1447

Winnie's Restaurant and Dairy Bar, 79 Parsons Street, 768–5539

STOCKHOLM
Eureka Hall Restaurant, 5 School Street, 896–3196

Index

INDEX

INDEX

About the Author

Wayne Curtis is a writer who moved to Maine from Washington, D.C., in 1987. Since arriving, he's explored the state by car, foot, canoe, mountain bike, ski, and sea kayak, the last of which he paddled 300 miles from Portland to Machias. As a freelance writer, Wayne has contributed stories to the *New York Times, Yankee, Outside Magazine, House Beautiful, Discovery Channel Online,* and *National Geographic Traveler.* Between 1993 and 1995 he was editor of *Casco Bay Weekly,* a 30,000-circulation alternative newspaper based in Portland. Wayne is also author of two other travel guides: *Frommer's Northern New England* and *Frommer's Nova Scotia, New Brunswick, and Prince Edward Island.* In 1998 he moved from the state's largest city (Portland) to its smallest (Eastport).

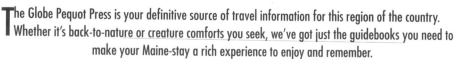